BOYS' BODIES

AC SS

Adolescent Cultures, School & Society

GENERAL EDITORS

Joseph L. DeVitis & Linda Irwin-DeVitis

Vol. 46

PETER LANG

New York • Washington, D.C./Baltimore • Bern
Frankfurt • Berlin • Brussels • Vienna • Oxford

BOYS' BODIES

Speaking the Unspoken

EDITED BY
Michael Kehler & Michael Atkinson

PETER LANG
New York • Washington, D.C./Baltimore • Bern
Frankfurt • Berlin • Brussels • Vienna • Oxford

Library of Congress Cataloging-in-Publication Data

Boys' bodies: speaking the unspoken /
edited by Michael Kehler, Michael Atkinson.
p. cm. — (Adolescent cultures, school and society; v. 46)
Includes bibliographical references and index.
1. Boys—Psychology. 2. Body image. 3. Masculinity.
4. Identity (Psychology) in adolescence. 5. Physical education and training—
Psychological aspects. I. Kehler, Michael.
II. Atkinson, Michael. III. Title.
HQ775.K44   305.23—dc22   2010016252
ISBN 978-1-4331-0626-2 (hardcover)
ISBN 978-1-4331-0625-5 (paperback)
ISSN 1091-1464

Bibliographic information published by **Die Deutsche Nationalbibliothek**.
Die Deutsche Nationalbibliothek lists this publication in the "Deutsche
Nationalbibliografie"; detailed bibliographic data is available
on the Internet at http://dnb.d-nb.de/.

FSC

Mixed Sources
Product group from well-managed
forests, controlled sources and
recycled wood or fiber

Cert no. SCS-COC-002464
www.fsc.org
©1996 Forest Stewardship Council

The paper in this book meets the guidelines for permanence and durability
of the Committee on Production Guidelines for Book Longevity
of the Council of Library Resources.

© 2010 Michael Kehler & Michael Atkinson
Peter Lang Publishing, Inc., New York
29 Broadway, 18th floor, New York, NY 10006
www.peterlang.com

Printed in the United States of America

Contents

Preface. Thinking about Boys, Bodies and Health – Michael Kehler and Michael Atkinson vii

Acknowledgements xvii

Part One: Reviewing the Intersections of Obesity, Body Image and Masculinity

Chapter One. Boys, Girls and the Prejudices of Obesity Research
Michael Gard.. 3

Chapter Two. Adolescent Males' Body Image: An Overview of Research on the Influence of Mass Media – Travis A. Ryan, Todd G. Morrison and Cormac Ó Beaglaoich.. 21

Chapter Three. The "Masculinity Vortex" of School Physical Education: Beyond the Myth of Hyper-masculinity – David Kirk 51

Part Two: Enforcing Masculinities

Chapter Four. Boys, Gyms, Locker Rooms and Heterotopia – Michael Atkinson and Michael Kehler.. 73

Chapter Five. Consuming Media, Constructing Masculinities: A Study of Youth Audiences and Physical Education in "Reflexively Modern" Times Brad Millington and Brian Wilson 91

Chapter Six. The Struggle for Recognition: Embodied Masculinity and the Victim-Violence Cycle of Bullying in Secondary Schools
James W. Messerschmidt 113

Chapter Seven. Soft Pedagogy for a Hard Sport: Disrupting Hegemonic Masculinity in High School Rugby through Feminist-Informed Pedagogy Richard Light and Jeanne Adèle Kentel 133

Part Three: Emerging/Contesting Masculinities

Chapter Eight. Negotiating Masculinities in PE Classrooms: Boys, Body Image and "Want[ing] to Be in Good Shape - Michael Kehler.................... 153

Chapter Nine. Marginalized Boys Speak Out: Insights from School Physical Education for the Obesity Crisis—Nate McCaughtry and Amy Tischler 177

Chapter Ten. Australian Young Men's Meanings of Physical Activity and Health: An Exploration of Social Class and Schooling - Jessica Lee 201

List of Contributors 223
Index.. 229

Thinking about Boys, Bodies and Health

Michael Kehler and Michael Atkinson

In the United States, Canada, Australia and the United Kingdom, parents, educators and health care professionals have expressed heightened concern about inactivity and obesity among youth. Current efforts to address obesity and inactivity among youth in schools have been remiss in acknowledging how cultured gendered identities play a role in both processes, and specifically the link between a culture of masculinity and an increased visibility of boys and their bodies. A little more than a decade ago, Kirk (1998) demonstrated a clear link between the practices of school sport and physical education, and broader public views of the body and gender-appropriate behaviour. In large part, this study and others (see Drummond, 2001; Gard, 2001; Gard & Meyenn, 2000; MacPhail, Gorely, & Kirk, 2003; Ricciardelli, McCabe & Ridge, 2006) considered school sport participation and the privilege associated with groups of boys. Wellard (2009) explains that school experiences of sport and physical education have a significant impact on adolescent development of a masculine identity as well as future participation in sports. The central positioning of the body and reading of the body among adolescents, particularly in confined and prescribed spaces such as a gymnasium or locker room, significantly impacts the way the masculine body is navigated and managed. There is an ongoing and understood status accorded to "the active, able bodied, athletic male body which in turn subordinates other bodies, particularly those which are associated with physical weakness" (Wellard, 2009, p. 110). Gard and Meyenn (2000) similarly acknowledged the body as one level at which new understandings of gender might emerge.

Given the extant, albeit spotted, research on boys, bodies and masculinities, current efforts to increase physical activity among youth has not fully addressed the bodily dividends and trade-offs associated with male participation in physical activity. This and other issues are raised in the following chapters as central to how educators might better engage and respond to all boys, not only those privileged by muscularity and physicality. We hope that by raising critical questions and proposing alternative ways for understanding inactivity among adolescent males in the physical health and education domain, educators may better respond to the valuing of bodies and particular ways for knowing and understanding masculine physical culture and its many dimensions.

The World Health Organization (2000) has identified gender (masculinity in particular) as a significant factor shaping body expectations, behaviours, and health practices. Yet, as we strive to illustrate in the chapters of this book, little is being done within the academy to address this relationship and its connection to a decline in participation in physical health education classes across many Western nations.

Considerable research has already established schools as a site of masculinising practices through which boys learn particular codes of masculinity. Practices of masculinity are directly related to beliefs, attitudes, and understandings of what it means to be a man from dominant, negotiated and marginalized cultural perspectives. The current physical culture of masculinity and climate of homophobia in many schools, for example, has a potentially damaging impact and further contributes to the suppression and silencing of anxieties about body image among men and boys. At the same time, school sport consistently exalts and elevates a particular brand of 'dangerous' and ruggedly traditional masculinity; namely, one of muscularity and competitiveness. In very public and visible ways, the schooled male body, not unlike the female body, becomes a representational marker in a gendering process that valorizes certain forms of masculinities while marginalizing others. Recent calls from institutional health communities have lobbied and pressured schools to implement practices that promote healthy and active life practices "for all." Our response to concerns for youth and specifically young men who struggle with the increased attention focused on physicality, masculinity and body image, has led us to canvass the insights and recent research of national and international scholars with varied experience and expertise regarding how boys' bodies are managed as matters of public order, cultural ritual and population health.

Contributing authors to this book reflect a diverse set of research interests and backgrounds. Each has added to this book with a shared understanding that the aim is to disengage from a mainstream health discourse that threatens to simplify both the practices and policies currently being developed to respond to inactivity among youth, masculine physical culture, concerns held by young boys about their bodies, and their marginalization within schools and elsewhere. As editors we offer this book as a vehicle for showcasing the relatively unexplored spaces of secondary school physical health and education as zones of male (physical) disciplining and contestation. Our aim is to probe the nooks and crannies of locker rooms to the recesses of the gymnasium for the narratives of a relatively unexplored population of men; namely, the boys who navigate in and out of the shadow of popular boys, and who have historically dominated and controlled these spaces. As such this book offers research-based evidence and compelling stories from the often unregulated zone of PE classrooms to provide a nuanced and textured analysis of policies, practices, and problems underlying the current rush to solve "the battle with blubber" among adolescent youth.

Given all of the above, our aims in developing this book are:

- To promote a critical examination of issues related to physical activity among adolescent youth, specifically, body image, masculinities and the intersection of these issues in the context of secondary schools.
- To foster a more nuanced and complicated picture of the types of responses to youth inactivity with a specific focus on media attention, education policy, and school curricular initiatives.
- To offer to teacher educators, teachers, policy makers, and health care professionals, a series of both practical and theoretical responses to the "obesity epidemic" debate.
- To provide an examination of the latest research-based evidence of body image research intersecting health, physical fitness, masculinities, and schooling.

In Canada, a recent report titled "It's time to unplug our kids" (2008), reflected a powerful message of how and why an increasing number of youth are inactive. Unplugging and (re)tuning our kids into a physical and vibrant world around them is imperative. The report, produced by Active Healthy Kids Canada, noted that while participation in *sport* among girls remains stable, rates of sport participation among boys is steadily decreasing. The decline of boys participating in sport, though modest, is nonetheless significant. The author speaks to sport participation. He notes that overall, in Canada, boys participate in sport at higher rates than girls. The trend, however, as youth enter teenage years, is that there is a decline in participation and an increase in inactivity among adolescent youth. The question the author raises is, "How do we engage children and youth who are already suffering with obesity, without creating anxiety around body image?" In the chapters that follow in this book we argue, in part, that we need to extend our view to include youth who struggle to participate in physical activity but who find the barriers too formidable to step onto centre court. Adolescent men routinely bear the brunt of knowing they are somehow not made for athletics. The ability or inability as it were to demonstrate a ripped, buff or shredded masculine body leaves many boys vulnerable and open to scrutiny by a privileged and powerful few. "The approval of and respect from other men, which is the ultimate accolade of masculinity, may be withheld if the boy cannot produce a body worked to a lean muscular form" (Frost, 2003, p.67).

It is not surprising, given the increased public preoccupation with why Canada, the United States and many other nations are seeing a reduced physical activity among youth, that a book such as this has emerged. What is perhaps surprising, though, is the fact that we address issues intersecting body image, masculinity and inactivity among adolescents amidst the current discourse swirling about an "obesity pandemic." Morgan (1993), reflecting on history and the ability to problematize the gendered or embodied subject, reminds us that "it is the relatively powerless who find themselves reflecting upon their identity in society. . .only under certain situations of crisis do the relatively powerful find themselves engaging in similar processes of reflection" (p. 73). He later explains that virtually all sites or arenas are embodied by the very fact that gender, power and bodies interact in those locations. The locker room, the physical health education arena and the like are just such sites intersecting men, bodies, and the power with which they are imbued. The private domain of the locker room, the open spaces of the gymnasium, school fields and fitness zones, and the public domain of the auditorium require different types of bodily performance. We will not debate here the distinctions between the private and public domains but rather want to suggest, similar to Morgan, that some sites are open to scrutiny and the form of surveillance that imposes, defines and restricts codes of masculinity through bodily performance and expressions. How and to what degree these spaces are gendered and embodied spaces is not up for debate. Our intent is to argue that in gendered spaces such as the locker room and gymnasium, the bodies of adolescent boys and young men is integral if not central to how and what forms of masculinities are negotiated. In describing the social and psychological price athletes pay for membership in their elite cultural club, Messner (2000) argues that institutionalized racism and class intersect in schools where poor and ethnic minority males are channeled into more dangerous and oftentimes combative sports. A masculine identity, it is argued is established though aggressive sport while privileged males tend to have more options available to them and thus gradually opt out of sport. In current times many adolescent young men are opting out of physical education health but this does not always reflect racialized or classed existences. In fact, while health reports routinely indicate a range of reasons for inactivity among youth, very little is being said about the intersection of masculinities as an explanatory factor why some boys are opting out. The prevailing assumption is that all boys enjoy gym and are actively engaged in physical education and health. Boys are *natural* athletes. Yet, as Messner (2000) reminds us, with the "decline in the practical need for physical strength in work and in warfare, representations of the muscular male body as strong, virile and powerful have taken on increasingly important ideological significance in gender relations. . .Though an athletic body is popularly thought of as natural, it is nevertheless the product of social practice" (p. 149)

In her examination of the contemporary connections and debates in physical education Penney (2007) draws further attention to the "ways in which young people are able to express gender identities in and through physical activity and sport and the pressures and expectations to express *particular* (emphasis in original) gender identities" as "highly significant aspects of the impact of physical education on lives, lifestyles and well-being" (p. 12). Her critique acknowledges a need for a greater level of inclusivity in which "physical education and sport need[s] to be a space and place within which young people are able and encouraged to openly express and celebrate their (gender, class, ethnic, cultural, sexual, embodied) identities" (p. 20). In a time when there is both private and public concern for the physical health and well-being of youth, it is not surprising that she relies on the professional responsibility of "physical education teachers and teacher educators as uniquely positioned to either disrupt or reaffirm established understandings of health, fitness, physical activity and physical abilities that typically fail to embrace the complexities of gender, ethnicity, class, and culture" (p. 20)

The first meta-section of our book concerns two main streams in physical cultural studies: obesity and body image. Chapters in the section home in on how boys in a variety of social locations and contexts internalize and embody codes of masculinity, and whether or not extant research and moral panicking about problematic (boys) bodies bears any empirical fruit. In chapter one, **Michael Gard** outlines the political dimensions of the obesity epidemic, and how the supposedly objective science of fatness is indeed replete with ideological sentiment and practice. To be sure, Gard's chapter sets an important critical and sceptical tone for the entire book. Gard carefully acknowledges worrying empirical trends in body shape and size in the United States and elsewhere, while illustrating how the rise in size and shift in body composition of some children is far more biologically, psychologically, socially and culturally complex than portrayed in pseudo-scientific obesity discourses.

Chapter two presents an impressive meta-analysis and quantitative study undertaken by **Ryan, Morrison, and Ó'Beaglaoich** on the relationship between boys, body image and personal development over the life-course. In particular, the authors critically analyze what constitutes contemporary knowledge about the effects of mass mediated images of masculinity on physical culture by administering the Male Body Image-related Media Messages [M-INT] amongst a sample of boys. Ryan, Morrison, and Ó'Beaglaoich conclude that the drive for muscularity among young boys shows an interesting correlation with their consumption of media messages about ideal men. Inasmuch, they advocate for increased media literacy interventions at the level of school system and elsewhere. In the final chapter of this section, **David Kirk** provides a useful historical examination of physical education teacher education in Britain. His snapshot from the 1930s to the 1970s is enriched by a reflective discussion of his own biographical experiences as a student of physical education during the 1970s. Kirk examines the "self-reproducing vortex of masculinity-making" that occurs in the shadows of dominant stereotypes of physical education teachers. His chapter usefully depicts a process of negotiated masculinities that have been historically tempered by contextual and curricular restraints.

The second sub-section of the book, Enforcing Masculinities, contains four chapters which separately and collectively document how incredibly stereotypical and mythic codes of masculinity institutionally and culturally reproduce young boys in a variety of physical education and health settings. In chapter four, **Atkinson and Kehler** take readers inside the high school gym locker room to illustrate how it is an institutional zone replete with fear for boys who do not measure up to proto-typical male body images and standards. The chapter presents findings from a larger qualitative examination of why boys in particular schools in Ontario, Canada, drop out of gym class in high school as soon as they are institutionally permitted. The authors present experiential accounts of the locker room as a heterotopic space of anxiety for boys on the fringe of accepted masculinity; ultimately pointing to how the largely understudied manners by which boys police boys through physical education is a contributory factor to poor body image and sedentary lifestyles. In chapter five, **Millington and Wilson** similarly start from the empirical "ground up" to reveal how youth are active consumers of media messages and negotiate these messages in the context of gym class. The authors present school boys as far more media savvy and sensitive than typically suggested in masculinity research. The intesectionality of race and class with masculinity codes and media interpretation in the gym setting is shown quite starkly by the researchers. Important is how Millington and Wilson show how the culture of aggression and dominance in gym class is juxtaposed rather ironically by the boys against media messages about hegemonic masculinity. **Messerschmidt's** chapter six reminds readers how bullying and victimization is indeed a part of the lived realities of far too many young boys and girls. Messerschmidt uncloaks the victimization process with emotionally moving qualitative data, and paints a chilling but familiar portrait of how physical activity, sport and school-based bullying comingle in complex and deeply gendered ways. What is especially significant about chapter six is Messerschmidt's analysis of the completely arbitrary, but massively consequential, nature of gender categories and their links with social, cultural and biological "worth" in school and elsewhere. The final chapter in this section addresses the contentious terrain of men simply "being men" in sport zones. **Light and Kentel** provoke us to reconsider the pedagogical practices of physical education, and specifically the possibilities for a non-genderist pedagogy within the context of a masculinist domain, that of sport and specifically rugby in the Australian context. Light and Kentel examine how a traditional coaching method and approach is underscored by a "dominant discourse of manliness," and thus creates a discomfort and tenuous acceptance or acquiescence among a team of rugby players to "put their bodies on the line." In this chapter they begin a dialogue that disentangles traditional pedagogical practices from normative masculinity. Building on the concept of "hard coaching" and player-centered "soft coaching," Light and Kentel raise questions from within a feminist pedagogical standpoint to propose broader possibilities in reconceived pedagogies that have the potential to unsettle particular discourses of masculinity.

The third and final sub-section of the book, Emerging/Contesting Masculinities, offers a series of international case studies examining how boys resist and contest dominant messages regarding and physical cultures of preferred masculinities. Each of the chapters in this section stresses how boys encounter and negotiate marginalized masculine identities as fringe males in cultures which still privilege historically rigid traditional masculine identities. Inasmuch, the chapters centrally engage a politics of hope regarding an acceptable, fuller panorama of masculine identities across the social landscape. In chapter eight, **Kehler** examines a sample of boys who are reluctant to participate in high school physical education. He argues that the experiences and impressions of less-than-dominant boys in grade nine PE classes highlight the tensions between wanting to be healthy while also negotiating normative and restrictive models of masculinity. Kehler highlights how codes of body idiom matter just as much for boys as they do for young girls, and how PE classes provide an important cultural battleground in the fight to produce more healthy, active and developmentally beneficial spaces for boys in the middle of a contemporary health crisis. **McCaughtry and Tischler** add a useful analysis of the experiences of young men marginalized by "privileged boys" who dominate many secondary school PE classes. In their analysis of physical health education programs at two suburban schools in the Midwestern United States, McCaughtry and Tischler examine "boys' bodies both as physical entities and simultaneously as manifestations and metaphors of the masculine self." Their insight to the experiences of the masculine body among young men is a compelling and troubling account of the routine anxiety and fears that prevented these boys from fully participating in this context. They provide a cautionary note regarding the current trend to enforce and impose physical health education without fully understanding how boys' experiences are variously constructed around and through the masculine body. Chapter Ten provides a case study of Australian males from different social, economic and geographical locations. In this final chapter of the book, **Jessica Lee** considers the intersection between masculinities, participation in physical activity, and engagement with physical culture. In her three-year study, young men from three different schools and spanning ages from 11 to 14 were interviewed to describe their past and present participation in physical activity. Lee includes interviews from several teachers along with an analysis of the school website and physical and health education and school sport policies. Her insight reveals the ways in which physical labour and the meanings associated with physicality are variously connected to classed and gendered realities in their everyday lives. Her chapter highlights the struggles of men who continue to work against the idealization of masculine bodies and the messy and unstable meanings associated with physical activity, health and fitness.

Our book is ultimately given as a partial response to absences in the current debate regarding how to encourage youth to become active, how to energise those feeling apathetic, how to mobilize the marginalized, and how to dislodge youth from whatever may prevent them from being physically active. Our intention in developing this book and collaborating with the contributors is to begin a project aimed at understanding how and why cultures of physical inactivity are mushrooming at a time when scientists, educators, policy makers, and general publics are all too aware of the health-related consequences of such activity among populations including young boys.

Bibliography

Active Healthy Kids Canada. (2008). It's time to unplug our kids. The active healthy kids Canada report card on physical activity for children and youth. Toronto, Ontario.

Drummond, M. (2001). Boys' bodies in the context of sport and physical activity: Implications for health. *Journal of Physical Education New Zealand, 34*(1), 53-64.

Frost, L. (2003) Doing bodies differently? Gender, youth, appearance and damage. *Journal of Youth Studies, (6), 1, pp. 53-70.*

Gard, M. (2001). "I like smashing people, and I like getting smashed myself": Addressing issues of masculinity in physical education and sport. In W. Martino & B. Meyenn (Eds), *What about the boys?: Issues of masculinity in schools* (pp. 222-235). Buckingham, UK: Open University Press.

Gard, M., & Meyenn, R. (2000). Boys, bodies, pleasure and pain: Interrogating contact sports in schools. *Sport, Education and Society, 5*(1), 9-34.

Kirk, R (1998) *Schooling bodies: Schooling practice and public discourse 1880-1950.* London: Leicester University Press.

MacPhail, A., Gorely, T., & Kirk, D. (2003). Young people's socialization into sport: A case study of an athletics' club. *Sport, Education and Society, 8*(2), 251-267.

Messner, M. (2000). When bodies are weapons. In M. Baca Zinn & Maxine Baca Zinn, Pierrette A. Hondagneu-Sotelo, Michael A. Messner (eds), *Through the prism of difference* (pp. 146-150). Upper Saddle River, NJ: Prentice Hall.

Morgan, D. (1993). You too can have a body like mine: Reflections on the male body and masculinities. In *Body matters: Essays on the sociology of the body* (pp. 69-88). London, UK; The Falmer Press.

Penney, D. (2007). Physical education, physical activity, sport and gender: Contemporary connections and debates. In I. Welland (Ed), *Rethinking gender and youth sport* (pp. 12-22). Abingdon, UK: Routledge.

Ricciardelli, L. A., McCabe, M. P., & Ridge, D. (2006). The construction of the adolescent male body through sport. *Journal of Health Psychology, 11*(4), 577-587.

Wellard, I. (2009). *Sport, Masculinites and the body.* New York; Routledge.

World Health Organization (2000). *What about boys?: A literature review on the health and development of adolescent boys.* Department of Child and Adolescent Health and Development.

Acknowledgements

We would like to express our appreciation to the boys and young men whose experiences in gym classes have often been overlooked and unheard. Your willingness to "speak the unspoken" to the researchers whose work is reflected in this collection of chapters is but one way of giving voice to the impact you leave on us and our effort to let that impact be heard and felt by others.

Michael Kehler would like to thank the endless support of his partner, Christena McKillop, who regardless of the day and time has always been willing to listen and support my every effort. To Claire and Matthew, thank you for being the life, the inspiration, and my joy. And to my mother, brothers, Bill and Doug thanks for understanding and always supporting me.

Michael Atkinson would like to thank his two boys, Eoghan and Finnegan, for constantly reminding him about the joys of being a boy. This book stems from an interest in providing boys like them with lighter and brighter cultural spaces to simply run, laugh and feel comfortable in their own bodies.

We would like to thank the Social Sciences and Humanities Research Council of Canada for generously supporting the three year study examining why some boys do not like participating in Grade nine Physical Health and Education and which is partially reflected in Chapters Four and Eight.

We are both thankful to a superb group of Research Assistants: Anne Watson, Vi Vo, and Terry Loerts, whose dedication and commitment to the research project and this book has been outstanding. Anne Watson in particular has left us both giving thanks that pales in comparison to the ongoing effort and vigour with which she has applied herself to some of the more laborious and fine detailed work of this book.

Finally, both Michaels thank Chris Myers and Sophie Appel at Peter Lang for guiding us through this process. Your encouragement and direction was always welcome. Thanks for the opportunity to work with you both and for always being available to us and ready to respond.

PART ONE

Reviewing the Intersections of Obesity, Body Image and Masculinity

CHAPTER ONE

Boys, Girls and the Prejudices of Obesity Research

Michael Gard

Despite the confident tone that often attaches to talk of an 'obesity epidemic', the field of obesity research is replete with uncertainty and confusion. And because it is has direct relevance to people's everyday lives, it is also an area of study that is particularly prone to the influence of stereotypes. In other words, because we all eat, move and think about the state of our own bodies, the world is full of obesity 'experts'. In previous research I have made the argument that there is a connection between the prevalence of social and cultural stereotypes, on the one hand, and the confused state of obesity science, on the other. Part of this connection seems to be explained by the simple fact that obesity researchers harbor the same kinds of prejudices as the rest of us. So, while academics in some fields might complain about how poorly the general public understands their area of expertise, my impression is that there is little to distinguish between popular scientific rhetoric when it comes to overweight and obesity. With respect to obesity, popular and scientific discourses are essentially one and the same thing.

The influence of prejudices and stereotypes is particularly marked in the area of childhood obesity. For example, a great deal of research energy has gone into problematizing the behavior and body weight of Western girls. In the work of many childhood obesity researchers girls are a particular problem because 'we know' teenage girls become less interested in physical activity and more interested in social networking and personal grooming as they get older. However, while it is true that research consistently shows girls' participation in certain forms of physical activity (such as organized sports) declining through the teenage years, it is not always clear that this leads to greater levels of obesity than boys or greater levels of obesity than men in later life.

The constant refrain in the obesity literature that girls are a bigger problem than boys runs parallel to the stereotype that today's children are a generation of technology addicted 'couch potatoes'. And although the problem of technology is not often cast in explicitly gendered terms, the images that are used to accompany media stories about 'couch potato' children are almost always male, usually featuring one or two children, remote controls in hand and bowls of potato chips nearby. Similar images are regularly used in scientific reports. But while there is some empirical support for the idea that boys use televisions, computers and other forms of electronic technology more than girls, again it is not immediately clear why this should be cause for concern. Research consistently shows that physical activity and technology use have very little to do with each other; less of one does not mean more of the other and many children manage to do lots or very little of both.

In short, what I will attempt to show in this chapter is how both public and scientific discourse has been poorly served by stereotypes. I show how research is generally ambiguous about whether Western boys are more overweight and obese than Western girls. I also show how research into the determinants of childhood overweight and obesity has been dogged by a priori assumptions about what boys and girls are like.

Before proceeding, a few points of clarification are necessary. I will use the term 'obesity research' and 'obesity researchers' to refer to the academic practice and community devoted to studying human body weight, with the obvious exception of those who explicitly study human underweight and related subjects such as eating disorders and body image. Obesity research encompasses a wide range of research endeavors and academic disciplines, such as paediatrics, epidemiology, physiology and health promotion. Except where I indicate otherwise, I use 'obesity' as a blanket term for the technical categories of 'overweight' and 'obese'. In using 'obesity' in this way I am aware that the conflation of overweight and obesity causes confusion and misunderstanding in both academic and popular discourse. In this chapter I distinguish between overweight and obesity when it is important to do so. In some cases, particularly when discussing childhood body weight research, I will use the term 'overweight' where 'overweight' is used by researchers to refer to all those children over a certain body weight cut-off, regardless of how much they exceed this cut-off by.

The Couch Potato Generation?

Many obesity researchers admit that they work from a severely limited and limiting knowledge base. This was true when concern about an 'obesity epidemic' began to morph into hysteria about ten years ago and it remains true today. This is important because, given that this chapter will devote a great deal of space to critiquing obesity research, I want to be clear about the kind of critique I am offering.

The rise of 'obesity epidemic' rhetoric has spawned a set of opposing discourses that includes what is sometimes called 'critical obesity studies'; the work of scholars who critique many of the alarmist claims of mainstream obesity research on empirical and/or ethical grounds. I have some misgivings about the term 'critical obesity studies' because it is not always clear how 'critical' some writers in this field of study are. In any case, whether a scholar's work is 'critical' or not is probably a value judgement and it is for this reason I opt instead to talk about obesity skepticism rather than critical obesity studies.

Some of the high profile North American obesity skeptics have tended to make the charges of incompetence, dishonesty and opportunism against mainstream obesity researchers. For example, writers like Paul Campos (2004) and J. Eric Oliver (2006) have argued that the 'obesity epidemic' is essentially a myth or, in fact, a grand hoax. They question the intelligence of obesity researchers and point to the money and prestige that is at stake in the study of obesity and the search for pharmaceutical interventions. In other words, their argument is that we are being told that there is an 'obesity epidemic' because it is in someone else's self-interest to do so.

As an obesity skeptic, I have tried to make a somewhat different case. While I do think that obesity researchers are mistaken about many things and that the flow of money into obesity research and obesity-related pharmaceuticals is significant, I do not smell a conspiracy. Rather, I have tended to focus on the *a priori* assumptions and prejudices that have been used to frame changing population obesity rates. That is, rather than viewing the idea of an obesity epidemic as a myth in need of exploding, I am more inclined to see it as a social movement in need of explanation. The significance of this distinction should, I hope, become clear as we begin to consider obesity research itself, particularly with respect to children.

I am aware of few writers who dispute the point that overweight and obesity have increased in many countries around the world over the last 30 years or so. And yet, those who see the idea of an 'obesity epidemic' as a hoax are basically locked into arguing that since nothing of substance has actually happened, nothing, therefore, need be said. In contrast, my argument here would be to acknowledge that something *is* going on and that the important task is to explain whatever this something is. In this context explanation means at least two things. First, it means explaining why these apparently widespread changes in human body weight happened. Second, and closer to my own research interests, it means explaining why these body weight changes were transformed into something called an 'obesity epidemic' and not, for example, something less dramatic.

In my view, we can at least begin to explain both of these aspects of the obesity epidemic by looking at the stereotypes, or what I have called 'prejudices', that have framed the phenomenon itself. For example, from the beginning of the 21st century, in both the academic and popular literature, obesity levels were constantly described as 'exploding'. But were they? It is at least arguable that what appeared to some as an explosive change in obesity levels was an artifact of the very low rates that existed in Western countries during the two or three decades after the Second World War. For example, Booth et al. (2003) have reported that obesity amongst ten-year-old Australian boys increased from 1.3% in 1985 to 4.1% in 1997. This is probably not the place to conduct a detailed statistical assessment of these numbers, but two points are worth registering. First, whether this change represents an explosive rise in obesity amongst ten-year-old boys is, I think, a matter of perspective. While in absolute terms it is an increase of only 2.8% over more than a decade, proportionally it represents an increase of over 200%.

Second, it should also be kept in mind that, because of the way body weight categories are calculated, the absolute amount of weight needed for a ten-year-old boy to move from, say, 'normal weight' to 'overweight' and then on to 'obese' is actually quite small. In other words, when we read that the number of Australian ten-year-old boys classified as obese more than trebled between 1985 and 1995, we still need to ask what this actually means in terms of actual body weight. Of course, we might also ask what this extra body weight means for a person's health except that no scientific answer to this questions exists or is ever likely to. Indeed, as Flegal, Tabak and Ogden (2006) put it:

> In children, there are no risk-based fixed values of BMI used to determine overweight, because it is unclear what risk-related criteria to use. The long time span before adverse outcomes appear and the small samples identifying cardiovascular risks in youth make finding risk-related cutoffs difficult (p. 756).

In other words, when researchers categorize children as 'normal weight', 'overweight' or 'obese', this is not done because there is clear evidence that children categorized as overweight or obese will suffer worse health consequences than other children, now or in the future. Rather than a measure of health, BMI categories for children, as well as adults, are mere statistical conveniences.

In the United States, data from the authoritative National Health and Nutrition Examination Survey (NHANES) data also help to problematise the idea of exploding childhood body weights. For example, in the period between the 1988-1994 and 1999-2000 surveys, there appear to have been significant increases in overweight amongst non-Hispanic black and Mexican American adolescents (12 to 19 years), for both boys and girls, but only small increases for non-Hispanic white adolescents (Ogden, Flegal, Carroll & Johnson, 2002). By 2000, non-Hispanic white American adolescents were clearly the least overweight ethnic group. Are body weights exploding here?

Similarly, in more recent data there appears to have been an interesting shift. From the 1999-2000 to the 2003-2004 surveys, overweight went up amongst non-Hispanic white 12- to 19-year-olds from 11.4% to 17.3%, while non-Hispanic blacks dropped from 23.1% to 21.8% and Mexican Americans dropped from 23.2% to 16.3%. In 1999-2000 overweight amongst Mexican American 12- to 19-year-olds was more than double that of non-Hispanic whites (23.2% and 11.4% respectively), but in 2003-2004 non-Hispanic white adolescents are slightly more overweight than Mexican Americans (17.3% and 16.3% respectively) (Ogden, Carroll, Curtin, McDowell, Tabak & Flegal, 2006). Once again, my sense is that whatever else we might say about these statistics, a generalized explosion of obesity would be a less-than-adequate account of the apparent changes in children's body weight. The overarching point to be made here is that changes in obesity levels, whether for children or adults, can be made to sound more or less alarming depending on how they are represented. On top of this, there is the long recognized controversy concerning the methods used for measuring fatness and classifying children. For example, it is very easy to derive very different levels of overweight and/or obesity in a population of children simply by using one of the many widely used measurement protocols (Luciano, Bressan, Bolognani, Castellarin and Zoppi, 2001).

What sense are we to make of alarmist rhetoric around childhood obesity? Unlike some obesity skeptics, I would at least concede that the charge of alarmism is not always easy to substantiate. No one really knows whether too much has been made of obesity and it will be years before the picture is clearer. In other words, I am reluctant to accuse mainstream obesity researchers of rank incompetence or fat hatred; after all, their alarmism may eventually turn out to be prescient or even conservative. Further, we need to remember that obesity levels *have* changed and it seems unlikely that these changes will have no medical consequences of any kind. I think it is more prudent to see obesity statistics as open to multiple interpretations. And while we may want to argue for one particular interpretation over others, there are no bedrock truths from which interpretations stray more or less egregiously.

Why changes in obesity levels, and particularly for children, have tended to be framed as an 'epidemic' or 'crisis' is also open to interpretation and disagreement. However, as media coverage of the 'obesity epidemic' became more frequent and intense during the first few years of the 21st century, it was noticeable that images were playing a central role in determining how obesity statistics were understood. Many readers will have seen newspaper reports about childhood obesity levels embellished with photographs of children sitting or lying transfixed in front of a television or computer screen, often with large amounts of high calorie food close by or in the process of being consumed. I have collected dozens of these images from newspapers and magazines and they are almost invariably of boys. More telling, I think, is that basically the same image is used over and over again, probably indicating that at least some people see lazy gluttonous children as an increasing and widespread malaise; the so-called 'couch potato generation'. In other words, these images are used because they are assumed to be culturally intelligible; they speak volumes for themselves, instantly capturing what are widely thought to be the reasons behind rising obesity levels. And although a difficult thing to prove, my sense is that these images are used also because they are what journalists and publishers would call 'strong images', offering the reader an embodiment of, and thus a target for, their fears and disgust.

Fear and disgust may be part of the explanation why increasing obesity statistics have been characterized as 'exploding' and the situation as an 'epidemic'. Oliver (2006) makes a convincing case that it was the use of images by the Centers for Disease Control and Prevention, in this instance a series of maps charting the 'spread', contagion style, of obesity across America over time, that marked a decisive shift towards the rhetoric of 'epidemic' and 'crisis' in the first years of the 21st century.

What we can say, I think, is that fear has been both an important cause *and* effect of the 'obesity epidemic'. Some examples, pertaining particularly to children, will help to illustrate this point.

The images of fat children lying on couches eating potato chips has not simply been a convenient way to decorate newspaper articles about childhood obesity. The image of the couch potato has also become a dominant framing mechanism for understanding young people in general. Despite what seem to me to be the obvious dangers of generalizing about 'all children', the technology-addicted, exercise-phobic young person has proved a stereotype too good for journalists and scientists to resist. For example, as far back as 2000, Canadian children were being described as the "first full Nintendo generation" (Arnold, 2000, p. A1). Sometimes the words are slightly different, but the idea remains the same; Scottish children are a "couch potato generation" (English 2005) and Australian children a "cotton-wool generation" (Powell, 2000, p. 6). While it is unclear how he came by this information, a recent former Governor-General of Australia was reported regularly complaining about the state of today's children who "were at risk from a 'fat lifestyle' and needed to be prized from their DVDs and Playstations and encouraged to play sport" (Hudson, 2004, p. 3).

On the one hand, we might think it unremarkable for adults to denigrate the generations that come after them as less industrious and virtuous as themselves; this is surely an age-old tendency. Still, on the other hand, the level of scorn and ridicule heaped on today's children seems, at least to me, unwarranted and excessive. This is particularly so given that secular trend research into children's physical activity has consistently been either inconclusive or counter to prevailing orthodoxies. For example, an assessment of physical activity trends amongst South Australian youth between 1985 and 2004 found:

> There is no consistent evidence of declining physical activity among South Australian youth. It is apparent that physical activity in some contexts has declined, while in other contexts levels are the same or higher than in 1985. This underscores the complex nature of physical activity and the influences on this behavior. (Lewis, Dollman & Dale, 2007, p. 418)

The research finding of generally stable or increasing participation in physically active leisure amongst young people has been repeated in a number of Western countries including Sweden between 1974 and 1995 (Westerståhl, Barnekow-Bergkvist, Hedbergand & Jansson, 2003), Canada between 1981 and 1998 (Eisenmann, Katzmarzyk & Tremblay, 2004), England between 1987 and 2003 (Schools Health Education Unit, 2004), and the United States between the mid 1960s and 1997 (Pratt, Macera & Blanton, 1999). Of course, we need here to concede that it is impossible to be sure about the 'real' secular trends in young people's physical activity anywhere in the world. The point to make, though, is that those who charge today's children with being a 'couch potato generation' almost always do so without consulting the existing evidence base, imperfect as is. In other words, the distance between the stereotype of the 'couch potato generation' and the state of empirical knowledge is very great indeed.

A similar picture emerges if we engage even more directly with the couch potato stereotype and consider the relationship between childhood obesity, the use of technologies such as televisions and computers, and physical activity. What evidence is there that modern technologies reduce the amount of physical activity that children do and, as a result, contribute to childhood obesity?

The empirical case against televisions and computers probably began with Dietz and Gortmaker (1985) who asked 'Do we fatten our children at the television set?' Since then, a large number of almost entirely cross-sectional studies have been conducted in the name of convicting television for rising childhood obesity. I will spare readers a detailed discussion of this literature and simply summarize what I take to be the result of 25 years of research in this area (for a more detailed account see Gard & Wright, 2005).

First, there is some evidence that high levels of television watching are associated with a higher risk of childhood obesity. However, very few studies have even attempted to determine whether this relationship is causational or simply correlational and the results of those that have are mixed. Second, studies have generally failed to show a robust statistical link between electronic technology usage and physical activity levels. While some studies have found that children who watch a lot of television tend to be fatter, their higher fatness levels is not explained by differences in their level of physical activity. Third, level of technology use appears to have little bearing on physical activity participation. This is an especially important research finding for boys since they tend to be higher users of technology, particularly computers. As a number of literature reviews have pointed out, many children report high technology use *and* high levels of physical activity (Marshall, Biddle, Gorely, Cameron & Murdey, 2004; Marshall, Biddle, Sallis, McKenzie, & Conway, 2002).

This set of findings is worth dwelling on for a moment. I am struck by how often published research papers in this area emphasize findings that conform to negative stereotypes about children, technology and obesity and de-emphasize those findings that do not. One of the more flagrant examples I have seen appears in Andersen, Crespo, Bartlett, Cheskin and Pratt (1998), a study of the behavior of 4,063 United States children between 1988 and 1994. As with other similar studies, this paper reports that children who watched the most television had higher BMIs and higher skinfold measurements than low television users. This finding figures prominently in the paper's abstract. We need to dig further into the paper to discover that the researchers also found that for boys, the more television they watched the more self-reported vigorous physical activity they did. For girls, there was no association between television and self-reported physical activity. Also, a very high proportion of children (80% in fact) met health guidelines for physical activity, although boys were higher than girls. Boys watched more television than girls but also did more physical activity. Girls tended to do less physical activity as they got older but physical activity was lowest (and TV watching highest) amongst black and Hispanic girls. Why were these interesting and, as far as dominant thinking about 'couch potato' children goes, counter-intuitive findings not given prominence in the paper's title or abstract? I can see no other reason than the grip of the couch potato stereotype. In fact, rather than rejecting the hypothesis that the study appears to have been based on—more television equals less physical activity equals higher obesity—the paper's abstract concludes meekly with a statement that might easily have been written before the study was conducted:

> Many US children watch a great deal of television and are inadequately active. Vigorous activity levels are lowest among girls, non-Hispanic Blacks and Mexican Americans. Interventions are needed to stem the adverse health consequences of inactivity. (Andersen et al., 1998, p. 938)

In other words, as in so much obesity research, the researchers appear simply to be uninterested in their own findings.

There is an interesting epilogue to my brief discussion here about the idea of a 'couch potato generation'. Following an 'obesity summit' convened by the government of the Australian state of New South Wales, a comprehensive study into the body weight of the states' children was commissioned. The study received some media attention when it was released in 2006 because it found that children were fitter and more active than they had been in the previous decade, one newspaper article describing the idea of increasingly inactive children as an 'urban myth' (Robotham & Lee, 2006, p. 1). The article goes on:

> But the children, aged four to 16, were exercising harder. More than 80 per cent in years 6 to 8 were adequately physically active—spending at least an hour a day in moderate or vigorous activity—compared with less than 60 per cent in 1997. 'This flies in the face of what I think was an urban myth that children were inactive,' said Dr Booth, who was so surprised that he ordered a recalculation. 'Like everyone else, I believed the urban myth.'

More recently, a large study (discussed further below) has recently claimed that increases in American childhood obesity can be explained by changes in diet *alone*. The authors of the study also suggested that there may have been *increases* in children's physical activity that have partially off-set weight changes caused by changing diets.

If there is one message to glean from my study of obesity research it is that very little can be concluded from single studies, no matter how well conducted the research or how well known the researchers; the field is awash with diametrically opposed findings and there is always a study with a counter-intuitive finding around the next corner. However, I think we can now safely say that a large enough body of evidence exists to cast serious doubt on the idea that modern children are lazy, addicted to technology and disinterested in physical activity. Moreover, it is now clear, at least to me, that the stereotype of the 'couch potato' prejudiced a large section of the obesity research community from the start of this research endeavor. That is, while we must accept that doing science necessarily involves mistakes and blind alleys, the grip of the 'couch potato' stereotype fascinated and transfixed a generation of researchers beyond all reasonable limits.

There are children for whom accessing and enjoying appropriate amounts of physical activity is difficult for a wide range of reasons. It is surely reasonable for researchers to seek to understand these reasons better so that something can be done. What is less reasonable, I think, is to start with a prejudice about all children and devote energy and resources to proving this prejudice in the face of an ever-growing body of disconfirming results.

Who Is the Fattest of Them All?

While very few obesity researchers seriously doubt the fundamental role played by food and physical activity in the regulation of human body weight, what their roles actually are has proved remarkably elusive. This confusion underlines an age-old tension, familiar in many fields of study, between what we might tentatively call 'common sense' and empirical science. Literally hundreds of published scientific research articles about obesity include a common sense statement to the effect that human body weight is simply a matter of the difference between energy consumed in the form of food and energy expended in the form of physical activity. To my knowledge, there are no plausible reasons to doubt the general efficacy of this formulation except in relatively rare cases of severe metabolic disturbance. But as secure as this common sense view of human body weight might seem, it is not at all clear whether it is of any use when trying to understand *changes* in human body weight. This is especially so when our unit of analysis moves from individuals to entire populations.

In the remainder of this chapter I want to pose the reader a question for which I will only offer a partial answer. The question is as follows: what is the reason for the apparently intractable controversy surrounding the relative contribution of food and physical activity to increasing body weights in Western countries? In other words, why does this question endure?

There are at least two potential answers. First, it could be that the problem itself is extremely difficult to research and it is for this reason that reliable information is scarce; the elusiveness of truth in this area of research is not due to shortcomings in the people doing the research.

A second potential answer might rest in the question itself. For example, does it make any sense to attempt to generalize about the determinants of body weight beyond the level of the individual? To take a striking example, a study presented at the 2009 European Congress on Obesity made the claim that increases in the body weight of United States children since the early 1970s could be explained *entirely* by changes in food intake and not physical activity. This conclusion was arrived at via estimates of such things as the total amount of food produced, the amount of food wasted and the amount fed to animals. However, each component in a calculation of this kind must be viewed with caution. After all, we do not really know how much food was fed to American animals during the 30-odd years covered by the study; all we can do is make an educated guess. Thus, the claim that food intake alone has led to increasing body weights amongst American children is little more than an accumulation of educated guesses.

My point here is to ask whether there is something fundamentally misguided about this kind of research. Does it make any sense at all to construct a study that seeks to say something concrete about a group as diverse as all American children who have lived since the early 1970s? To return to the original question I posed above, is it possible that the problem of trying to explain the causes of rising childhood obesity endures precisely because it is not a question that can be answered? For example, if it were actually the case that childhood body weight was determined largely by personal or geographically local or socially specific factors (such as educational level or socio-economic class), then generalizations about 'all American children' would be essentially meaningless.

Let me pursue this line of reasoning by considering research into the body weight of boys and girls around the world. In doing so, I want to make clear that my purpose here is to demonstrate how obesity research yields few robust generalizable findings.

If we begin in the United States, most researchers take their lead from the long-standing National Health and Nutrition Examination Survey (NHANES), preceded by the National Health Examination Survey (NHES), data usually reported by researchers at the Centers for Disease Control and Prevention. Although initial NHES sample sizes were much smaller than later NHANES surveys, childhood overweight data goes back to the early 1960s. Children between 6 and 11 years old were the only age group reported from the 1963-1965 NHES survey. Here, the prevalence of overweight for boys (4.0%) and girls (4.5%) is, at least in absolute terms, tiny (Ogden, Flegal, Carroll & Johnson, 2002). As subsequent surveys were conducted, other age groups were included and these produced only small deviations from gender parity; in some age groups boys recorded higher overweight prevalence rates but not others.

For the 1999-2000 survey, the percentage of Americans aged between 2 and 19 years classified as overweight was 13.9%. Interestingly, in this survey boys between 12 and 19 years recorded exactly the same level of overweight as girls, 15.5%. By the 2003-2004 survey, overweight prevalence for 2- to 19-year olds had increased to 17.1%; boys were slightly higher–18.2% (up from 14.0% in 1999-2000)—and girls slightly lower–16.0% (up from 13.8%) (Ogden et al., 2006). In the 2003-2004 survey, non-Hispanic white boys aged 2 to 19 years (17.8%) were more likely to be overweight than non-Hispanic white girls (14.8%). For non-Hispanic blacks the picture was reversed; boys (16.4%, lower than white boys) scored considerably lower than non-Hispanic black girls (23.8%, higher than white girls). This situation was reversed again for Mexican American young people, with boys (22.0%) appearing to be much more overweight than girls (16.2%).

A great many more United States statistics could be quoted here. Whether more numbers serve to improve or erode clarity is probably a matter of perspective. For example, NHANES childhood body weight statistics can be subdivided into smaller categories such as Mexican American boys between 2 and 5 years or non-Hispanic white girls between 6 and 11 years. These 'reveal' a series of curious fluctuations and disparities for which a range of explanations are no doubt possible. For example, the relatively high rates of overweight among black girls and Mexican American boys have been attributed by some people to cultural rather than economic factors, while there are only very small differences between the prevalence of overweight amongst all other American 2- to 19-year-olds.

In my view it is difficult to know what sense to make of this kind of data, particularly but not only if one's concern is to draw comparisons between groups of children. This is obviously the case if we keep our categories broad, such as all boys versus all girls where there are only small differences. But drilling down further into ethnic and age-related data sub-sets produces only more questions. For example, while overweight prevalence for Mexican American boys is higher than all other groups except non-Hispanic black girls, this situation has turned around somewhat by adulthood. The 2003-2004 NHANES survey showed very little difference in obesity prevalence amongst all men, regardless of ethnicity, and non-Hispanic white women. In what is now an often-replicated research finding, obesity prevalence is highest amongst non-Hispanic black and Mexican American women (Ogden et al., 2006).

In summary, for the most researched country in the world, Wang and Beydoun (2007) offer the following about the body weights of American children:

> The overall national average prevalence is similar among boys and girls; however, large gender differences exist in some racial/ethnic groups. In 1999–2000 and 2003–2004, the prevalence of both outcomes showed a larger gender gap among non-Hispanic Blacks and Mexican-American children and adolescents compared with non-Hispanic Whites (pp. 14-15).

Elsewhere there are equally ambiguous data. In Britain, some data suggest that infant boys tend to be less overweight than infant girls but that this situation is reversed by the later teenage years (Jebb, Rennie & Cole, 2003). This is despite the consistent research finding that girls self-report increasingly lower levels of physical activity participation as they get older compared with boys. Interestingly, Stamatakis, Primatesta, Chinn, Rona and Falascheti (2005) paint a slightly different picture for English only children, with 5 to10-year-old girls scoring higher overweight and obesity levels from the 1970s through to 2003. However, they also show that the differences between boys and girls vary significantly depending on which of the different available methods for calculating childhood overweight and obesity is used. Rennie and Jebb's (2005) review also suggests that English girls tend to be higher than boys in both overweight and obesity by a few percentage points:

> There are few data available on the prevalence of obesity in children, particularly using the International Obesity Task Force cut-offs. Data from three independent cross-sectional surveys (1974, 1984 and 1994) showed that there was little change in the prevalence of overweight in 4–11 years children from 1974 to 1984. However, overweight increased from 5–6% in boys and 9–10% in girls in 1984 to 9–10% in boys and 13–16% in girls in 1994. More recent data from the HSE [Health Survey for England] in 2002 suggest a further increase in 2- to 15-year-olds, with 5.5% of boys and 7.2% of girls obese and 22% and 28% overweight or obese (p. 11).

In Australia there is now a patchwork of empirical sources to draw on, most of which suggest that there have been, and continue to be, only small differences in overweight or obesity between boys and girls (Booth et al. 2003; Magarey, Daniels & Boulton, 2001). In O'Dea (2003), differences between boys and girls were generally lower than differences between children from different socio-economic class groups. More recently, some researchers have reported small early signs of a divergence of overweight and obesity levels between Australian boys and girls, with girls perhaps dropping below boys (Booth, Dobbins, Okely, Denney-Wlson & Hardy, 2007). On the other hand, O'Dea's (2008) study of nearly 8,000 Australian children showed only minor gender differences:

> Prevalence of obesity was 6.4% of males and 5.6% of females in primary school students (P = 0.34). More high school males were obese than females (7.7% vs. 5.7%, P = 0.001). Obesity was more prevalent among students from Pacific Islander backgrounds. Adolescents who were most likely to be obese were boys and girls of low SES or Pacific Islander or Middle Eastern/Arabic background. The least likely to be obese were Anglo/ Caucasian or Asian students and in particular, the girls (p. 282).

There is probably little point in laboring the point with further examples. Taking an international view, it is not at all clear how important gender is to understanding changing childhood obesity levels. Perhaps the most challenging aspect of studying obesity is that it is not a field from which powerful generalizing truths regularly emerge. So, while we might (or might not) reach the conclusion that gender is not a significant determining factor, it is not the case that strong alternatives are ready to suggest themselves. For example, while many researchers have studied the role of ethnicity and socio-economic class, these appear to be significant only in some countries and in some contexts. Socio-economic class, in particular, seems generally to negatively correlate with female body weight but be much less statistically significant for males.

Of course, one of the dangers of failing to find a statistical 'smoking gun' to explain changes in childhood and adult obesity levels is that we simply assume that obesity affects everyone everywhere to roughly the same degree. This is a point of view I have argued strongly against (Gard & Wright, 2005). Rather, the challenge of studying changes in obesity levels turns out to be the ability to manage intellectually the paradox of a real and generalized epidemiological phenomenon that needs to be understood with an, at times, frustratingly tedious attention to specific, local social circumstances. Although the phenomenon of increasing obesity is a generalized phenomenon, generalizations simply do not work as an explanation for it.

Childhood Body Weight and Health

A great deal has been written about how worried we should be about changing childhood body weights. For the purposes of this chapter the question might be reworked to ask to what extent we should be worried about differences between the body weights of boys and girls. This is not an easy question to answer. For example, it is not clear how the behaviors of childhood lead to specific body weight and health outcomes in adulthood. So, given that there is a quite consistent finding across the Western world that women tend to outnumber men in the obese category but the opposite is true for mere overweight (Cameron et al., 2003; Hensrud & Klein, 2006; Joint Health Surveys Unit, 1999), how should we respond?

We might ask similar questions about the research finding that Western girls appear to become less involved in organized physical activity, particularly sport, as they get older. A huge amount of research energy has gone into this phenomenon without producing anything like a sound knowledge base from which to act. The difficulties multiply when we take into account the fact that women live longer than men and, as they age, seem to engage in health enhancing physical activity with at least the same enthusiasm as men.

There is now a great deal of enthusiasm for using schools as a kind of front line in the 'war on obesity'. Is this reasonable? Should schools be expected to monitor and manage children's body weight on top of all the other things they are expected to do? I have tried to show in this chapter that many of the things that people assume to be true about childhood obesity— such as the role played by technology or the amount of physical activity today's children are (or are not) doing—are either uncertain or just untrue. And I have also argued that obesity statistics are open to many different interpretations.

Taken together, these points lead, I think, to some new questions. For example, how should schools treat the bodies of students? After all, there are now schools that periodically weigh children, send reports home to parents warning about their child being too fat and even require students to pass fitness tests in order to graduate (see Parry, 2008). To what extent do these kinds of policies make schools more or less emotionally safe places for children? Are these policies likely to have the intended effect or some unexpected negative effect? Are they based on sound science? I want to conclude this chapter by suggesting that fighting obesity in schools is an idea generated by scientists and, by extension, politicians responding to pressure to take action on obesity. I find it hard to believe that some of the more strange and disturbing things happening in schools in the name of fighting obesity, such as public weigh-ins, would have been chosen by parents or teachers or children by themselves. This is a reminder, I think, that schools are many things, including a place where the power of particular groups of people, such as scientists and politicians, is visited upon the bodies of children, whether they like it or not.

Bibliography

Andersen, R. E., Crespo, C. J., Bartlett, S. J., Cheskin, L. J., & Pratt, M. (1998). Relationship of physical activity and television watching with body weight and level of fatness among children: Results from the Third National Health and Nutrition Examination Survey. *Journal of the American Medical Association, 279*(12), 938-942.

Arnold, T. (2000, November 27). Obesity rate triples for boys. *National Post*, p. A1.

Booth, M. L., Chey, T., Wake, M., Norton, K., Hesketh, K., Dollman, J., & Robertson, I. (2003). Change in the prevalence of overweight and obesity among young Australians, 1969-1997. *American Journal of Clinical Nutrition, 77*(1), 29-36.

Booth, M. L., Dobbins, T., Okely, A. D., Denney-Wlson, E., & Hardy, L. L. (2007). Trends in the prevalence of overweight and obesity among young Australians, 1985, 1997, and 2004. *Obesity, 15*(5), 1089-1095.

Cameron, A. J., Welborn, T. A., Zimmet, P. Z., Dunstan, D. W., Owen, N., Salmon, J., Dalton, M., Jolley, D., & Shaw, J. E. (2003). Overweight and obesity in Australia: The 1999-2000 Australian Diabetes, Obesity and Lifestyle Study (AusDiab). *Medical Journal of Australia, 178*(9), 427-432.

Campos, P. (2004). *The obesity myth: Why America's obsession with weight is hazardous to your health.* New York: Gotham Books.

Dietz, W. H., & Gortmaker, S. L. (1985). Do we fatten our children at the television set? Obesity and television viewing in children and adolescents. *Pediatrics 75*(5), 807–812.

Eisenmann, J. C., Katzmarzyk, P. T., & Tremblay, M. S. (2004). Leisure-time physical activity levels among Canadian adolescents, 1981-1998. *Journal of Physical Activity and Health, 1*(2), 154-162.

English, S. (2005). The fattest children in the world. *Times Online*. Retrieved October 10, 2006, from http://www.timesonline.co.uk/article/0,,8126-1922831,00.html

Flegal, K. M., Tabak, C. J., & Ogden, C. L. (2006). Overweight in children: Definitions and interpretation. *Health Education Research, 21*(6), 755-760.

Gard, M., & Wright, J. (2005). *The Obesity epidemic: Science, morality and ideology.* London: Routledge.

Hensrud, D. D., & Klein, S. (2006). Extreme obesity: A new medical crisis in the United States. *Mayo Clinic Proceedings, 81*(10 Suppl), S5-S10.

Hudson, P. (2004, May 30). $60m fight against 'fat lifestyle'. *The Sunday Age*, p. 3.

Jebb, S. A., Rennie, K. L., & Cole, T. J. (2003). Prevalence of overweight and obesity among young people in Great Britain. *Public Health Nutrition, 7*(3), 461-465.

Joint Health Surveys Unit (1999). *Health Survey for England 1998.* London: The Stationary Office.

Lewis, N., Dollman, J., & Dale, M. (2007). Trends in physical activity behaviours and attitudes among South Australian youth between 1985 and 2004. *Journal of Science and Medicine in Sport, 10*(6), 418-427.

Luciano, A., Bressan, F., Bolognani, M., Castellarin, A., & Zoppi, G. (2001). Childhood obesity: Different definition criteria, different prevalence rate. *Minerva Pediatrica, 53*(6),

537-541.

Magarey, A. M., Daniels, L. A., & Boulton, T. J. C. (2001). Prevalence of overweight and obesity in Australian children and adolescents: Reassessment of 1985 and 1995 data against new standard international definitions. *Medical Journal of Australia, 174*(11), 561-564.

Marshall, S. J., Biddle, S. J. H., Gorely, T., Cameron, N., & Murdey, I. (2004). Relationships between media use, body fatness and physical activity in children and youth: A meta-analysis. *International Journal of Obesity, 28*(10), 1238-1246.

Marshall, S. J., Biddle, S. J. H., Sallis, J. F., McKenzie, T. H., & Conway, T. L. (2002). Clustering of sedentary behaviors and physical activity among youth: A cross national study. *Pediatric Exercise Science, 14*(4), 401-417.

O'Dea, J. (2003). Differences in overweight and obesity among Australian schoolchildren of low and middle/high socioeconomic status. *Medical Journal of Australia, 179*(1), 63.

O'Dea, J. A. (2008). Gender, ethnicity, culture and social class influences on childhood obesity among Australian schoolchildren: Implications for treatment, prevention and community education. *Health and Social Care in the Community, 16*(3), 282-290.

Ogden, C. L., Carroll, M. D., Curtin, L. R., McDowell, M. A., Tabak, C. J., & Flegal, K. M. (2006). Prevalence of overweight and obesity in the United States, 1999-2004. *Journal of the American Medical Association, 295*(13), 1549-1555.

Ogden, C. L., Flegal, K. M., Carroll, M. D., & Johnson, C. L. (2002). Prevalence and trends in overweight among US children and adolescents, 1999-2000. *Journal of the American Medical Association, 288*(14), 1728-1732.

Oliver, J. E. (2006). *Fat politics: The real story behind America's obesity epidemic.* Oxford: Oxford University Press.

Ogden, C. L., Flegal, K. M., Carroll, M. D., & Johnson, C. L. (2002). Prevalence and trends in overweight among US children and adolescents, 1999-2000. *Journal of the American Medical Association, 288*(14), 1728-1732.

Parry, S. K. (2008). High school students face state mandated fitness testing. Retrieved January 19 January, 2009, from
http://ww.uniontrib.com/uniontrib/20080412/news_lz1mc12fitnes.html

Powell, S. (2000, May 27-28). One in four Australian children is overweight. Slower, stiffer, heavier – they are the cotton-wool generation'. *Weekend Australian*, 'Review' section, p. 6-8.

Pratt, M., Macera, C. A., & Blanton, C. (1999). Levels of physical activity and inactivity in children and adults in the United States: current evidence and research issues. *Medicine and Science in Sports and Exercise, 31*(11), S526-S533.

Rennie, K. L., & Jebb, S. A. (2005). Prevalence of obesity in Great Britain. *Obesity Reviews, 6*(1), 11-12.

Robotham, J., & Lee, J. (2006, April 22-23). Shocking truth of childhood obesity. *The Sydney Morning Herald*, p. 1.

Schools Health Education Unit (2004). *Trends – Young people and physical activity: Attitudes to and participation in exercise and sport 1987-2003.* Exeter: SHEU.

Stamatakis, E., Primatesta, P., Chinn, S., Rona, R., & Falascheti, E. (2005). Overweight and obesity trends from 1974 to 2003 in English children: What is the role of socioeconomic factors? *Archives of Disease in Childhood, 90*(10), 999-1004.

Wang, Y., & Beydoun, M. A. (2007) The obesity epidemic in the United States–gender, age, socioeconomic, racial/ethnic, and geographic characteristics: A systematic review and meta-regression analysis. *Epidemiologic Reviews, 29*(1), 6-28.

Westerståhl, M., Barnekow-Bergkvist, M., Hedbergand, G., & Jansson, E. (2003). Secular trends in sports: participation and attitudes among adolescents in Sweden from 1974 to 1995. *Acta Paediatrica, 92*(5), 602-609.

CHAPTER TWO

Adolescent Males' Body Image: An Overview of Research on the Influence of Mass Media

Travis A. Ryan, Todd G. Morrison
and Cormac Ó Beaglaoich

B ody image is the "multifaceted psychological experience of embodiment, especially but not exclusively one's physical appearance," comprising "body-related self-perceptions and self-attitudes, including thoughts, beliefs, feelings, and behaviors" (Cash, 2004, p. 1). Typically, researchers focus on two dimensions of body image: evaluation and investment. Body image evaluation refers to how (dis)satisfied people are with their appearance or body and includes associated evaluative beliefs and emotions (Cash, Jakatdar, & Williams, 2004; Hargreaves & Tiggemann, 2006). In contrast, body image investment concerns the "degree of cognitive and behavioral importance" that people assign to their body and appearance (Cash & Pruzinsky, 2002, p. 510).

Historically, social scientists who researched these body image constructs focused predominantly on female populations (Cash, 2007). In particular, attention has been directed to eating disturbances (e.g., Stice, Orjada, & Tristan, 2006; Thompson et al., 2007); the desire to become thinner (e.g., Ahern, Bennett, & Hetherington, 2008; Wiederman & Pryor, 2000); and objectification (e.g., Grippo & Hill, 2008; Harper & Tiggemann, 2008). Until recently, male body image received comparatively little research attention (Cash, 2007; Olivardia, 2007a) and social scientists were slow to study muscularity, focusing instead on body fat and associated constructs (e.g., the drive for thinness) (Cash, 2007; McCabe & Ricciardelli, 2001; Thompson & Cafri, 2007).

The glorification of male bodily attractiveness is not a new phenomenon. A lean, muscular male form was idealized in ancient Greece and Rome, as evident from their literature and artwork (Labre, 2002), and in non-mainstream media since the 1880s (Waugh, 1996). However, it wasn't until the 1980s and 1990s that mainstream media started to celebrate this mesomorphic physique (Labre, 2002). According to Waugh (1996), non-mainstream media's celebration of the muscular physique gradually changed hegemonic media's beliefs surrounding the use of scantly clad men in advertising: once considered homoerotic, current mainstream advertising campaigns embrace aesthetically pleasing images of naked male bodies to sell products[1]. Indeed, research has demonstrated the prevalence of media images of idealistic male bodies (e.g., Frederick, Fessler, & Haselton, 2005; Morrison & Halton, 2009; Soulliere & Blair, 2006).

This ideal, the muscular mesomorphic physique, is characterised by broad shoulders, a muscular stomach, chest and arms, and a narrow waist (Grogan & Richards, 2002; Kimmel & Mahalik, 2004; Labre, 2005; Ridgeway & Tylka, 2005). Kimmel and Mahalik's (2004) Masculine Body Ideal Distress Scale, which measures distress resulting from "failing" to achieve the ideal male body, delineates the constituent elements of this physique. Its 8 items focus on being fat, lacking muscle definition, and having "love handles," a stomach without the requisite "six pack," flabby pectorals, small biceps, and scrawny legs. Although this body is the hegemonic ideal (i.e., the physique that is predominantly idealized by society), the degree to which males adopt it as a personal goal and standard (i.e., internalization [Jones, 2004]) is varied (Ryan & Morrison, in press-b; Ryan & Morrison, 2009).

While researchers investigating male body image have often used samples of children (e.g., Harrison & Bond, 2007; Moriarty & Harrison, 2008) and adults (e.g., McDonagh, Morrison, & McGuire, 2008; Morrison, Morrison, & Hopkins, 2003), adolescent boys have received the most empirical scrutiny[2] (McCabe & Ricciardelli, 2004b). This focus is intuitive because body image is "an important aspect of self-representation and self-evaluation during adolescence" (Jones, 2001, p. 645)—a period of development commonly operationalized as between 10 and 19 years of age (World Health Organization, 2008).

The adolescent years are critical in the development of body image (Levine & Smolak, 2002) as boys experience substantial social, physical, and cognitive changes and evidence heightened investment in their physical appearance (Ata, Ludden, & Lally, 2007; Dittmar et al., 2000). They enter puberty and their shoulders broaden; secondary sexual characteristics develop (e.g., increased genital size and pubic hair); their voices deepen; they grow taller;

and, perhaps most importantly, they acquire an ability to gain muscle mass and become stronger.

Body image may be particularly salient for boys who reach puberty later than their peers as pubertal-induced muscle growth brings boys in closer proximity to the physique exalted by mainstream society (Cafri, van den Berg, & Thompson, 2006). Research findings on the relationship between puberty and boys' body image are mixed (Cafri et al., 2005; McCabe & Ricciardelli, 2006). McCabe and Ricciardelli (2004a) found that, compared to on-time and late-maturing boys, boys who matured early were more satisfied with their bodies and less likely to engage in strategies to increase muscularity or use food supplements. Cross-sectional research has found that pubertal growth was positively associated with body image importance and the use of food supplements (McCabe & Ricciardelli, 2003). However, longitudinal research has found that pubertal growth did not predict tendencies to think about and engage in uncontrollable overeating, exercise dependence, use of food supplements or steroids to lose weight and/or increase muscle, or the pursuit of thinness (McCabe & Ricciardelli, 2006). Cafri et al. (2005) explained the mixed findings regarding puberty and body image by suggesting that pubertal timing rather than growth is critical. Similarly, Ricciardelli and McCabe (2007) stated that compared to their on-time counterparts, early- and late-maturing boys may experience more problems due to the deviancy of their pubertal development.

The body image investment (Ata et al., 2007) and body dissatisfaction (Littleton & Ollendick, 2003) that has been documented among adolescent boys may be attributable to their heightened sensitivity to sociocultural standards of body image and pressures to achieve lean muscularity (Ricciardelli & McCabe, 2007). Smolak, Murnen, and Thompson (2005) argued that unlike childhood, early adolescence is characterized by an expectation to enter puberty and gain muscle mass and, therefore, become "big and strong"—a key component of the idealistic male form. In accordance with this proposition, Kostanski, Fisher, and Gullone (2004) compared male children (M age = 8.4) and adolescents (M age = 14.66) and found that the latter were more dissatisfied with their bodies. Critically, in underweight adolescent boys, dissatisfaction was attributable to being "too thin" whereas, among their overweight counterparts, it was attributable to being "too fat." Thus, deviation from the muscular ideal—in either direction—appears to be perceived as problematic.

Although adolescent boys experience sociocultural pressures to conform to the muscular ideal, and those whose pubertal timing deviates from that of their peers may be at risk for body dissatisfaction (Ricciardelli & McCabe, 2007), a measurement problem permeates male body image research. That is, the magnitude of body dissatisfaction and investment among boys may be underestimated because discussion about the male body is verboten. Indeed, findings have suggested that, on average, boys do not report body image concerns (e.g., Bearman, Presnell, Martinez, & Stice, 2006; Hargreaves & Tiggemann, 2006; Nishina, Ammon, Bellmore, & Graham, 2006; Presnell, Bearman, & Stice, 2004). These findings are likely influenced by a reluctance to admit body image problems due to pressures to conform to masculine norms and/or a desire to avoid distress arising from non-conformity (Hargreaves & Tiggemann, 2006; Pope, Philips, & Olivardia, 2000; Ryan & Morrison, 2009).

Recent qualitative findings (Ryan & Morrison, 2009) support the contention forwarded by Pope et al. (2000) that males' body image problems constitute a "secret crisis." In focus groups and interviews, Irish heterosexual males identified body image as an "effeminate" or "gay" topic and admitted to monitoring their disclosure of body image opinions for fear of appearing gay. Congruent with this point, a focus group of gay males emphasized the social unacceptability of discussing body image concerns, especially for heterosexual males. Discussants reported that such conversation likely would result in reprimands from other men in the form of insults. According to these males, body image concerns exist privately. If so, then studies using pen-and-paper indicators of body image satisfaction/dissatisfaction should be interpreted with caution as they may underestimate the magnitude of negative body image evaluation among males. To investigate this issue, researchers should examine whether responses to male body image questionnaires relate to scores on indices of impression management, which are designed to assess the purposeful manipulation of responses to create a more favorable social image (Paulhus, 1991).

In summary, body image constitutes a critical aspect of boys' sense of identity (e.g., Cafri et al., 2006; Dittmar et al., 2000) and, therefore, demands empirical attention. Despite social pressures to hide body image concerns, it is not uncommon for adolescent males to report being dissatisfied with their physical appearance (e.g., Cohane & Pope, 2001). The next three sections briefly examine whether this age group regards a muscular mesomorphic physique as ideal, both culturally and individually, and illustrate why body image evaluation and investment may be important has for boys' development.

Adolescent Boys' Recognition of Lean Muscularity as Ideal

Research in which boys are asked to particularize the specific features of "optimal" male bodies, has demonstrated awareness that a lean and muscular male body is the hegemonic ideal. Dittmar et al. (2000) conducted focus groups and interviews with 28 adolescent boys from England (age range = 12-

16 years) about the qualities of an "ideal man." The boys' conversations reflected the ideal male body promoted by media, with muscular, strong, powerful, athletic, and hard-bodied emerging as the most commonly used body image related adjectives. In a follow-up quantitative study, 79 adolescent boys were asked to choose adjectives that described someone they would like to be like, or a pop star or a sports person. A well-developed and athletic male body emerged as ideal.

McCabe, Ricciardelli, and Ridge's (2006) qualitative investigation with 40 Australian adolescent boys (M age = 15.98, SD = 0.66) reflected a similar understanding of the constituent elements of the ideal male form. Results revealed that interviewees dissatisfied with their bodies typically identified increased muscle mass and/or weight loss as personal goals. The authors also reported that strength and size, key features of the muscular ideal, emerged as major themes in boys' body image discussions

Similarly, Ricciardelli et al.'s (2007) semi-structured interviews with 24 Indigenous Fijian (M age = 16.27, SD = 1.88), 24 Indo-Fijian (M age = 15.67, SD = 1.52), and 24 Tongan (M age = 16.63, SD = 1.81) boys indicated a perceived ideal male body that was lean and muscular. While most boys discussed their body image evaluation and investment in broad terms (e.g., body strength and size), other boys' conversations were more detailed revealing, for example, a desire to have more muscular biceps and abdominal muscles.

Adolescent Boys' Body Image Evaluation

Studies (e.g., Bearman et al., 2006; Nishina, et al., 2006; Paxton, Neumark-Sztainer, Hannan, & Eisenberg, 2006; Presnell et al., 2004) have documented that boys' scores on measures of body dissatisfaction approximated scale midpoints (suggesting neutrality). Further, self-reports of body satisfaction were stable across time and did not differ as a function of ethnicity (i.e., Caucasian, African American, Latino, Asian, and Multiethnic [Nishina et al., 2006]).

However, studies also revealed that a notable minority of adolescent participants reported body dissatisfaction (Bearman et al., 2006; Presnell et al., 2004). For example, Bearman and associates (2006) conducted a prospective study of 181 boys (M age = 13.57) from the United States by distributing a questionnaire pack thrice, 12 months apart annually. They found that, each year, a minority of boys (i.e., 23% [time 1]; 19% [time 2] and 16% [time 3]) reported experiencing moderate or extreme body dissatisfaction). In this study, the body mass indices (BMI) of satisfied and dissatisfied males were comparable (Ms = 21.98 and 21.72, respectively). However, unlike their female counterparts, boys' body image dissatisfaction did not follow a linear association with BMI. Instead, at Time 1 and in accord with other studies (Falkner et al., 2001; Jones & Crawford, 2006; Kostanski et al., 2004), a U-shaped model was deemed most appropriate. While normal weight participants reported low body dissatisfaction, underweight (e.g., non-muscular) or overweight (e.g., fat) adolescent boys experienced greater body dissatisfaction. These findings suggest that body dissatisfaction is constituted by negative assessments of body fat and/or muscularity and that both components need to be examined.

Psychological correlates of negative body image evaluation have been well documented. Studies have reported an inverse relationship between self-esteem and body dissatisfaction among boys (e.g., Davison & McCabe, 2006; Polce-Lynch, Myers, Kilmartin, Forssmann-Falck, & Kliewer, 1998; Seidah & Bouffard, 2007). Other studies have revealed that, among this age group, body dissatisfaction has been positively related to negative affect (Chen & Jackson, 2009), depressive symptoms (Chaiton et al., 2009), suicidal ideation and suicide attempts (Crow, Eisenberg, Story, & Neumark-Sztainer, 2008) and dieting, unhealthy weight control practices, and binge eating (Neumark-Sztainer, Paxton, Hannan, Haines, & Story, 2006).

Adolescent Boys' Body Image Investment

As adolescent boys typically desire enhanced muscle mass and leanness, a combination of body investment strategies is often used (e.g., dieting and weight lifting; Smolak et al., 2005). Researchers have documented the different types of behaviors adolescent boys employ to change their bodies and the frequency with which these behaviours are used (e.g., Crow, Eisenberg, Story, & Neumark-Sztainer, 2006; Field et al., 2005; Irving, Wall, Neumark-Sztainer, & Story, 2002; Jones & Crawford, 2005; Kindlundh, Hagekull, Isacson, & Nyberg, 2001). For example, research has shown that minorities of adolescent boys report consuming products aimed at increasing muscle mass and/or reducing body fat (e.g., Field et al., 2005; Irving et al., 2002; Kindlundh et al., 2001). Field et al. (2005) assessed the use of products to improve appearance or strength among a sample of 4,237 adolescent sons of nurses[3] (M age = 15.0, SD = 1.6) from the United States and found, for example, that 10.2% of boys reported some use of protein powder or shakes in the past year.

Moving outside the behavioral realm, Jones and Crawford (2005) investigated body image investment attitudes in a sample of sixty-nine 8th-grade (M age = 13.6) and fifty-nine 11th-grade (M age = 16.6) adolescent males from the USA. Investment indices examined were drive for muscularity attitudes (i.e., the desire to attain an idealized muscular physique [Morrison & Harriman, 2005]) (range = 4 – 20), drive for thinness attitudes (range = 6 – 36), appearance conversations with friends (range = 5 – 25), and muscle-building conversations with friends (range = 5 – 25). While descriptive statistics suggested that, on average, participants invested little in their body image (e.g., drive for thinness [M = 8.91, SD = 4.40] and appearance conversations [M = 7.57, SD = 3.15]), indices of investment in muscularity were higher (i.e., drive for muscularity attitudes [M = 11.32, SD = 3.89] and engagement in muscle-building conversations [M = 11.17, SD = 5.05]).

The correlates of body image investment, which is defined in multifarious ways such as dieting and steroid use, have been scrutinized. These include: greater suicidal ideation (Kim, 2009; Kim & Kim, 2009); greater number of past suicide attempts (Irving et al., 2002); low self-esteem (Crow et al., 2006; Davison & McCabe, 2006; Irving et al., 2002); body dissatisfaction (Crow et al., 2006); depressive symptoms (Crow et al., 2006; Irving et al., 2002); poor other-sex relations (Davison & McCabe, 2006); poor attitudes toward, and low concern about, health and nutrition (Irving et al., 2002); less knowledge about healthy nutrition (Irving et al., 2002); and more recent cigarette, alcohol, marijuana, and other drug (e.g., cocaine) use (Irving et al., 2002). Also, adolescent males using steroids to gain muscle mass have been shown to report binge eating and being told by a physician they have an eating disorder more often (Irving et al., 2002).

Summary

Research has suggested that modest proportions of adolescent boys report being dissatisfied with and invested in their physical appearance. Gender role norms prohibiting body image conversation (Ryan & Morrison, 2009) may attenuate self-reports of body image concerns. That is, given body image's feminine or gay connotations, adolescent boys may dismiss the subject as irrelevant to avoid distress arising from non-conformity to masculine norms. Despite the taboo nature of male body image, minorities of boys have admitted negative evaluation and substantial investment in their physique. Importantly, self-reports of evaluation and investment have correlated with key indicants of and psychological well-being such as dieting and self-esteem.

Sociocultural Theory

The aforementioned studies do not address a key question: why do some adolescent boys evidence greater levels of dissatisfaction and investment than other boys?[4] To account for such inter-individual variations, researchers have employed diverse theoretical frameworks; the most commonly used being sociocultural theory.

Sociocultural theory[5] proposes that Western society, consisting of mass media, peer groups, friends, and family, sets unrealistic standards for physical attractiveness, which are unattainable by most people. It is important to note that, despite sociocultural agents disseminating the message that the muscular mesomorphic body is attainable via exercise, diet, supplements, and a host of other advertised products, it remains elusive and, therefore, results in dissatisfaction among males who want (and invariably fail) to achieve this physique (Dittmar, 2005; Thompson, Heinberg, Altabe, & Tantleff-Dunn, 1999). Researchers testing this theory initially focused on women and the sociocultural pressures they experience to become thin (Thompson et al., 1999). However, sociocultural theorists are increasingly focusing on men, a trend whose importance is underscored by society's wide dissemination of messages about muscularity and masculinity (Cash, 2007) and increasing sociocultural pressures on men to achieve a muscular body (Leit, Pope, & Gray, 2000; Thompson & Cafri, 2007).

Researchers have investigated relations between adolescent males' body image and non-media sociocultural agents (e.g., peers [e.g., Jones, 2001] and family [e.g., Meesters, Muris, Hoefnagels, & van Gemert, 2007]). However, given this chapter's focus, the subsequent discussion will be limited to research on media. When applied to males, Morrison, Kalin, and Morrison (2004b) contended that the core tenets of Sociocultural Theory are: a) mass media promote a muscular body ideal; b) the promotion of this ideal transmits the message that what is muscular is attractive, desirable, and masculine; and c) internalization of this message has implications for body image evaluation and investment.

In recent years, internalization has emerged as critical in understanding males' body image. Research has shown that compared to simple awareness of media standards of male physical attractiveness, internalization accounts for greater variance in body image indices (e.g., Smolak, Levine, & Thompson, 2001; Warren, 2008). Further, when persons internalize media messages, the influence of idealistic imagery on their sense of self is heightened as they are more likely to compare themselves to unrealistic body ideals (Jones, Vigfusdottir, & Lee, 2004). Indeed, Ryan and Morrison (in press-b) proposed that it is only when media messages are internalized that they significantly affect males' body image. Media images are theorized to harm adolescents affected by body image problems and disordered eating because they seek out media with idealistic imagery, internalize their messages, and use them as information resources in attempts to improve their body image (Littleton & Ollendick, 2003). Research pertaining to each tenet of Sociocultural Theory, as articulated by Morrison et al. (2004b), will be reviewed briefly.

Tenet A: Media & the Muscular Ideal

Studies have demonstrated that magazines targeting a male readership are rife with images of idealistic male bodies, articles about muscularity and leanness, and advertisements for products purported to increase the aesthetic value of the male body (e.g., Alexander, 2003; Frederick et al., 2005; Labre, 2005; Law & Labre, 2002). To illustrate, after content analyzing a purposeful sample of 15 Men's Health and 15 Men's Fitness magazines published between 1999 and 2003, Labre (2005) found that 96% of male images were characterised by low body fat levels and 97% were characterised as muscular. Images of non-muscular or fat men were presented negatively, often as stimuli to advertise weight loss and/or muscle building supplements.

The idealistic male physique promoted by magazines has been demonstrated in other cultural artifacts. Pope, Olivardia, Gruber, and Borowiecki (1999) noted that male action figures have become progressively more muscular over time, with the authors highlighting that if the recent incarnation of one model, GI Joe Extreme, were transformed to the height of the average man, his biceps would be larger than any bodybuilder in history. In an extension of Pope et al.'s work, Baghurst, Hollander, Nardella, and Haff (2006) compared the neck, chest, arm, waist, thigh, and calf circumferences of Batman, GI Joe, The Hulk, Spiderman, and Superman over a 25-year period after scaling each figure to a height of 70 inches. Compared to the originals, the latest versions of these toys had necks, chests, arms, thighs, and calves that were (in order): 52.5%, 55.4%, 63.7%, 60%, and 70.4% larger.

Tenet B: Muscularity Is Good

Soulliere and Blair (2006) analyzed for content 118 episodes of World Wrestling Entertainment (WWE) programming, which is particularly popular among male adolescent audiences (Labre, 2002), between August 2001 and August 2002. They found that the ideal male body was big, lean, muscular, and strong and most of the wrestlers were in excess of 6 feet in height, weighing approximately 240 to 280 pounds. Their muscular physiques were routinely construed as beneficial and desirable with commentators explicitly idealizing wrestlers' physiques (e.g., "[He] probably has 8 or 9 percent body fat. That's impressive").

In a recent study, Morrison and Halton (2009) analyzed for content how muscular versus non-muscular characters were depicted in top-grossing action films, a genre that is popular among adolescent males. Focusing on a random selection of titles released between 1980 and 2006, the authors reviewed 42 motion pictures. Of the 159 characters coded, most were muscular (76%) and had low body fat (65.4%). The authors also found that those categorized as muscular evidenced greater levels of physical aggression, and were more likely to be objectified, engage in sexual relations, and experience a favorable outcome at the climax of the film.

Tenet C: Internalization of Media Ideal & Body Image

Two primary categories of research have attempted to examine whether internalization of the muscular ideal presented in mass media has implications for consumers' body image evaluation and investment. These categories are: associative (i.e., correlational) and experimental. The former is advantageous because it permits more naturalistic assessments of media exposure; however, its chief disadvantage is that it does not allow causal inferences to be made. The latter addresses this limitation but at the cost of being somewhat artificial; that is, the viewer's "relationship" with media is removed from its "natural" context (traditionally, the home) and function (typically, the provision of entertainment). Representative examples of associative and experimental studies are detailed below.

Associative Research

Jones (2004) examined the utility of variables (e.g., internalization) to predict changes in body dissatisfaction in 158 early adolescents (88 girls, 70 boys, Time 1 M age = 12.5) and 146 mid-adolescents (77 girls, 69 boys, Time 1 M age = 15.5) from the USA. Participants completed questionnaires one year apart, one of which was a modified, muscularity-focused 5-item version of the Internalization subscale of the Sociocultural Attitudes Towards Appearance Questionnaire$_6$ (SATAQ-I; Heinberg, Thompson, & Stormer, 1995). Two items appearing in the original SATAQ-I and measuring social comparison to persons in the media (e.g., "I tend to compare my body to people in magazines and on TV") were dropped to form a "conceptually consistent scale" (p. 827).

Multiple regression analysis revealed that Time 1 body dissatisfaction and internalization scores emerged as statistically significant predictors of boys' body dissatisfaction change over the one-year period. That is, boys who were more body dissatisfied and evidenced greater internalization of sociocultural standards of appearance at Time 1 were more likely to experience heightened body dissatisfaction at Time 2. Although a weaker predictor than Time 1 body dissatisfaction, Jones emphasized the importance of internalization of societal standards of appearance and hypothesized that it marks adolescent boys' entry into appearance culture.

Halliwell and Harvey (2006) examined the relationship between internalization and dieting and food preoccupation among 257 male adolescents aged 11 to 16 years from England. The original 8-item

Internalization subscale of the SATAQ-I was employed (i.e., wording was not modified for adolescent boys but, rather, focused on thinness). Internalization was associated positively with appearance comparison to friends, dieting and food preoccupation, and perceived body-related pressures from sociocultural agents (i.e., mother, father, siblings, friends, and media), and negatively with body satisfaction. Structural equation modeling (SEM) revealed that body dissatisfaction was predicted by internalization, which, in turn, was predicted by perceived pressures from sociocultural agents and appearance comparison to friends. Also, the association between internalization and dieting and food preoccupation was mediated by body dissatisfaction. These findings suggested that boys who perceived body image related pressures from people and the media, and compared their appearance to that of their friends, were more likely to internalize sociocultural standards of appearance. Such internalization may have led to feelings of body dissatisfaction and, ultimately, dieting and being preoccupied with food.

Knauss, Paxton, and Alsaker (2007) employed a modified version of the SATAQ-I (Heinberg et al., 1995; Smolak et al., 2001), distributing it to a sample of 1,610 adolescents (819 boys, 791 girls, M age = 14.9, SD = 0.73) from Switzerland. The modifications were akin to those employed by previous researchers (Smolak et al., 2001) in an effort to make the scale more relevant to males (i.e., "muscular" replaced "thin" throughout). Two items identified as repetitive in a pilot study (i.e., "I would like to look like the models in the magazines" and "I wish I looked like a swimsuit model") were dropped and replaced by "I wish I looked like a model." Findings revealed that internalization predicted body dissatisfaction and was positively related to BMI and perceived pressures to meet societal standards of appearance.

Other studies of adolescent males have employed different permutations of the SATAQ-I (e.g., Jones, Bain, & King, 2008; Knauss, Paxton, & Alsaker, 2008; Knauss, Paxton, & Alsaker, 2009; McVey, Tweed, & Blackmore, 2005; Smolak & Levine, 2001; Smolak et al., 2001; Tiggemann, 2005; Wilksch, Tiggemann, & Wade, 2006) and have found that levels of internalization have correlated positively with: appearance magazine exposure (Jones et al., 2004); appearance conversations with friends (Jones et al., 2004); appearance criticism from peers (Jones et al., 2004); viewing specific categories of television programs such as soap operas (Tiggemann, 2005); watching television for the purposes of social learning or easing negative affect (Tiggemann, 2005); muscularity concern (Smolak et al., 2001); weight and eating concerns (Knauss et al., 2009); drive for thinness (Jones et al., 2008; Knauss et al., 2009); body surveillance and body shame (Knauss et al., 2008); self-reported engagement in muscle-building behaviors (McVey et al., 2005; Smolak et al., 2001); and body dissatisfaction (Jones et al., 2004; Jones et al., 2008; Knauss et al., 2008; Knauss et al., 2009). As well, levels of internalization have been found to be inversely associated with body esteem (Smolak et al., 2001) and watching educational television programs (Tiggemann, 2005).

Experimental Research

Researchers have seldom conducted experiments on the effects of idealistic media imagery on male adolescents' body image (for notable exceptions, see Farquhar & Wasylkiw, 2007; Hargreaves & Tiggemann, 2004; Humphreys & Paxton, 2004). Of these, only Humphreys and Paxton focused on internalization when investigating the impact of idealized images of male bodies on the body satisfaction, anxiety, and depression of 100 adolescent boys from Australia (M age = 15.6, SD = 0.6). There were two conditions: experimental (i.e., exposure to 10 images of ideal male bodies) and control (i.e., exposure to images without bodies). One week prior to participating in the experiment, the boys completed a questionnaire packet (including the SATAQ-I; Smolak et al., 2001) and were randomly assigned to a condition. During the experiment, participants first completed Visual Analogue Scales (VASs) measuring depression, anxiety, body satisfaction, the desire to change their body shape, and the desire to have a toned body. Then, boys viewed images with or without ideal male bodies. To ensure attendance to the images presented, participants were asked questions about each image before proceeding to the next one. After presentation of all images, the VASs were completed again.

There were no differences between the groups on mood, the desire to have a toned body, or the desire to change one's body shape. Further, contrary to expectation, compared to boys in the control condition, participants who viewed the idealistic imagery reported higher body satisfaction. However, some boys were negatively affected by the images of muscular bodies (i.e., 22% of participants liked their body shape less, 24% wanted to change their body shape more, and 28% desired a more toned body) and internalization scores helped explain these self-reports. That is, internalization predicted decrements in reported liking of one's body shape and increments in desires to have a more toned body and change one's physique.

Key Limitation

The research conducted to date has improved understanding of the relationship between the media adolescent boys (potentially) consume and their corporeal attitudes and behavioral practices. Internalization of the ideal male body also has been identified as an important psychological mechanism. However, we contend that a measurement problem—applicable to both experimental and non-experimental work—permeates the research literature and needs to be addressed to attain a more accurate understanding of the role internalization plays in boys' body image.

The Sociocultural Attitudes Towards Appearance Questionnaire (SATAQ: Heinberg et al., 1995) was originally developed to "assess women's recognition and acceptance of societally sanctioned standards of appearance" (p. 81). Thus, rote application of its Internalization subscale (SATAQ-I) to examine males' internalization of sociocultural influences constitutes poor psychometric practice. Additionally, the SATAQ-I possesses other limitations that warrant mention. First, ambiguous terms are used (e.g., "appearance" may refer to non-body constructs such as clothing) as are double-barreled statements (e.g., one item asks whether magazines and television are social comparison stimuli—see, for example, Knauss et al., 2009). With respect to the latter issue, how does a participant respond if he compares his body to people on television only? Second, this type of item may not measure internalization of media standards (i.e., a male may compare his body to the physiques of males appearing on television and reject, as a personal goal and standard, the body depicted by this medium). Third, some permutations of the SATAQ-I include the word "bodybuilder," which is surprising given research suggesting that, compared to muscular images, hypermuscularity is considered to be less desirable/attractive, further removed from the male ideal, and less attainable (Arbour & Martin Ginis, 2006). Fourth, some of the items conflate internalization and social comparison (e.g., "I often read magazines like Muscle & Fitness, Sports Illustrated, and GQ, and compare my appearance to the male models in the magazine"—see, for example, Smolak et al., 2001). This imprecision is problematic as internalization and social comparison reflect conceptually distinct constructs: the former characterizes adoption of media ideals as a personal goal whereas the latter denotes one mechanism through which individuals make determinations about their appearance. Fifth, and most importantly, the actual content of modified versions of the SATAQ-I (e.g., Jones, 2004; Smolak et al., 2001) have not been adequately informed by male body literature. We believe that changing words like "thin" to "muscular" does not comprehensively sample the domain of content relevant to males and their physical appearance.

Critically, no one measure of internalization is employed consistently, with researchers making alterations to items on an ad hoc basis. Thus, the accumulation of a coherent body of knowledge is compromised. For example, while Tiggemann (2005) employed 3 items "loosely based" on the SATAQ-I (Heinberg et al., 1995), which were modified to ensure gender non-specificity (e.g., "people" replaced "women"), Jones and colleagues (2008) used 5 items from the SATAQ-I that were changed to reflect the importance of muscularity to male body image.

Given these psychometric concerns, we developed a new measure of internalization of media-disseminated body image standards (Internalization of Male Body Image-related Media Messages [M-INT]—see Appendix A), which adhered to best practices in scale development. A comprehensive account of the measure's development (i.e., item construction, removal, and refinement), dimensionality, and construct validity is provided in Ryan and Morrison (in press-b).[7] Unlike the various forms of the SATAQ-I used by researchers, the M-INT does not conflate different sociocultural influences; it is specific to media. In the next section, we focus on the psychometric properties of the M-INT, when distributed to samples of late adolescent boys (ages 18-19). Particular attention is paid to scale score reliability and convergent validity.

Study 1

Fifty-nine boys aged 18 (45.8%) or 19 years old (54.2%) completed the 9-item M-INT (Ryan & Morrison, in press-b). Most were Irish (76.3%), followed by English (8.5%), American (3.4%), and Northern Irish (3.4%). Similarly, a majority (81.4%) lived in Ireland, followed by Northern Ireland (5.1%), England (5.1%) and America (5.1%). Most boys self-identified as heterosexual (69.5%), with 15.3% identifying as gay, 11.9% as bisexual, and 1.7% as "other" (one boy skipped this item). In relation to employment status, participants mostly identified as undergraduate college students (64.4%) or secondary school students (20.3%). In this sample, the M-INT's alpha coefficient was excellent (α = .93, 95% CI: .90 – .95).

To assess the convergent validity of the M-INT, several hypotheses were tested. Means, standard deviations, and alpha coefficients for all validation measures are provided in Table 1.

Table 1

Study 1 Validation Measures

Measure	Alpha (95% CI)	Mean (SD)	Possible Range	Attained Range
DMAQ	.83 (.75-.89)	26.29 (6.05)	8-40	11-37
MB	.81 (.72-.88)	13.38 (5.46)	7-35	7-29
RSE	.86 (.80-.91)	37.67 (6.89)	10-50	21-49
SDS-17	.74 (.63-.84)	50.54 (7.57)	16-80	37-70

Note: DMAQ = Drive for Muscularity Attitudes Questionnaire (8 items: Morrison et al., 2004b); MB = Muscle-Oriented Behavior subscale (7 items: McCreary & Sasse, 2000); RSE = Rosenberg Self-Esteem Scale (10 items: Rosenberg, 1965); SDS-17 = Social Desirability Scale (16 items: Stöber, 2001)

Hypothesis 1

Previous research has found a positive association between drive for muscularity attitudes and media exposure (e.g., Morrison et al., 2003). Therefore, it seemed reasonable to posit that scores on the M-INT would correlate positively with scores on the Drive for Muscularity Attitudes Questionnaire (DMAQ; Morrison, Morrison, Hopkins, & Rowan, 2004c). This hypothesis was confirmed: M-INT and DMAQ, $r(49) = .73$, $p < .001$. Thus, adolescent boys who internalized the media messages disseminated about the ideal male body also evidenced stronger body image investment, as measured by the drive for muscularity.

Hypothesis 2

Morrison and Morrison (2006) found that male participants' self-reported engagement in muscle-building activities correlated positively with their exposure to media containing idealistic representations of the male body (i.e., fitness magazines). Based on this finding, it was predicted that scores on the Muscularity Behavior (MB) subscale of the Drive for Muscularity Scale (McCreary & Sasse, 2000) would be positively associated with scores on the M-INT. This prediction was confirmed: M-INT and MB, $r(50) = .44$, $p < .002$. Therefore, individuals who reported greater internalization of media-disseminated ideals also were more likely to report engaging in behaviors designed to build muscle mass.

Hypothesis 3

Research suggests that men's internalization of media messages regarding the idealistic male form is inversely associated with their level of self-esteem (e.g., Cahill & Mussap, 2007). Thus, it was hypothesized that scores on the M-INT would correlate negatively with scores on the Rosenberg Self-Esteem Scale (Rosenberg, 1965). This prediction was supported: M-INT and RSE, $r(53) = -.39$, $p < .004$.

Hypothesis 4

It has been suggested that gay men's elevated risk for eating disorders and body dissatisfaction (e.g., Morrison, Morrison, & Sager, 2004a) may be attributed, in part, to the emphasis placed by gay culture on physical attractiveness (e.g., Williamson, 1999). Therefore, it was hypothesized that participants who self-identified as gay or bisexual would obtain higher scores on the M-INT in comparison to heterosexual participants.[8] An independent samples t-test supported this prediction: M-INTGAY OR BISEXUAL = 27.38 (SD = 9.15) versus M-INTSTRAIGHT = 22.31 (SD = 7.93), t (55) = 2.08, p < .05, d = .59.

Finally, a correlation was computed between scores on the M-INT and social desirability bias. The result was not statistically significant, r(49) = -.27, p = ns.

Study 2

Participants included 90 late-adolescent males aged 18 (58.9%) or 19 (41.1%) years old, the majority of whom were Irish (83.3%), followed by Scottish (7.8%), and Northern Irish (5.6%). (Three boys self-identified as Welsh, Argentine, and Asian, respectively.) Ireland represented the country of residence for 86.7% of the boys. Most boys self-identified as heterosexual (85.5%), with smaller proportions self-identifying as bisexual (6.7%), gay (5.6%) or "other" (2.2%). Most participants were undergraduate college students (71.1%), followed by secondary school students (15.6%), and employed persons (10.0 %). The alpha coefficient for the M-INT coefficient was very good (α = .85, 95% CI: .80 - .90).

To assess the convergent validity of the M-INT, the following hypothesis was tested.

Hypothesis 1

Muscle dysmorphia (MD) is a condition characterized by a person's pathological preoccupation and obsession with the belief that his or her body is insufficiently lean and muscular and consequent clinically significant distress or impairment in social, occupational, and/or other vital areas of functioning (Olivardia, 2001, 2007b). Media are identified as a probable etiological factor in the development of MD (e.g., Grieve, 2007; Grieve & Helmick, 2008; Olivardia, 2007b). Thus, it was predicted that scores on the M-INT would correlate positively with scores on a measure of MD symptoms. The latter variable was assessed using the revised, 6-item version (see Ryan & Morrison, in press-a) of the Muscle Appearance Satisfaction Scale (MASS;

Mayville, Williamson, White, Netemeyer, & Drab, 2002): M = 11.19 (SD = 4.25), α = .79 (95% CI = .75-.82). This hypothesis was supported: M-INT and MASS-6, r(69) = .26, p < .05. Thus, male adolescents evidencing greater levels of internalization also reported greater symptomatology characteristic of muscle dysmorphia.

The authors also tested the relationship between scores on the M-INT and social desirability bias, as measured by the Social Desirability Scale-17 (SDS-17; Stöber, 2001): M = 52.86 (SD = 7.58), α = .77 (95% CI = .68-.84). As noted in Study 1, a statistically non-significant association was observed, r(67) = -.16, p = ns.

General Discussion

Our review suggests that adolescent boys' body image is a complex, multi-faceted construct whose myriad psychological correlates underscore its importance. When examining this population's body image, most researchers have adopted the sociocultural paradigm, with many investigating the role of mass media, and, more recently, highlighting the importance of internalization of the ideal male body. However, research efforts have been handicapped by their inclusion of different forms of the SATAQ-I (Heinberg et al., 1995), all of which share certain psychometric limitations. As recommended by DeVellis (2003), future work should "strive for an isomorphism between the theoretical constructs in which [researchers] have an interest and the methods of measurement they use to operationalize them" (p. 12).

Our research indicated that late adolescent boys, who evidenced greater internalization of the idealistic body standards promulgated by mass media, as measured by the M-INT, reported lower levels of self-esteem, and a stronger drive for muscularity (measured both attitudinally and behaviorally). We also found that males self-identifying as gay or bisexual evidenced greater levels of internalization in comparison to heterosexual respondents. An additional study suggested that adolescent boys' level of internalization was positively associated with muscle dysmorphic symptomatology such as feeling addicted to weightlifting, and compulsively checking one's muscularity. These strands of evidence attest to the convergent validity of the M-INT. As well, alpha coefficients for the M-INT ranged from very good to excellent, with 95% confidence intervals suggesting that alpha values less than .80 were unlikely. Based on these findings, we recommend that researchers wishing to examine adolescent boys' internalization of media standards of the muscular mesomorphic ideal use the M-INT.[9]

As validation is an incremental process (Morrison & Morrison, 2006), further work is needed. The current research findings pertained to male adolescents aged 18 or 19 years, who volunteered to participate in a lengthy survey examining body image. Thus, different populations of adolescent males (e.g., early, mid, and late) should be targeted, and the M-INT should be subjected to exploratory and confirmatory factor analysis, test-retest reliability, and assessments of divergent validity.

Outside the realm of psychometrics, the findings from our study have clinical implications. Specifically, we documented positive relationships between scores on the M-INT and scores on a measure of symptoms of muscle dysmorphia (Ryan & Morrison, under review). Historically conceptualized as "reverse anorexia" (Pope, Katz, & Hudson, 1993), MD may lead to constant, involuntary thinking and anxiety about physical appearance, cognitive distortions (e.g., perceiving oneself as small and weak despite being large and muscular), general distractibility (e.g., not being able to concentrate at work), excessive exercise and weight lifting, extremely strict dieting, social avoidance, interpersonal relationship problems, the use of anabolic steroids, and muscle checking (Olivardia, 2007b). Research has suggested that, on average, the onset of symptoms begins in late adolescence (M = 19.4; Olivardia, Pope, & Hudson, 2000) and according to Grieve (2007), internalization may be one of the most important factors contributing to the onset of muscle dysmorphia.

Longitudinal studies investigating the magnitude of associations between M-INT and MASS scores may increase understanding of both the development of symptoms and the role, if any, played by internalization of media-promoted body ideals. Further, given uncertainty regarding which etiological factors are most predictive of muscle dysmorphia (Olivardia, 2007b) and recommendations to examine non-media etiological factors (Grieve, 2007; Olivardia, 2007b), it may be useful to gauge the ability of scores on the M-INT versus other variables to predict symptoms of muscle dysmorphia.

If internalization of media messages regarding idealistic male embodiment emerges as important, this will inform prevention and treatment techniques. According to Olivardia (2007b), treatment should commence with "psychoeducation about realistic body image ideals, proper nutrition, the dangers of steroids, and a critical analysis of media images" (p. 135). As males scoring higher on the M-INT are more susceptible to media images, they may be more likely to have unrealistic body image ideals. Similarly, such males may be more vulnerable to media messages promoting "fad diets" and/or the use of steroids. Therefore, M-INT scores may help identify males who should be targeted for psychoeducational programming.

Olivardia (2007b) also identified cognitive behavioral therapy as potentially beneficial given the problematic thoughts and actions of males with muscle dysmorphia. If internalization proves pertinent, a patient may be encouraged to change his cognitions surrounding media-disseminated ideal bodies (e.g., a boy may be helped to adopt a more realistic body image target and accurately perceive the discrepancy [if any] between that body type and his own). Similarly, a patient's behavior in relation to media should be addressed. For example, it may be advantageous to suggest that the patient reduces his exposure to idealistic media (e.g., fitness magazines).

Given aforementioned relations of M-INT scores to body image and self-esteem, similar interventions (e.g., media literacy campaigns) may help improve adolescent males' body satisfaction and self-esteem by reducing their internalization of unrealistic body image ideals (Richardson, Paxton, & Thomson, 2009; Wilksch et al., 2006). However, the ability of psychoeducational programs to decrease adolescent boys' internalization of media standards of male embodiment is unclear, with studies reporting mixed findings (e.g., McVey, Tweed, & Blackmore, 2007; Richardson et al., 2009; Wilksch et al., 2006; Wilksch, & Wade, 2009). For example, Richardson and colleagues (2009) investigated the efficacy of a body image and self-esteem program for adolescents widely disseminated in schools (i.e., BodyThink). Participants were 277 Australian students (M age = 12.67 years, SD = 5.58 months) and males completed a 14-item modified version of the SATAQ-1 (Smolak et al., 2001). Following the BodyThink program, boys in the intervention group (n = 85) reported improved media literacy (e.g., knowledge about digital manipulation of images) and body satisfaction (i.e., a general measure of, for example, weight, appearance, and body) compared to males in the control group (n = 65). However, no differences in scores on body dissatisfaction (a measure specific to body parts [e.g., biceps, shoulders, and chest]) or its risk factors (e.g., internalization) emerged across conditions. Additional research is needed to determine the robustness of these findings.

Future experimental research should explore the ability of boys' scores on the M-INT to moderate/mediate the effects of media on body image variables. For example, a researcher might randomly expose adolescent participants to experimental primes (i.e., images of ideal male bodies) or control primes (e.g., images of landscapes). Then, he or she might ask participants to complete state measures of body image evaluation and the M-INT while providing them with an opportunity to consume candy. In such a scenario, internalization may strengthen (or weaken) the consequences of exposure to idealistic media images (i.e., scores on the M-INT would serve as a moderator).

Conclusion

Due to psychometric weaknesses associated with measures commonly used in body image research with adolescent boys, we believe that scientists' ability to determine the pertinence of media vis-à-vis boys' body image evaluation and investment has been compromised. We highlight internalization of the muscular ideal disseminated by media as key to enhancing knowledge of males' physical appearance attitudes and behaviors. Limitations central to the study of internalization have been outlined in this chapter, and we have offered a new questionnaire, the M-INT, which was developed in accordance with stringent psychometric practice, and possesses good scale score reliability and validity. Lastly, we believe that the M-INT will prove beneficial to researchers examining the relationship between media and adolescent males' body image.

Appendix A

Internalization of Male Body Image-Related Media Messages (M-INT)

1. When I see male actors on television without their shirts, I feel that I should do more sit-ups.

2. When I see men on the covers of fitness magazines, I feel that I should get in better shape.

3. I feel that I should exercise more when I see male models in underwear advertisements.

4. Seeing male porn stars with muscular bodies makes me feel that I should work out more.

5. When I see the buttocks of male models in advertisements, I feel I should have more muscular buttocks.

6. I want an upper body like that of men advertising cosmetic surgery procedures.

7. I want an upper body like professional athletes who take their jerseys off after sporting events.

8. I want my chest to be as muscular as the chests of men appearing in fitness magazines.

9. When I see male professional athletes, I feel that I should exercise more to increase the muscularity of my body.

Notes

1. Waugh (1996) noted a paucity of documentation on why mainstream media embraced the naked idealistic male form that was once prohibited given its homoerotic connotations. Given this omission, Waugh's discussion is

restricted to relevant context (e.g., technological advances in the production and popular dissemination of media imagery) and artifacts (e.g., early 20th-century postcards that feature topless muscular and lean men).

2. Smolak (2004) noted that most research on the body image of minors involves participants who are white and American, British, or Australian.

3. However, as the boys' mothers were all nurses and, presumably, may have been more aware of the dangers associated with consumption of such products, these findings may underestimate the use of substances to enhance musculature.

4. As the traditional male role in Western culture demands adherence to particular standards and expectations (Pleck, 1995), most boys likely experience similar pressures to conform to masculine norms.

5. For a more extensive overview of sociocultural theory, please refer to Thompson et al. (1999).

6. While non-specific to media influence, the majority of items in the Sociocultural Attitudes Towards Appearance Questionnaire (SATAQ; Heinberg et al., 1995) and its later revisions (i.e., SATAQ-R; Cusumano & Thompson, 1997; SATAQ-3; Thompson, van den Berg, Roehrig, Guarda, & Heinberg, 2004) focus on the role of media and, therefore, research using modified versions of these questionnaires is included to articulate media influence on adolescent boys.

7. The internalization measure developed by Ryan and Morrison (M-INT; in press-b) is a subscale of the Media Influences on Male Body Image Scale (MMBI). Given the chapter's focus on internalization, only information relating to the M-INT is detailed. Additionally, it should be noted that all data were collected in accordance with ethical standards for research using human participants. More extensive information about the recruitment of participants, attainment of informed consent, and debriefing was provided by Ryan and Morrison (in press-b).

8. There is a lack of empirical data examining the ways in which the body is represented in media targeting gay youth. However, inspection of one youth-oriented publication (XY magazine), which has an average readership age of 18, suggested an emphasis on muscularity and leanness characteristic of "older" gay culture.

9. Although pornography is consumed by adolescent males (Peter & Valkenburg, 2006; Ybarra & Mitchell, 2005) and therefore may be a legitimate source of internalization, some researchers may decide to omit the item relating to pornography performers. Omission of this item does not produce an appreciable decrement in alpha (e.g., Study 1: α = .92) and does not compromise the measure's validation coefficients. For example, similar associations were observed between the 8-item M-INT and the DMAQ (r 50] =

.73, p < .001), MB (r[50] = .43, p < .002), RSE (r[54] = -.42, p < .002), SDS-17 (r[50] = -.27, p = ns), and the MASS-6, (r[69] = .26, p < .05).

10.   For items 1, 2, 3, 4, 5, and 9, the response format is: Never, Rarely, Sometimes, Often, and Always. For items 6, 7, and 8, the response format is: Strongly Agree, Agree, Neither Agree nor Disagree, Disagree, and Strongly Disagree. We recommend that the response options be switched periodically (e.g., Strongly Disagree → Strongly Agree for some items and Strongly Agree → Strongly Disagree for other items – see Barnette [2000]).

Bibliography

Ahern, A.L., Bennett, K.M., & Hetherington, M.M. (2008). Internalization of the ultra-thin ideal: Positive implicit associations with underweight fashion models are associated with drive for thinness in young women. *Eating Disorders, 16,* 294-307.

Alexander, S.M. (2003). Stylish hard bodies: Branded masculinity in *Men's Health* magazine. *Sociological Perspectives, 46,* 535-554.

Arbour, K.P., & Martin Ginis, K.A. (2006). Effects of exposure to muscular and hypermuscular media images on young men's muscularity dissatisfaction and body dissatisfaction. *Body Image, 3,* 153-161.

Ata, R.N., Ludden, A.B., & Lally, M.M. (2007). The effects of gender and family, friend, and media influences on eating behaviors and body image during adolescence. *Journal of Youth & Adolescence, 36,* 1024-1037.

Baghurst, T., Hollander, D.B., Nardella, B., & Haff, G.G. (2006). Change in sociocultural ideal male physique: An examination of past and present action figures. *Body Image, 3,* 87-91.

Barnette, J.J. (2000). Effects of stem and Likert response option reversals on survey internal consistency: If you feel the need, there is a better alternative to using those negatively worded stems. *Educational and Psychological Measurement, 60,* 361-370.

Bearman, S.K., Presnell, K., Martinez, E., & Stice, E. (2006). The skinny on body dissatisfaction: A longitudinal study of adolescent girls and boys. *Journal of Youth and Adolescence, 35,* 229-241.

Cafri, G., Thompson, J.K., Ricciardelli, L., McCabe, M., Smolak, L., & Yesalis, C. (2005). Pursuit of the muscular ideal: Physical and psychological consequences and putative risk factors. *Clinical Psychology Review, 25,* 215-239.

Cafri, G., van den Berg, P., & Thompson, J.K. (2006). Pursuit of muscularity in adolescent boys: Relations among biopsychosocial variables and clinical outcomes. *Journal of Clinical Child & Adolescent Psychology, 35,* 283-291.

Cahill, S., & Mussap, A.J. (2007). Emotional reactions following exposure to idealized bodies predict unhealthy body change attitudes and behaviors in women and men. *Journal of Psychosomatic Research, 62,* 631-639.

Cash, T.F. (2004). Body image: Past, present, and future. *Body Image, 1,* 1-5.

Cash, T.F. (2007). Foreword. In J.K. Thompson & G. Cafri (Eds.), *The muscular ideal: Psychological, social, and medical perspectives* (pp. ix-x). Washington, DC: American Psychological Association.

Cash, T.F., Jakatdar, T.A., & Williams, E.F. (2004). The Body Image Quality of Life Inventory: Further validation with college men and women. *Body Image, 1,* 279-287.

Cash, T.F., & Pruzinsky, T. (2002). Future challenges for body image theory, research, and clinical practice. In T.F. Cash & T. Pruzinsky (Eds.), *Body image: A handbook of theory, research, and clinical practice* (pp. 509-516). NY: Guilford Press.

Chaiton, M., Sabiston, C., O'Loughlin, J., McGrath, J.J., Maximova, K., & Lambert, M. (2009). A structural equation model relating adiposity, psychosocial indicators of body image and depressive symptoms among adolescents. *International Journal of Obesity, 33,* 588-596.

Chen, H., & Jackson, T. (2009). Predictors of changes in body image concerns of Chinese adolescents. *Journal of Adolescence, 32*, 977-994.

Cohane, G.H., & Pope, H.G., Jr. (2001). Body image in boys: A review of the literature. *International Journal of Eating Disorders, 29*, 373-379.

Crow, S., Eisenberg, M.E., Story, M., & Neumark-Sztainer, D. (2006). Psychosocial and behavioral correlates of dieting among overweight and non-overweight adolescents. *Journal of Adolescent Health, 38*, 569-574.

Crow, S., Eisenberg, M.E., Story, M., & Neumark-Sztainer, D. (2008). Suicidal behavior in adolescents: Relationship to weight status, weight control behaviors, and body dissatisfaction. *International Journal of Eating Disorders, 41*, 82-87.

Cusumano, D.L., & Thompson, J.K. (1997). Body image and body shape ideals in magazines: Exposure, awareness, and internalization. *Sex Roles, 37*, 701–721.

Davison, T.E., & McCabe, M.P. (2006). Adolescent body image and psychosocial functioning. *The Journal of Social Psychology, 146*, 15-30.

DeVellis, R.F. (2003). *Scale development: Theory and applications* (2nd ed.). Thousand Oaks, CA: Sage.

Dittmar, H. (2005). Vulnerability factors and processes linking sociocultural pressures and body dissatisfaction. *Journal of Social and Clinical Psychology, 24*, 1081-1087.

Dittmar, H., Lloyd, B., Dugan, S., Halliwell, E., Jacobs, N., & Cramer, H. (2000). The "body beautiful": English adolescents' images of ideal bodies. *Sex Roles, 42*, 887-915.

Falkner, N.H., Neumark-Sztainer, D., Story, M., Jeffery, R.W., Beuhring, T. & Resnick, M.D. (2001). Social, educational, and psychological correlates of weight status in adolescents. *Obesity Research, 9*, 32-42.

Farquhar, J.C., & Wasylkiw, L. (2007). Media images of men: Trends and consequences of body conceptualization. *Psychology of Men & Masculinity, 8*, 145-160.

Field, A.E., Austin, S.B., Camargo, C.A., Jr., Taylor, C.B., Striegel-Moore, R.H., Loud, K.J. et al. (2005). Exposure to the mass media, body shape concerns, and use of supplements to improve weight and shape among male and female adolescents. *Pediatrics, 116*, 214-220.

Frederick, D.A., Fessler, D.M.T., & Haselton, M.G. (2005). Do representations of male muscularity differ in men's and women's magazines? *Body Image, 2*, 81-86.

Grieve, F.G. (2007). A conceptual model of factors contributing to the development of muscle dysmorphia. *Eating Disorders, 15*, 63-80.

Grieve, R., & Helmick, A. (2008). The influence of men's self-objectification on the drive for muscularity: Self-esteem, body satisfaction and muscle dysmorphia. *International Journal of Men's Health, 7*, 288-298.

Grippo, K.P., & Hill, M.S. (2008). Self-objectification, habitual body monitoring, and body dissatisfaction in older European American women: Exploring age and feminism as moderators. *Body Image, 5*, 173-182.

Grogan, S., & Richards, H. (2002). Body image: Focus groups with boys and men. *Men and Masculinities, 4*, 219-232.

Halliwell, E., & Harvey, M. (2006). Examination of a sociocultural model of disordered eating among male and female adolescents. *British Journal of Health Psychology, 11*, 235-248.

Hargreaves, D.A., & Tiggemann, M. (2004). Idealized media images and adolescent body image: "Comparing" boys and girls. *Body Image, 1*, 351-361.

Hargreaves, D.A., & Tiggemann, M. (2006). "Body image is for girls": A qualitative study of boys' body image. *Journal of Health Psychology, 11*, 567-576.

Harper, B., & Tiggemann, M. (2008). The effect of thin ideal media images on women's self-objectification, mood, and body image. *Sex Roles, 58*, 649-657.

Harrison, K., & Bond, B.J. (2007). Gaming magazines and the drive for muscularity in preadolescent boys: A longitudinal examination. *Body Image, 4*, 269-277.

Heinberg, L.J., Thompson, J.K., & Stormer, S. (1995). Development and validation of the Sociocultural Attitudes Towards Appearance Questionnaire. *International Journal of Eating Disorders, 17*, 81–89.

Humphreys, P., & Paxton, S.J. (2004). Impact of exposure to idealised male images on adolescent boys' body image. *Body Image, 1*, 253-266.

Irving, L.M., Wall, M., & Neumark-Sztainer, D., & Story, M. (2002). Steroid use among adolescents: Findings from project EAT. *Journal of Adolescent Health, 30*, 243-252.

Jones, D.C. (2001). Social comparison and body image: Attractiveness comparisons to models and peers among girls and boys. *Sex Roles, 45*, 645-664.

Jones, D.C. (2004). Body image among adolescent girls and boys: A longitudinal study. *Developmental Psychology, 40*, 823-835.

Jones, D.C., Bain, N., & King, S. (2008). Weight and muscularity concerns as longitudinal predictors of body image among early adolescent boys: A test of the dual pathways model. *Body Image, 5*, 195-204.

Jones, D.C., & Crawford, J.K. (2005). Adolescent boys and body image: Weight and muscularity concerns as dual pathways to body dissatisfaction. *Journal of Youth and Adolescence, 34*, 629-636.

Jones, D.C., & Crawford, J.K. (2006). The peer appearance culture during adolescence: Gender and body mass variations. *Journal of Youth and Adolescence, 35*, 257–269.

Jones, D.C., Vigfusdottir, T.H., & Lee, Y. (2004). Body image and the appearance culture among adolescent girls and boys: An examination of friend conversations, peer criticism, appearance magazines, and the internalization of appearance ideals. *Journal of Adolescent Research, 19*, 323-339.

Kim, D.S. (2009). Body image dissatisfaction as an important contributor to suicidal ideation in Korean adolescents: Gender difference and mediation of parent and peer relationships. *Journal of Psychosomatic Research, 66*, 297-303.

Kim, D.S., & Kim, H.S. (2009). Body-image dissatisfaction as a predictor of suicidal ideation among Korean boys and girls in different stages of adolescence: A two-year longitudinal study. *Journal of Adolescent Health, 45*, 47-54.

Kimmel, S.B., & Mahalik, J.R. (2004). Measuring masculine body ideal distress: Development of a measure. *International Journal of Men's Health, 3*, 1-10.

Kindlundh, A.M.S., Hagekull, B., Isacson, D.G.L., & Nyberg, F. (2001). Adolescent use of anabolic-androgenic steroids and relations to self-reports of social, personality and health aspects. *The European Journal of Public Health, 11*, 322-328.

Knauss, C., Paxton, S.J., & Alsaker, F.D. (2007). Relationships amongst body dissatisfaction, internalisation of the media body ideal and perceived pressure from media in adolescent girls and boys. *Body Image, 4,* 353-360.

Knauss, C., Paxton, S.J., & Alsaker, F.D. (2008). Body dissatisfaction in adolescent boys and girls: Objectified body consciousness, internalization of the media body ideal and perceived pressure from media. *Sex Roles, 59,* 633-643.

Knauss, C., Paxton, S.J., & Alsaker, F.D. (2009). Validation of the German version of the Sociocultural Attitudes Towards Appearance Questionnaire (SATAQ-G). *Body Image, 6,* 113-120.

Kostanski, M., Fisher, A., & Gullone, E. (2004). Current conceptualization of body image dissatisfaction: Have we got it wrong? *Journal of Child Psychology and Psychiatry, 45,* 1317–1325.

Labre, M.P. (2002). Adolescent boys and the muscular male body ideal. *Journal of Adolescent Health, 30,* 233-242.

Labre, M.P. (2005). The male body ideal: Perspectives of readers and non-readers of fitness magazines. *The Journal of Men's Health & Gender, 2,* 223-229.

Law, C., & Labre, M.P. (2002). Cultural standards of attractiveness: A thirty-year look at changes in male images in magazines. *Journalism & Mass Communication Quarterly, 79,* 697-711.

Leit, R.A., Pope, H.G., Jr., & Gray, J.J. (2000). Cultural expectations of muscularity in men: The evolution of *Playgirl* centerfolds. *International Journal of Eating disorders, 29,* 90-93.

Levine, M.P., & Smolak, L. (2002). Body image development in adolescence. In T.F. Cash & T. Pruzinsky (Eds.), *Body image: A handbook of theory, research, and clinical practice* (pp. 74-82). NY: Guilford Press.

Littleton, H.L., & Ollendick, T. (2003). Negative body image and disordered eating behavior in children and adolescents: What places youth at risk and how can these problems be prevented? *Clinical Child and Family Psychology Review, 6,* 51-66.

Mayville, S.B., Williamson, D.A., White, M.A., Netemeyer, R.G., & Drab, D.L. (2002). Development of the Muscle Appearance Satisfaction Scale: A self-report measure for the assessment of muscle dysmorphia symptoms. *Assessment, 9,* 351-360.

McCabe, M.P., & Ricciardelli, L.A. (2001). Parent, peer, and media influences on body image and strategies to both increase and decrease body size among adolescent boys and girls. *Adolescence, 36,* 225-240.

McCabe, M.P., & Ricciardelli, L.A. (2003). Sociocultural influences on body image and body changes among adolescent boys and girls. *The Journal of Social Psychology, 143,* 5-26.

McCabe, M.P., & Ricciardelli, L.A. (2004a). A longitudinal study of pubertal timing and extreme body change behaviors among adolescent boys and girls. *Adolescence, 39,* 145-166.

McCabe, M.P., & Ricciardelli, L.A. (2004b). Body image dissatisfaction among males across the lifespan: A review of past literature. *Journal of Psychometric Research, 56,* 675-685.

McCabe, M.P., & Ricciardelli, L.A. (2006). A prospective study of extreme weight change behaviors among adolescent boys and girls. *Journal of Youth and Adolescence, 35,* 425-434.

McCabe, M.P., Ricciardelli, L.A., & Ridge, D. (2006). "Who thinks I need a perfect body?" Perceptions and internal dialogue among adolescents about their bodies. *Sex Roles, 55,* 409-419.

McCreary, D.R., & Sasse, D.K. (2000). An exploration of the drive for muscularity in adolescent boys and girls. *Journal of American College Health, 48,* 297-304.

McDonagh, L.K., Morrison, T.G., & McGuire, B.E. (2008). The naked truth: Development of a scale designed to measure male body image self-consciousness during physical intimacy. *The Journal of Men's Studies, 16,* 253-265.

McVey, G., Tweed, S., & Blackmore, E. (2005). Correlates of weight loss and muscle-gaining behavior in 10- to 14-year-old males and females. *Preventive Medicine, 40,* 1-9.

McVey, G., Tweed, S., & Blackmore, E. (2007). Healthy Schools-Healthy Kids: A controlled evaluation of a comprehensive universal eating disorder prevention program. *Body Image, 4,* 115-136.

Meesters, C., Muris, P., Hoefnagels, C., & van Gemert, M. (2007). Social and family correlates of eating problems and muscle preoccupation in young adolescents. *Eating Behaviors, 8,* 83-90.

Moriarty, C.M., & Harrison, K. (2008). Television exposure and disordered eating among children: A longitudinal panel study. *Journal of Communication, 58,* 361-381.

Morrison, M.A., Morrison, T.G., & Sager, C-L. (2004a). Does body satisfaction differ between gay men and lesbian women and heterosexual men and women? A meta-analytic review. *Body Image, 1,* 127-138.

Morrison, T.G., & Halton, M. (2009). Buff, tough, and rough: Representations of muscularity in action motion pictures. *Journal of Men's Studies, 17,* 57-74.

Morrison, T.G., & Harriman, R.L. (2005). Additional evidence for the psychometric soundness of the Drive for Muscularity Attitudes Questionnaire (DMAQ). *The Journal of Social Psychology, 145,* 618-620.

Morrison, T.G., Kalin, R., & Morrison, M.A. (2004b). Body-image evaluation and body-image investment among adolescents: A test of sociocultural and social comparison theories. *Adolescence, 39,* 571-592.

Morrison, T.G., & Morrison, M.A. (2006). Psychometric properties of the Swansea Muscularity Attitudes Questionnaire (SMAQ). *Body Image, 3,* 131-144.

Morrison, T.G., Morrison, M.A., & Hopkins, C. (2003). Striving for bodily perfection? An exploration of the drive for muscularity in Canadian men. *Psychology of Men & Masculinity, 4,* 111-120.

Morrison, T.G., Morrison, M.A., Hopkins, C., & Rowan, E.T. (2004c). Muscle mania: Development of a new scale examining the drive for muscularity in Canadian males. *Psychology of Men & Masculinity, 5,* 30-39.

Morrison, M.A., Morrison, T.G., & Sager, C-L. (2004c). Does body satisfaction differ between gay men and lesbian women and heterosexual men and women? A meta-analytic review. *Body Image, 1,* 127-138.

Neumark-Sztainer, D., Paxton, S.J., Hannan, P.J., Haines, J., & Story, M. (2006). Does body satisfaction matter? Five-year longitudinal associations between body satisfaction and health behaviors in adolescent females and males. *Journal of Adolescent Health, 39,* 244-251.

Nishina, A., Ammon, N.Y., Bellmore, A.D., & Graham, S. (2006). Body dissatisfaction and physical development among ethnic minority adolescents. *Journal of Youth and Adolescence, 35,* 189-201.

Olivardia, R. (2001). Mirror, mirror on the wall, who's the largest of them all? The features and phenomenology of muscle dysmorphia. *Harvard Review of Psychiatry, 9,* 254-259.

Olivardia, R. (2007a). Body image and muscularity. In J.E. Grant & M.N. Potenza (Eds.), *Textbook of Men's Mental Health* (pp. 307-324). Washington, DC: American Psychiatric Publishing.

Olivardia, R. (2007b). Muscle dysmorphia: Characteristics, assessment, and treatment. In J.K. Thompson and G. Cafri (Eds.), *The muscular ideal: Psychological, social, and medical perspectives* (pp. 123-140). Washington, DC: American Psychological Association.

Olivardia, R., Pope, H.G., Jr., & Hudson, J.I. (2000). Muscle dysmorphia in male weightlifters: A case-control study. *American Journal of Psychiatry, 157,* 1291-1296.

Paulhus, D.L. (1991). Measurement and control of response bias. In J.P. Robinson, P. R. Shaver, & L.S. Wrightsman (Eds.), *Measurement of personality and social psychological attitudes* (pp. 17-59). San Diego, CA: Academic Press.

Paxton, S.J., Neumark-Sztainer, D., Hannan, P.J., & Eisenberg, M.E. (2006). Body dissatisfaction prospectively predicts depressive mood and low self-esteem in adolescent girls and boys. *Journal of Clinical Child and Adolescent Psychology, 35,* 539-549.

Peter, J., & Valkenburg, P.M. (2006). Adolescents' exposure to sexually explicit material on the Internet. *Communication Research, 33,* 178-204.

Pleck, J.H. (1995). The gender role strain paradigm: An update. In R.F. Levant & W.S. Pollack (Eds.), *A new psychology of men* (pp. 11-32). NY: Basic Books.

Polce-Lynch, M., Myers, B.J., Kilmartin, C.T., Forssmann-Falck, R., & Kliewer, W. (1998). Gender and age patterns in emotional expression, body image, and self-esteem: A qualitative analysis. *Sex Roles, 38,* 1025-1048.

Pope, H.G., Jr., Katz, D.L., & Hudson, J.I. (1993). Anorexia nervosa and "reverse anorexia" among 108 male bodybuilders. *Comprehensive Psychiatry, 34,* 406-409.

Pope, H.G., Jr., Olivardia, R., Gruber, A., & Borowiecki, J. (1999). Evolving ideals of male body image as seen through action toys. *International Journal of Eating Disorders, 26,* 65-72.

Pope, H.G., Jr., Philips, K.A., & Olivardia, R. (2000). *The Adonis complex: The secret crisis of male body obsession.* NY: Free Press.

Presnell, K., Bearman, S.K., and Stice, E. (2004). Risk factors for body dissatisfaction in adolescent boys and girls: A prospective study. *International Journal Eating Disorders, 36,* 389–401.

Ricciardelli, L.A., & McCabe, M.P. (2007). Pursuit of muscularity among adolescents. In J.K. Thompson and G. Cafri (Eds.), *The muscular ideal: Psychological, social, and medical perspectives* (pp. 199-216). Washington, DC: American Psychological Association.

Ricciardelli, L.A., McCabe, M.P., Mavoa, H., Fotu, K., Goundar, R., Schultz, J., et al. (2007). The pursuit of muscularity among adolescent boys in Fiji and Tonga. *Body Image, 4*, 361-371.

Richardson, S.M., Paxton, S.J., & Thomson, J.S. (2009). Is *BodyThink* an efficacious body image and self-esteem program? A controlled evaluation with adolescents. *Body Image, 6*, 75-82.

Ridgeway, R.T., & Tylka, T.L. (2005). College men's perceptions of ideal body composition and shape. *Psychology of Men & Masculinity, 6*, 209-220.

Rosenberg, M. (1965). *Society and the adolescent self-image.* Princeton, NJ: Princeton University Press.

Ryan, T.A., & Morrison, T.G. (in press-a). Psychometric properties of the Muscle Appearance Satisfaction Scale among Irish and British men. *Body Image.*

Ryan, T.A., & Morrison, T.G. (in press-b). Men's body image evaluation and investment: A review of key theoretical frameworks. In C. Blazina & D.S. Shen-Miller (Eds.), *An international psychology of men: Theoretical advances, case studies, and clinical innovations.* NY: Routledge.

Ryan, T.A., & Morrison, T.G. (2009). Factors perceived to influence young Irish men's body image investment: A qualitative investigation. *International Journal of Men's Health, 8*, 213-234.

Seidah, A., & Bouffard, T. (2007). Being proud of oneself as a person or being proud of one's physical appearance: What matters for feeling well in adolescence? *Social Behavior and Personality, 35*, 255-268.

Smolak, L. (2004). Body image in children and adolescents: Where do we go from here? *Body Image, 1*, 15-28.

Smolak, L., & Levine, M.P. (2001). A two-year follow-up of a primary prevention program for negative body image and unhealthy weight regulation. *Eating Disorders, 9*, 313-325.

Smolak, L., Levine, M.P., & Thompson, J.K. (2001). The use of the Sociocultural Attitudes Towards Appearance Questionnaire with middle school boys and girls. *International Journal of Eating Disorders, 29*, 216-223.

Smolak, L., Murnen, S.K., & Thompson, J.K. (2005). Sociocultural influences and muscle building in adolescent boys. *Psychology of Men & Masculinity, 6*, 227-239.

Soulliere, D.M., & Blair, J.A. (2006). Muscle-mania: The male body ideal in professional wrestling. *International Journal of Men's Health, 5*, 268-286.

Stice, E., Orjada, K., & Tristan, J. (2006). Trial of a psychoeducational eating disturbance intervention for college women: A replication and extension. *International Journal of Eating Disorders, 39*, 233-239.

Stöber, J. (2001). The Social Desirability Scale-17 (SDS-17): Convergent validity, discriminant validity, and relationship with age. *European Journal of Psychological Assessment, 17*, 222-232.

Thompson, J.K., & Cafri, G. (2007). The muscular ideal: An introduction. In J.K. Thompson and G. Cafri (Eds.), *The muscular ideal: Psychological, social, and medical perspectives* (pp. ix-x). Washington, DC: American Psychological Association.

Thompson, J.K., Heinberg, L.J., Altabe, M.N., & Tantleff-Dunn, S. (1999). *Exacting beauty: Theory, assessment, and treatment of body image disturbance.* Washington, DC: American Psychological Association.

Thompson, J.K., Shroff, H., Herbozo, S., Cafri, G., Rodriguez, J., & Rodriguez, M. (2007). Relations among multiple peer influences, body dissatisfaction, eating disturbance, and self-esteem: A comparison of average weight, at risk of overweight, and overweight adolescent girls. *Journal of Pediatric Psychology, 32,* 24-29.

Thompson, J.K., van den Berg, P., Roehrig, M., Guarda, A.S., & Heinberg, L.J. (2004). The Sociocultural Attitudes Towards Appearance Scale-3 (SATAQ-3): Development and validation. *International Journal of Eating Disorders, 35,* 293-304.

Tiggemann, M. (2005). Television and adolescent body image: The role of program content and viewing motivation. *Journal of Social and Clinical Psychology, 24,* 361-381.

Warren, C.S. (2008). The influence of awareness and internalization of Western appearance ideals on body dissatisfaction in Euro-American and Hispanic males. *Psychology of Men & Masculinity, 9,* 257-266.

Waugh, T. (1996). *Hard to imagine: Gay male eroticism in photography and film from the beginnings to stonewall.* NY: Columbia University Press.

Wiederman, M.W., & Pryor, T.L. (2000). Body dissatisfaction, bulimia, and depression among women: The mediating role of drive for thinness. *International Journal of Eating Disorders, 27,* 90-95.

Wilksch, S.M., Tiggemann, M., & Wade, T.D. (2006). Impact of interactive school-based media literacy lessons for reducing internalization of media ideals in young adolescent girls and boys. *International Journal of Eating Disorders, 39,* 385-393.

Wilksch, S.M., & Wade, T.D. (2009). Reduction of shape and weight concern in young adolescents: A 30-month controlled evaluation of a media literacy program. *Journal of the American Academy of Child & Adolescent Psychiatry, 48,* 652-661.

Williamson, I. (1999). Why are gay men a high risk group for eating disturbance? *European Eating Disorders Review, 7,* 1-4.

World Health Organization. (2008, September). *10 facts on adolescent health.* Retrieved April 17, 2009, from http://www.who.int/features/factfiles/adolescent_health/en/index.html

Ybarra, M.L., & Mitchell, K.J. (2005). Exposure to Internet pornography among children and adolescents: A national survey. *CyberPsychology & Behavior, 8,* 473-486.

CHAPTER THREE

The "Masculinity Vortex" of School Physical Education: Beyond the Myth of Hyper-masculinity

David Kirk

"It is most unlikely that a lad with an unsatisfactory record of behaviour and attitude will find a locker in our dressing rooms ... I believe ... (that) the force of example in teachers is all important. In such things as speech, dress, personal cleanliness we are constantly under the keen scrutiny of that hypercritical section of the community – the school boy ... Constantly I am reminding myself that we are charged with the task of training *men* to teach *boys*. This is a purely masculine sphere. Training *must* at all times be strong, must be virile." (Hugh "The Bomber" Brown, Principal, Scottish School of Physical Education, 1958, p. 93)

(The physical education teacher is a) "dominant competitive, aggressive, not-too-bright individual...(the) companionable 'man of action', but not someone with whom to engage in professional dialogue." (Whitehead and Hendry, 1976, p.75)

When sociologists have in the past written about the social construction of the body or the part played by sport in the construction of gender, school physical education is rarely mentioned (e.g., see Scraton, 1990), a situation that has only in the last decade begun to improve (e.g., see Gard & Meyenn, 2000; Hickey, 2008). Physical education sometimes attracts only passing reference, sometimes the terms "physical education" and "sport" are used interchangeably. This is unfortunate, since physical education may very well be, in Connell's (2008) words, one of the "masculinity vortices" of the school in which the masculinity-making agenda is closer to the surface and more explicit than in many other areas of the curriculum. Connell argues that all of schooling is part of and contributes to the gender order, but that some curriculum activities may play a more specialised and explicit part in this process than others.

We need pause for only a short time to reflect, along with physical education researchers such as Flintoff (1994), Brown and Rich (2002) and Williams and Bedward (1999), on why this might be. To begin with, few other school subjects require children to undress in order to participate. Schools vary in degrees of freedom they allow children in what they might wear for physical education, but whether they don tracksuits, swimsuits, or skimpy tops, shorts or skirts, this act of undressing in front of others sets physical education apart from most other school activities. The act of undressing relocates what is usually a private act into the semi-public space of the school changing-room (O'Donovan & Kirk, 2007). The changing-room ritual signals to children the commencement of a period of activity in which the body, their bodies, will be the centre of attention. There are few places to hide in physical education classes set as they are on playing fields, courts, in swimming pools and gymnasia. Physical competence or lack of it is there for all to see. More than this, hockey balls and sticks hurt when they hit, some people will bump and push, bodies collide and there is an ever-present danger of falling or being knocked over, some teachers will shout or make sarcastic comments, and some children will try desperately to be the best, to win, and get very upset when they don't.

Given the centrality of the body to physical education, given this drawing into public space of an otherwise relatively private undressed and exposed physical self, it is no surprise to learn that gender matters (in) physical education (Paetcher, 2003). It is indeed only recently that children have begun to be taught in co-educational classes in England, though single-sex physical education remains commonplace nonetheless, as it does also in many private schools in countries such as Australia and the USA where co-ed physical education in the state school sector was introduced in the 1970s. While some authors marvel at how long it has taken for co-education to become common practice in England (Williams & Bedward, 2001), equally we might wonder how boys and girls have ever come to be in the same physical education lessons. Long before sociologists discovered a connection between sport and masculinity, private schools for boys in England during the Victoria and Edwardian periods codified and developed games as a medium for the construction of a particular form of masculinity suited to the needs of the times and of the social class groups the schools served. As Mangan (1981) noted, the games ethic and the cult of athleticism were central to the resurrection of the English Public School for the sons of the emerging bourgeoisie in the mid 1800s, and the accoutrements of games playing such as extensive and manicured playing fields were the visible symbols of exclusivity and privilege. Moreover, in the parallel world of gymnastics, which formed the basis of the earliest school physical training programs in government schools in England from the 1880s, the division of the sexes was of overwhelming importance, a division that was alive and well in British physical education teacher education well into the 1970s.

Stepping back from physical education and taking a wider-angled lens to the school, we can note Philip Corrigan's (1988) meditation on the (for him) poignant fact that "bodies matter in schooling" and how "terror, fear, bodily turmoil" can be integral to some children's experiences of schools as particular kinds of institutions. We might also reflect that of all curriculum activities, physical education is most likely to carry forward the regulatory regime of schools as custodial institutions in the form of felt, lived experience. And in this context, of omission or only superficial attention from sociologists and other educational researchers, it is possible to understand how the physical education teacher might come to be viewed as a one-dimensional cardboard cut-out stereotype, either as the competitive, self-aggrandising bully of the film *Kes*, or as the hyper-masculine, militaristic disciplinarian of *Kindergarten Kop*. All of this is to suggest, then, there is every possibility that school physical education might be a masculinity vortex in the school, a place where the masculinity-making agenda is played out not just more explicitly than in some other areas of the curriculum, but in a powerfully visceral fashion, as a lived embodied experience.

Because, of course, all stereotypes contain some grain of truth; physical education teachers could not have achieved the reputation for being "dominant competitive, aggressive, not-too-bright" individuals, as hyper-masculine and homophobic, without there being some basis in reality. If we are to take seriously the possibility that school physical education contributes to the gender regime and that it may, possibly, be a masculinity vortex in the school, then we need a better and more widespread understanding of this marginal school subject and the marginal people who teach it (Hendry, 1976). If our lives, as Greg Dening (1993) put it, are "a double helix of past and present," then we need to understand in particular the continuities and discontinuities of the past in the present of physical education and in physical education teacher education.

In this chapter I will draw selectively on the historical record of men's physical education teacher education in Britain, focusing particularly on the period from the 1930s to the 1970s, and on my own biography of experience as a student of physical education in the mid-1970s, to suggest that this field has indeed been a masculinity vortex, not just in schools but in British society more broadly. At the same time, I want to challenge the simplification of the nature of the masculinities associated with this field, and to argue that even in the early period of the development of physical education teacher education, the stereotype grossly misrepresents the variety of masculinities prevalent

during this time. I will also suggest that more recent developments, set in motion in Britain in the 1970s with the academicisation of the physical activity field in higher education, provide a view of contemporary physical education and its teachers which is significantly different from our view of their past. At the same time, I suggest that the residue of the past and physical education's strong institutionalisation in the "industrial age school" (Lawson, 2009) contemporaneously, require a view of the physical education teacher to be continually re-made in the shadow of the stereotype, a process to which physical education teachers themselves actively if not always intentionally contribute, creating something that may well be a self-reproducing vortex of masculinity-making.

Continuity and Discontinuity in Physical Education Teacher Education

The first specialist colleges of physical training for men were established in Britain in the 1930s, some 40 years after the emergence of colleges for women in the 1890s (Kirk, 1992). Prior to the 1930s, a small number of men who gained professional qualifications in this field trained in Sweden, and one or two enrolled as private students in women's colleges such as Dunfermline (McIntosh, 1968). In contrast to the women's colleges and to the Scottish School of Physical Education (SSPE) in Glasgow, Carnegie College of Physical Training in Leeds and the specialist section of the Teacher Training College at Loughborough, both founded in the early to mid 1930s, required students to have already completed a two-year teachers' certificate or a three-year university degree before they could commence their one-year specialist course. This meant that the average age of students at Carnegie, for example, was 22 years from the 1930s through to the end of the 1950s. Leeds and Loughborough arguably more than the SSPE did much to set the early "gold standard" for male physical education in Britain, and the facts of the location of all three colleges within or on the same site as larger colleges of teacher education and, in the case of Carnegie and Loughborough, the age profile of the students, were both highly significant matters.

These early Colleges' location within or on the same site as colleges of teacher training could only have served to emphasise the fact that men and women student teachers of physical education trained separately, and that physical education was as a consequence somewhat different from other aspects of the school curriculum. While women were in a majority in general teacher training (a ratio of around 5:2 at City of Leeds Training College during this period), men and women nevertheless trained together. The women's physical training colleges were, in contrast, by and large entirely separate private institutions until the 1950s, a factor Fletcher (1984) recognised contributed to the fashioning of a unique feminine culture. While the men's colleges shared some facilities and some aspects of teacher training with the general training colleges that hosted them, they had along with their female counterparts enormous freedom to develop the curriculum as they saw fit.

The age profile of students in the two colleges in England was also significant since it meant their students were already physically mature and experienced in some aspects of physical activity before they began their training. Consistent with the women's colleges, the largest component of this training in the 1930s and 1940s was Swedish gymnastics, a system of free-standing exercises that sought the harmonious and balanced development of the body. Vaulting and agility work also featured in the men's courses from their beginning. A photograph of one of the gymnasia from the 1937-8 Carnegie Handbook (figure A) provides some evidence of the nature of the gymnastics work in this era. In addition to wall-bars for strengthening and stretching exercises and ropes and benches for climbing and balancing which were common place in Swedish gymnastics, there are bars for swinging, pommels and two vaulting horses. Along with the emphasis on Swedish gymnastics, the inclusion of vaulting and agility meant that there was a particular physique that was suited to training to be a physical education teacher. Photographs and film from this era show a considerable uniformity of height and body shape; men physical educators were from the beginning of this specialist era uniformly mesomorphic, agile, of only average height, but strong, with a good strength-weight ratio.

While games and other sports complemented gymnastics in the women's colleges, the men placed greater emphasis on these activities. Indeed by the mid-1950s games had displaced gymnastics as the main activities in the men's colleges. Students arrived at Carnegie and Loughborough as already experienced, expert and specialised gymnasts and sportsmen by virtue of their school, college and university education. From their inception, Carnegie and Loughborough held keenly contested annual matches in Rugby, Athletics, and various other competitive sports. Writing in retrospect in the Carnegie Research papers series in 1966, the first Warden of Carnegie Physical Training College Mr Ernest Major observed that

> During the period 1919-1939 the scope and conception of Physical Education in the schools were considerably broadened to include not only Physical Training in the narrow sense, but also games, swimming, dancing and athletics, and in many areas camping was also introduced. (Major, 1966, p.5)

The emphasis the men placed on games and sports was highly significant, and it led by the 1950s in Britain to a profound and irreversible shift in the field from gymnastics as its core to a sport-based form of the subject, a configuration of the field that has survived in schools to this day (Kirk, 2010). At the same time, as Whitehead and Hendry (1976) noted, the attitude to physical prowess during these formative years of male physical education was surprisingly ambivalent. During the opening of Carnegie College in 1933, several speakers emphasised the point that the new course was intended to produce teachers of physical training who had been educated in mind, body and soul, who were rounded exponents of "cultural physical education" and not, as Sir George Newman put it, mere "acrobats" or, in the words of the President of the College Board of Education, "super-experts" (Connell, 1983, p. 22). Hugh Brown (1958), a vociferous advocate for games over gymnastics as the core activity of physical education, nevertheless argued that the emphasis at the SSPE during his tenure as Principal was "first, last and all the time, *teaching*" (Brown, 1958, p. 93).

This ambivalence about sporting prowess notwithstanding, the men's specialist physical training colleges of this era, from their establishment in the 1930s until well into the 1970s, were (to paraphrase Brown) "first, last and all the time, *embodied*." The culture of the colleges was a *physical* culture, and the male body was its tool, the subject matter upon which it worked, its principal medium of expression. Not only was there a particular uniformity of body type during this era, there was also a strict ethic of appropriate manliness. As Brown (1958) insisted, training was at all times to be "strong" and "virile." The regular exposure of the body, naked except for shorts in the gymnasium or swimming trunks in the pool, and dressed in shorts and singlet or shirt for outdoor activities and only rarely in tracksuits, required, too, an ethic of compulsory heterosexuality. The colleges could only be so thoroughly embodied as long as there was no admission to even the slightest possibility of homosexuality. Moreover, Swedish gymnastics demanded "correctness of performance" (Kirk, 1998) in uniform movement of the group. There was no room whatsoever for individual interpretation or expression.

Uniformity of mass movement, of physique, virility and sexuality was the order of the day during the formative period of the life of the men's colleges. After WW2, the quasi-military style of instruction and of interaction that was intrinsic to this masculine physical culture received a boost. Peter Morris, one member of staff at Carnegie from 1968 for 30 years, recalled in an interview [i] that

> When the men came in after the war they were accustomed to discipline and had a regard for high standards. They worked hard with a clear focus on simple objectives. There was a sense of achievement through co-operation, a common purpose and identity, and a pride in membership of what was seen as a special group. They may have been "elitist" but through their own making. The staff at that time were ex-high ranking officers with war and combat experience. (Interview, P. Morris, 2008)

In this context, matters such as uniformity and appropriateness of dress, for example, were of immense importance.

> When the students arrived they were given an extensive list of clothing. Walking-out dress was the blazer or best "teddy bear" (sic) suit with brown shoes to match. There was a correct outfit for every occasion. This was strictly adhered to and the kit immaculately kept. You would be dismissed from a group session if any item was below standard. (Interview, Morris)

Bernard White, who joined the staff in 1959, in another interview provides an anecdote that further illustrates these characteristics of the culture of the colleges during and beyond the post Second World War period.

> There were some quite strong characters amongst the staff, and of course in the early years talking about John Dodd and Douglas Scott and Mr. Bouffler they were all ex-army people. They had all done military service during the war. Scotty was a Major at some fantastically young age and won himself an MC, he had a distinguished military career, and so these were people that I think were all looked up to by the students, and you didn't put a foot wrong. I actually remember in my early years I was going out to take a rugby session. It was morning break and I'd got my rugby shorts on and I'd got a rugby shirt on and over that I'd got a cricket sweater. I thought it's terribly Public School and I thought I was being terribly proper. I went in to get a coffee and Scotty came and stood by me and said "You want to get your bloody self properly dressed."   And I thought I had done the right thing and his comments were a bit harsh but you learn. (Interview, B. White, 2008)

Harsh they may have been, but not unexpected by those who were familiar with the culture of physical education colleges up to the 1970s. For anyone lacking physical self-confidence and, indeed, even for men who were physically talented, physical education colleges of this era could be scary places. They were not, in any case, for the faint-hearted, as I will elaborate momentarily.

At the same time, I suggest that it would be a mistake to read off from this account I have provided so far a simple message about a dominant form of masculinity. To be sure, the men's physical education colleges were creatures of their time in the period from the 1930s through to the end of the 1950s. Class divisions in British society, both economic and cultural, remained strong and explicit, and in schools a hierarchy of subjects ranging from academic to practical was unchallenged. It was in this era that the stereotype of the "dominant competitive, aggressive, not-too-bright individual" was born, the enthusiastic man of action, the practical man. But there were many men who did not fit this stereotype. We need to recall that many of the Carnegie and Loughborough students were already university graduates in an era when only a tiny, socially elite minority of the population attended university, while the rest were already qualified teachers. Those who went on to become leaders in their respective fields, as academics such as Peter McIntosh and Tony Mangan, authors and administrators such as AD Munrow and RE Morgan, sports commentators such as Ron Pickering and Bill McLaren, or coaches of elite sports teams such as Walter Winterbottom, Frank Dick and Ian McGeechan, were merely the super-elite of an articulate, well-educated and physically talented community of male physical educators.

Despite the presence of these and other exceptionally talented men within the community of physical educators, there appears nonetheless to have been something of a Pygmalion Effect working down through these years. Physical educators then and (as I will argue later in this chapter) now seemed keen to confirm the expectations of others that physical education teachers would conform to stereotype. For example, in the foreword to a book on curriculum planning in physical education by Gordon Underwood, Joe Jagger (1983) wrote

> Perhaps the practical emphasis that is so characteristic of our efforts indicates that we like doing things at which we are good, and basically we are excellent practitioners, highly capable of dealing adequately with direct teaching situations and with appropriate content of lessons. If criticism can be levelled at us, it can possibly be directed towards some inadequacies regarding the planning and development of syllabuses, and statements about outcomes and objectives associated with our courses and the accurate assessment of our levels of success. It may be assumed by us that any weaknesses in organized planning can be counterbalanced by enthusiasm displayed towards the practical (...) (p. xi)

Jagger (1983) was very much a spokesman for his generation of physical educators, practical men who knew what they were good at and were not afraid to say so, trusting that their energy and enthusiasm could offset their reluctance to theorise about curriculum planning and objective setting. But he was far from being a rank-and-file teacher. He was not only a successful school teacher and university lecturer, but he was also a leading light of outdoor education and is generally credited with popularising basketball during its early years in Britain. He was also father of the famous snake-hipped Rolling Stone Sir Mick, who claimed that his success owed much to the example his father set him in terms of self-discipline, while his father's physical prowess was responsible for Sir Mick's well-known athleticism and stamina on stage. My point is that even physical education's leaders in this era responded to the Pygmalion Effect, convincing themselves that they were indeed the practical men of the general public's expectation when in fact they were, many of them, rather more than the one-dimensional stereotypes Jagger's comments might suggest.

Physical Educator as *Homo Academicus* and the Multi-masculinisation of Physical Education Teaching

Alan Skelton's (1993) paper is one of the few theorised biographical accounts of "becoming a male physical education teacher." In it he fully accepts and seeks to evidence the notion that a hegemonic form of masculinity was both celebrated and reinforced during his physical education teacher education, particularly through the informal culture of the students which ran in direct opposition to his college's official endorsement of child-centredness and along with it a(n implied) softer form of masculinity. The "college" in question was Carnegie (though Skelton in this paper refers to it as "Major PE College"), by the time of his attendance there reduced to the status of a School within the gargantuan Leeds Polytechnic. Skelton's analysis is so powerful because it contains a juxta-positioning of sophisticated social theory with a first-hand account of two specific, student-run social events in his first year. He clearly found these events traumatic and he provides them as evidence to confirm his argument, that a dominant and particularly ugly form of masculinity continued to disfigure male physical education teaching which was, moreover, tacitly endorsed by some members of the college staff, in stark contrast to an official and more enlightened child-centred approach.

The two incidents he recounts, "Entertainments Night" and "The Greyhound Inn." are shocking to be sure. He is undoubtedly correct, intellectually, in his identification of these events as initiation rites typical of male-dominated institutions which mark the passage from "boy to man," and involve conformity to older male authority, external control of behaviour, the endurance of pain, and disrespectful behaviour towards women. And he is in my view equally correct, emotionally, in responding with disgust and abhorrence to the practices he describes. But despite my agreement on these points, intellectually and emotionally, I am led to ask whether these incidents provide evidence of the continuing domination of a particular (extreme and obnoxious) form of masculinity characteristic of male physical education teaching?

I do so, in part, on the basis of my arguments so far, that there was a form of masculinity characteristic of physical education teachers constructed during the early years of the history of male physical education colleges which formed the basis of a myth, but that in reality was much more nuanced and varied than the stereotype would suggest. I do so, too, on the basis of my reading of the historical record of physical education up to and beyond the time that Skelton attended Carnegie, and my own memories of becoming a physical education teacher some five years earlier than him. Notwithstanding my endorsement of his intellectual and emotional responses, I will argue that his evidence for the perpetuation of a form of hegemonic masculinity in physical education teaching is inconclusive and misleading. Why is this so?

First, we need to understand what was happening to physical education teacher education in Britain and elsewhere from around the late 1960s onwards, both institutionally and in terms of its curriculum. As I have shown (eg. Kirk, 1992; Kirk, 2000), by the end of the 1970s in countries such as Australia and Britain (earlier in the USA, later in other places), the sub-degree diploma which was the basic qualification to become a physical education teacher had been replaced by the four-year Bachelor of Education degree. This event was part of a wider process of the academicisation, scientisation, specialisation and ongoing and eventual fragmentation of the physical activity field in higher education (Lawson, 1991). The practical man of physical education teaching myth was gradually replaced by *homo academicus*, the academic man. As the field developed and new degrees emerged in sports science, leisure studies, and so on, physical education teaching, once the centre-piece of the field in higher education, was gradually pushed to the margins. Despite their degree-level qualifications and relatively easy access to masters and doctoral study compared with previous generations, physical education teachers through the 1980s and 1990s suffered from a double dose of marginality, the traditional form in schools as teachers of a practical subject in an academic curriculum, and as the educationalists and practitioners in a scientific and theoretical discipline (e.g., see Locke, 1998). We should note, along with Flintoff (1994), Brown and Rich (2002) and my own analysis in Kirk (1992) that these processes of academicisation and the earlier sportfication of physical education teaching were in themselves gendered processes in which women were, arguably, disadvantaged and disempowered (see also Fletcher, 1984).

When I entered the Glasgow-based Scottish School of Physical Education (SSPE) in October 1975 as a member of the first-year cohort of a new Bachelor of Education degree, I experienced this transitional moment of academicisation and its immediate consequences first hand. The SSPE was still at this time a single-sex "college," though it was housed in the larger Jordanhill College of Education which trained female and male teachers for primary and secondary schools as well as speech therapists and social and youth workers, among other professions. The senior cohorts of students at the SSPE were completing the college's own three year Diploma in Physical Education. These men gained entry to their course, by and large, with high school qualifications just below the norm for university entrance in Scotland at this time. In contrast, my cohort was selected very explicitly with a more academic curriculum in mind, a fact that was most certainly decisive in terms of my own success in gaining a place on the course. Indeed, my year group was called mockingly by the diploma students "Bernie's Book Boys." The SSPE

Principal was Bernard Wright, an Englishman new in post in 1974, and relatively unknown to the diploma students. The reference to "Book Boys" was a pun on the Glaswegian description of thugs as "boot boys" (because they typically wore Doctor Martin boots). Since "boot boys" were at the time symbols of a hyper-masculine under-class, "Bernie's Book Boys" was a put down that operated at a number of levels.

Some months before the course began in October 1975, several hundred of the 800 young men who had applied attended Jordanhill to be interviewed for one of 80 places on the course and to undergo a test of physical skills to assess our suitability to teach physical education, just as the diploma students had done in years previously. There was no question, though, that the overall standard of physical ability expected of my year group was lower than had been expected in the past, and the course I experienced reinforced what was, with historical hindsight, the beginning of a profound shift in the knowledge base of physical education teaching, in which practical knowledge and expertise in physical activities was to be significantly reduced (see Siedentop, 2002a). Just as one example among many, the students on the three-year diploma course practised gymnasts every day for the entire three years of their course. My cohort had one two-hour session once per week for two of four years. This shift in the knowledge base had a range of significant consequences, one of which was a much more diverse range of physiques among student teachers. As a non-gymnast, 800m runner with poor upper body strength, I would almost certainly not have been selected onto the diploma course a year earlier, nor would many of the other men in my BEd cohort who similarly possessed relatively strong academic qualifications but only mediocre physical capabilities.

My memory of my year group during our four years at Jordanhill contrasts markedly with Skelton's account of his experience of Carnegie. Yes, there was a group of men, most of whom I recall (though I may be wrong in this) were rugby players and from private school backgrounds, who seemed to enjoy drinking games in the college bar in which at least one of their group regularly ended up revealing some part of his body to all and sundry, a group that was also fond of leading the singing of "Swing Low Sweet Chariot" in the communal showers, accompanied by associated obscene gestures. This group's behaviour seems to me to come closest to the rituals described by Skelton, though my recollection is that the behaviour was restricted solely to this group. There were other recognisable sub-cultures within my cohort, such as a small group of semi-professional footballers, while other groups were formed around regional identities, such as the "Fifers" from the east coast of Scotland. There were musicians aplenty (I was one of them), some individuals who were active in student politics, and even a group of dancers (to which I also belonged) who specialised in modern dance in the third year of our course. My memory of my own experience of the SSPE between 1975 and 1979 was that there was no dominant group and thus the following description by Skelton (1992) is unrecognisable to me:

> Those small number of individuals who were not part of the dominant group of male PE students found it very difficult to articulate their educational ideas and values. This was, essentially, because their contributions were perceived, when set against the hegemonic form of PE, to be deviant: products of a personal deficit and not legitimate responses which deserved to be heard and considered for the sake of educational debate. This was both damaging to the quality of the training provided by the college and damaging for the professional development of these individuals. Gradually they became more and more passive, saying little in public, and keeping to themselves. They began to question their own beliefs and preferred practices and found it increasingly difficult to preserve a sense of self-esteem. (Skelton, 1993)

There was certainly a sense of tradition at the SSPE in the 1970s, and great pride in the College's achievements. But the era of passive acceptance of this tradition and the kind of masculinity/ies it inscribed could not be sustained in the face of this influx of *homo academici*. This is not to say that there was a sudden change of culture, since the new BEd degree was part of a transitional moment, nor that there were not some individuals, staff and students, who lived the myth of the "dominant competitive" individual. But my memory is that rather than being intimidated by the "he-men" of my college era, many of my cohort openly laughed scornfully at the antics of the rugby group and often mocked aspects of tradition. To be sure, I remember being called to Bernard Wright's office and being dressed down on a number of occasions for various offences against tradition. I remember writing a what was meant to be satirical essay modelled on the *Last Days of Ivan Denisovich* for a required outdoor activities weekend course widely unwelcomed by us as fourth-year students which was probably too clever by half and not well received by the lecturer in charge, Roy Small (or "Smalleski" as he was dubbed in the essay). I remember how many of us were shocked by the crude speech at our Graduation Dinner given by Craig Brown, son of The Bomber, former physical education teacher, Craigie College lecturer and yet-to-become Scotland football manager, who misjudged his audience by a wide margin. My recollection too is that many of the older college staff were themselves in turn shocked by what the new BEd degree and their policy of foregrounding academic ability in the selection process had unleashed. But there were other staff who were specifically recruited to support the new degree program and who themselves had active research careers, who were not unsympathetic and indeed were sometimes overtly supportive of the students' refusals to accept and reproduce the hegemonic masculinity myth.

The transitional moment I am describing was in its early days in mid-1970s Britain. By the mid-1980s when I completed a doctorate at

Loughborough University and took up my first academic appointment at the University of Queensland, the culture of physical education teacher education had changed irreversibly. For instance, in both institutions from the early 1980s men and women trained together (though without doubt at the cost of the disappearance, again it would seem irreversibly, of a "female tradition" [Fletcher, 1984]). The academicisation of the field was already well-advanced in both institutions, ahead indeed of the SSPE, and the place of practical knowledge and physical expertise was already highly problematic. Along with this devaluation of practical knowledge came a further exaggeration of the varieties of student teachers' physiques, interest and dispositions. Some twenty years later still, we can see very clear evidence that the kind of hegemonic masculinity Skelton (1993) described as occurring in the early 1980s can be viewed as anachronistic. With the invention of the physical education teacher as *homo academicus*, this stereotype formed in the 1930s through to the 1960s has not disappeared without trace from collective memory, and continues to survive in schools for reasons I will explain momentarily, but it has effectively been erased from the actual practices of physical education teacher education and the proliferation of masculinities it now embraces. This said, current PETE culture in most places in my experience stops short of embracing multiple sexualities, particularly among men, a problematic matter that suggests that there remain powerful continuities with the past in relation to compulsory heterosexuality, even if the stress on uniformity in other respects has weakened.

To complete this section and ahead of drawing this chapter to a conclusion, I want to return briefly to Skelton's (1993) evidence for the perpetuation of hegemonic masculinity in male physical education, set in opposition to the official curriculum of Carnegie. At the SSPE, there were no student residences, and the men either lived at home or in rented accommodation. At Carnegie, students were required to live in all male university campus accommodation. I suggest that it is the residential aspect of Skelton's account that is the decisive factor in the legitimation and persistence of the incidents he recounts, rather than the fact of the students involved being physical educators alone. This is not to suggest that physical education culture and sport culture more broadly do not provide a context in which obnoxious forms of masculinity can thrive. But student residences come closer to the "total institution" than most young people are ever likely to experience at any other time in their lives, and the kinds of behaviour Skelton described are commonplace in student residences regardless of field of study. Indeed, it is significant that the examples he uses to demonstrate that Carnegie was not unusual in housing these practices are also from residential settings in the USA (Rutgers University), while he draws on very few examples indeed from his course (though no doubt it might be argued that these experiences of hegemonic masculinity may have been more subtle and less dramatic and thus less persuasive than the examples he provides). But we might ask, as I conclude this chapter, why physical educators as much as others (such as the researchers Skelton cites) seem so willing to accept the legitimacy of the stereotype of the hyper-masculine physical education teacher?

Sport and the School as Interacting Institutions

It seems to me that there are two key institutions that come together in physical education to create the possibility of this subject acting as a masculinity vortex: sport and the school. As many sociologists of sport and gender have concluded, sport as an institution contributes to the social construction of gender as a complex relation of power and to the reproduction of gender inequality. Sport-based forms of physical education that have dominated the practice of the subject in schools in economically advanced countries since at least the 1950s have embedded in their routine practices these gender relations. Their effects are all the more powerful since they are accepted by many young people, their parents and their teachers as "natural." However, the socially reproductive effects of sport through physical education are neither straightforward nor entirely predictable.

As Lois Bryson (1990) helps us to understand, sport as an institution is not all of a piece. It is a highly complex, multi-layered, amorphous and deeply contradictory. We cannot, then, read-off the nature of "sport" from a small number of high-profile male professional sports such as football, rugby, baseball and basketball. These sports are undoubtedly sites for the display and reproduction of hyper-masculinity and while they impact on the "locker-room talk" of some men (Curry, 2002), they no less represent a hegemonic form of masculinity as the various parodies of hyper-masculinity represented by the "little big men" of body building (Klein, 1990) or the Hulk Hogans of wrestling. Badminton, slalom canoeing, figure skating and cross-country cycling, for example, may each contain highly competitive individuals who are driven to win, but they offer different media from contact sports such as Gridiron or Australian Rules Football or Rugby League for the display of masculinity. Indeed, we need only place Hulk Hogan in any one of the sports listed earlier (badminton, etc.), along with many others, to make this point that his particular version of masculinity would be ineffective and appear absurd, grotesque in these contexts.

Where physical education in schools conforms to the multi-activity model of curriculum (Ennis, 1999), which is the most common configuration of the subject practised in economically developed countries (Kirk, 2009), a wide range of sports are sampled and, for the reasons just proposed, there is no one settled form of masculinity that applies to these many activities. More than this, because of the way in which the school timetable invariably works, physical education is most often reduced to the practice of de-contextualised sports techniques rather than the full-blooded playing of intact sports. It is here, indeed, that the school as an institutional form plays a decisive part in providing certain kinds of gendered experiences available to young people in and through physical education. As Siedentop (2002b) among others has noted, physical education does not "do sport" particularly well. The kinds of embodied experiences of young people in physical education are then as much or more a product of the school as an institution as they may be of sport.

Lawson (2009) proposes that contemporary schools are highly problematic in a digital age while they retain an institutional form shaped by the logic of a past industrial age, with its heavy emphasis on standardization, centralization, specialization and bureaucratization (see also Fernandez-Balboa, 2003). And as Brown (1999) has noted, the prioritization of control over learning that is such a feature of the industrial age school as an institution is not simply a matter of choice for teachers. Teachers' concern for management and control of student behaviour ahead of learning of subject matter has a gendered dimension and, indeed, there is an expectation that "good" physical education teachers will display particular kinds of behaviour consistent with dominant forms of, in the case of his study, masculinity. Brown (1999) reflected that

> There is a very real concern for controlling classes and trying to fit into such a strongly regulated institution such as a school. Children, teachers and parents often demand strongly gendered displays from male PE teachers if they are to be considered legitimate and worthy. Given this combination of factors, even well meaning male PE teachers such as Joe and Derek, are likely to be drawn towards demonstrating complicit masculine teaching identities, and so remain active intermediaries in the reproduction of the gender order (p.156).

Brown and Evans (2004) developed this argument, suggesting that particular dispositions in new teachers can be traced to relationships with other physical education teachers, especially those experienced in a pupil-teacher and athlete-coach relationship. They suggested that these relationships may be viewed as intergenerational links which form key moments in the process of cultural production, in particular the production of gendered forms of physical education. Lawson (1983; 1988) has drawn on research into occupational socialization to argue that this intergenerational reproduction is how institutionalized forms of professional practice sustain themselves. Young physical education teachers, if they are to be judged as competent, must live up to the expectations of others. Those who cannot or will not, leave teaching (Macdonald, 1999). Those who remain are drawn inevitably and irresistibly into "acts of curriculum maintenance" (Lawson, 1988). Even in an era of *homo academicus*, these reproductive acts are shaped by a socialisation process that unfolds in the shadow of the mythical stereotype of the hyper-masculine physical education teacher.

Conclusion

My purpose in this chapter has been to challenge a stereotypical and relatively superficial view of physical education and physical education teachers that might provide a pat explanation as to why this school subject could be regarded, in Connell's terms, as a "masculinity vortex" in schools. My argument is that there are good reasons to suppose physical education does make a relatively more explicit contribution than other school subjects to constructing gender and reproducing gender relations, but not necessarily for reasons commonly supposed, based on this stereotype (Skelton, 1993; Parker, 1996; Wedgwood, 2005). I sought to show through a brief examination of the historical record the conditions from which this stereotype emerged, some of the lines of continuity and discontinuity between present and past, and how physical educators have themselves been complicit in the reproduction of the myth of the "dominant competitive, aggressive, not-too-bright" individual, in the process masking the nuanced variations of masculinity present during the formative period of development of the men's colleges between the 1930s and the 1970s. Since the 1970s, I argued (drawing again on the historical record and also my own experience of physical education teaching studentship) that the earlier sportification of physical education and then the academicisation of the physical activity field introduced *homo academicus* to replace the practical man of action of the earlier era. These processes I argued in turn lead to the multi-masculinisation of physical education, but also to processes of socialisation that take place in the shadow of the myth, and which are flavoured strongly by the institutional form of the industrial age school and its requirement for teachers to prioritize control over learning.

My point in all of this is that the gender-making that takes place in physical education classes, for girls as well as boys, is as much influenced by the school as an institution as it is by the subject matter of physical education. Indeed, it is the coming together of the two institutions of "sport" and "school" in physical education lessons that leads me to agree with Connell that this curriculum activity may indeed be a masculinity vortex. This point is not, I think, well understood in the sociology literature, on sport, on education, on gender, or on masculinity more specifically. Schooling is an immensely powerful socialising process and, as Corrigan (1988) among others has shown, is a more profoundly *embodied* experience than is commonly supposed. Schools require particular forms of embodiment of pupils and their teachers in order to function as industrial age institutions. The regulation of bodies in time and space, the social construction of bodies for productive though malleable citizenship, these are the basic tasks of the industrial age school (see for an elaboration Channan & Gilchrist, 1974; Lawson, 2009; Kirk, 1998; Kirk, 2010). Physical education lessons are merely the more visible and explicit manifestations of this industrial age logic.

In this context, the reform of school physical education cannot be brought about either through multi-masculinisation or de-masculinisation of physical education teacher education. The increasingly anachronistic character of the stereotype of the male physical education teacher does not signal triumphant progress in gender relations as some writing on gender and physical education seems to suppose. Just as the practical man of action has been replaced by *homo academicus*, some valuable aspects of physical education have been lost. The processes of sportification and academicisation have led to an irreversible shift in the knowledge configuration of the field. A unique female tradition has all but disappeared, surviving perhaps only in some corners of the private school sector. Physical education teachers are arguably now better qualified academically than they have ever been but ironically and paradoxically know less about their subject in terms of practical knowledge than the generations of teachers who preceded them.

Part of the explanation as to why we have reached this impasse, in which there is widespread recognition of a growing crisis in school physical education and fears for physical education futures is, as I have argued elsewhere (Kirk, 2010), a failure to understand the specific nature of the problem of physical education, in particular a failure to understand how past and present interact and intertwine, and to locate school physical education in relation to the broader physical culture of societies. Physical educators could not afford to do this given the subject's tenuous place in the competitive academic curriculum of the school. We need more research on gender and on masculinity in particular which has the capacity to capture these nuances and to avoid the simplicities and stereotypes that surround physical education and PETE which can, among other things, assist physical educators to struggle against the reproduction of identities in the shadow of an imagined past.

Notes
1. Interviews were conducted by researchers from Leeds Metropolitan University in 2008 as part of a project to commemorate the 75th anniversary of Carnegie Physical Training College.
2. Accessed online as HTML document with no pagination.

Bibliography

Brown, D. (1999). Complicity and reproduction in teaching physical education. *Sport, Education and Society, 4*, 143-159.

Brown, D., & Evans, J. (2004). Reproducing gender? Intergenerational links and the male PE teacher as a cultural conduit in teaching physical education. *Journal of Teaching in Physical Education, 23*, 48-70.

Brown, D., & Rich, E. (2002). Gender positioning as pedagogical practice in teaching physical education. In D. Penney (Ed.), *Gender and physical education: Contemporary issues and future directions* (pp.80-100). London: Routledge.

Brown, H.C. (1958). The training of the man teacher of physical education. *Physical Education, 50*, 91-94.

Bryson, L. (1990). Challenges to make hegemony in sport. In M.A. Messner & D.F. Sabo (Eds.), *Sport, men and the gender order: Critical feminist perspectives* (pp.173-184). Champaign: Human Kinetics.

Chanan, G., & Gilchrist, L. (1974). *What school is for.* London: Methuen.

Connell, L. (1983). *Carnegie: A history of Carnegie College and School of Physical Education 1933-1976.* Leeds: University Printing Service.

Connell, R. (2008). Masculinity construction and sports in boys' education: A framework for thinking about the issue. *Sport, Education and Society, 13*, 131-145.

Corrigan, P. (1988). The making of the boy: Meditations on what grammar school did with, to, and for my body. *Journal of Education, 170*, 142-61.

Curry, I. (2002). Fraternal bonding in the locker room: A profeminist analysis of talk about competition and women, in S. Scraton & A. Flintoff (Eds.), *Gender and sport: A reader* (pp.169-188). London: Routledge.

Dening, G. (1993). *Mr Bligh's bad language: Passion, power and theatre on the Bounty.* Cambridge: Cambridge University Press.

Ennis, C. D. (1999). Creating a culturally relevant curriculum for disengaged girls. *Sport, Education and Society, 4*, 31-50.

Fernandez-Balboa, J-M. (2003). Physical education in the digital (postmodern) era. In A. Laker (Ed.), *The future of physical education: Building a new pedagogy* (pp.137-152). London: Routledge.

Fletcher, S. (1984). *Women first: The female tradition in English physical education 1880-1980.* London: Althone.

Flintoff, A. (1994). Sexism and homophobia in Physical Education: The challenge for teacher educators. *Physical Education Review, 17*, 97-105.

Gard, M., & Meyenn, R. (2000). Boys, bodies, pleasure and pain: Interrogating contact sport in schools. *Sport, Education and Society, 5*, 19-34.

Hendry, L.B. (1976). Survival in a marginal role: The professional identity of the physical education teacher. In N. Whitehead & L.B. Hendry (Eds.), *Teaching physical education in England* (pp.). London: Lepus.

Hickey, C. (2008). Physical education, sport, and hyper-masculinity in schools. *Sport, Education and Society, 13*, 147-161.

Jagger, J. (1983). Foreword. In G.L. Underwood, *The Physical Education curriculum in the secondary school: Planning and implementation* (pp.xi-xiii) Lewes: Falmer.

Kirk, D. (1992). *Defining physical education: The social construction of a school subject in postwar Britain.* London: Falmer.

Kirk, D. (1998). *Schooling bodies: School practice and public discourse 1880-1950.* London: Leicester University Press.

Kirk, D. (2000). The reconfiguration of the physical activity field in Australian higher education, 1970-1986. *Sporting Traditions: Journal of the Australian Society for Sports History, 16*, 17-38.

Kirk, D. (2010). *Physical education futures.* London: Routledge.

Klein, A.M. (1990). Little big man: Hustling, gender narcissism and bodybuilding subculture. In M.A. Messner & D.F. Sabo (Eds.), *Sport, men and the gender order: Critical feminist perspectives* (pp.127-140). Champaign: Human Kinetics.

Lawson, H. (1983). Toward a model of teacher socialization in physical education: the subjective warrant, recruitment, and teacher education. *Journal of Teaching in Physical Education, 2*, 3-16.

Lawson, H. (1988). Occupational socialization, cultural studies and the physical education curriculum. *Journal of Teaching in Physical Education, 7*, 265-288.

Lawson, H. (1991). Specialization and fragmentation among faculty as endemic features of academic life. *Quest, 43*, 280-295.

Lawson, H. (2009). Paradigms, exemplars and social change. *Sport, Education and Society, 14*, 77-100.

Locke, L.F. (1998). Advice, stories and myths: the reactions of a cliff jumper. *Quest, 50*, 23-248.

Macdonald, D. (1999). Teacher attrition: A review of literature. *Teaching and Teacher Education, 15*, 835-848

Major, E. (1966). The development of physical education in England during the present century with special reference to gymnastics. *Carnegie Old Students Association Conference Papers, 1*, 1-9.

Mangan, J.A. (1981). *Athleticism in Victorian and Edwardian Public schools.* Cambridge: Cambridge University Press.

McIntosh, P.C. (1968). *PE in England since 1800* (2nd ed.). London: Bell.

O'Donovan, T.M. & Kirk, D. (2007). Managing classroom entry: An ecological analysis of ritual interaction and negotiation in the changing room. *Sport, Education and Society, 12*, 399-413.

Paetcher, C. (2003). Power, bodies and identity: How different forms of physical education construct varying masculinities and femininities in secondary schools. *Sex Education, 3*, 47-59.

Parker, A. (1996). The construction of masculinity within boys' physical education. *Gender and Education, 8*, 141-158.

Scraton, S.J. (1990). *Gender and physical education.* Geelong: Deakin University Press.

Siedentop, D. (2002a). Content knowledge for physical education. *Journal of Teaching in Physical Education, 21*, 368-377.

Siedentop, D. (2002b). Junior sport and the evolution of sport cultures. *Journal of Teaching in Physical Education, 21*, 392-401.

Skelton, A. (1993). On becoming a male physical education teacher. *Gender and Education, 5*, 289-303.

Wedgwood, N. (2005). Just one of the boys? A life history case study of a male physical education teacher. *Gender and Education, 17*, 189-201.

Whitehead, N., & Hendry, L.B. (1976) *Teaching physical education in England*. London: Lepus.

Williams, A., & Bedward, J. (1999) *Games for the girls—The impact of recent policy on the provision of physical education and sporting opportunities for female adolescents*. Winchester: King Alfred's College.

Williams, A., & Bedward, J. (2001). Gender, culture and the generation gap: Student and teacher perceptions of aspects of National Curriculum Physical Education. *Sport, Education and Society, 6*, 53-66.

Wright, J. (2002). Physical education teacher education: Sites of progress or resistance. In D. Penney (Ed.), *Gender and physical education: Contemporary issues and future directions* (pp.190-207). London: Routledge.

PART TWO

Enforcing Masculinities

CHAPTER FOUR

Boys, Gyms, Locker Rooms and Heterotopia

Michael Atkinson and Michael Kehler

Previous research has established schools, and physical education classes in particular, as a site of masculinizing practices through which boys learn, embrace and embody, or are damaged by particular codes of dominant masculinity (Connell, 2000; Kehler, 2007; Kehler & Martino, 2007). Two trends serve as empirical points of departure in this paper. The first is the burgeoning trend of anti-gym/exercise ideologies among young boys, and the proliferation of an anti-jock movement in Canada (Atkinson & Young, 2008, Wilson, 2006). The second, and clearly related trend, is growing attrition rates in grade nine physical education classes in Ontario, Canada. In the first instance, young boys are developing decisively anti-sport and PE attitudes. In the second instance, they are choosing to withdraw from gym class as soon as they are institutionally allowed in Ontario as a reaction to a victimizing jock culture in gym settings. Ontario schools have responded to concerns of youth attrition with curricular initiatives that mandate primary-junior schools to include 30 minutes of physical activity per day. In response to the public outcry and increased medical research associated with youth inactivity, the provincial government in Ontario has proposed a number of initiatives beyond the "30 minute rule" to help promote the importance of activity and fitness across the life-course. However, institutional methods to address the culture of dominant/jock masculinity in Ontario schools remain undeveloped.

Among the least addressed zones of boys' victimization and jock masculinity policing is the gym locker room. The locker room is a context of male surveillance and bio-political maneuvering, where anti-gym and anti-jock

(Wilson, 2006) mentalities among boys within grade nine health and physical education contexts ferment. Kehler, Davison and Frank, (2005), among others, have shown how degrees of gender/masculinity variation are monitored in situations where boys and young men face constant surveillance and policing by other boys. The relatively laissez-faire attitude coaches, physical education instructors and others in the educational field possess toward the locker room and its gender/power dynamics exacerbates the situation for boys who do not live up to stereotypical masculinities. The governmental logic (Foucault, 1979) and architecture underpinning the geography of the locker room, the institutional policies regulating and shaping locker room use, and the connection between masculine fear in the locker room and contemporary rates of attrition among boys in health, exercise and sport practices must be questioned.

Building on past studies of masculinities, bodies and the education settings, this paper draw on qualitative interviews undertaken with a sample of boys aged 14-16 who have voluntarily withdrawn from physical education in a selection of Ontario schools. [1] Attention is given to the ostracism and derision some boys experience as marginal males in the locker room setting. The locker room is a curious social space within the physical education context, as a zone wherein boys are sequestered from social control agents, and thus aggressively dominant boys are presented with an opportunity to police the preferred sorts of masculinity mainly reified in sports settings. Through the discussion of locker room and its relationship to the policing of masculinity in school, the space is dissected as a youth *heterotopia* (Foucault, 1967) for boys on the outside or fringes of normative masculinity. Heterotopia (Foucault, 1967) refers to a space outside of other, and perhaps more mainstream, institutional zones within which a person finds predictable order, cultural comfort and social normalcy. Heterotopia can be a zone where identities, maps of cultural meaning, relations of power and technical uses of the body are enforced in both traditional and non-traditional ways. In using Foucault's (1967) ideas regarding heterotopia, it is argued that locker rooms are places of liminal doubt and existential confusion; where boys' masculine identities are enforced and monitored among themselves in largely hidden, anxiety-producing, and ritual ways that have no ostensible (or inherent link) to the pedagogy of physical education itself.

Heterotopia as a Liminal Space

Heterotopia is a word coined by Foucault (1967), referring to a space outside of traditionally normative or dominant institutional zones of power. One's internalized cultural identities, maps of meanings and physical abilities are suspended or negated in these zones. Foucault (1967) articulates several possible types of heterotopic spaces: i) "Crisis heterotopia" as a separate space like a boarding school or a motel room where activities like coming of age or a honeymoon take place out of public sight; ii) "Heterotopias of deviation" as institutions where individuals are sequestered whose behaviour is outside the norm (hospitals, asylums, prisons, rest homes, cemetery; iii) "Heterotopia" in general as a pastiche place juxtaposing and re-contextualizing several spaces (a garden, for example, is a heterotopia because it is often meant to be a microcosm of different environments with plants from around the world); iv) "Heterotopias of time" like museums that enclose objects from various periods and epochs; and, v) "Heterotopias of ritual or purification" as (sub)cultural rite of passage spaces not freely accessible to outsiders.

Escalating numbers of physical education experts in North America and elsewhere articulate the high school gym setting as a blend of crisis heterotopia and heterotopia of ritual. Immersion in a crisis or ritual heterotopia situates a person in a place of uncertain regulation, emptiness, fear, uncertainty, physical risk and alienation. It is in many respects a space with physical boundaries, but where one's normal identity boundaries may be temporarily erased or crossed in a ritualistic manner. Heterotopic experiences are mainly private rather than public, and generally involve a liminal rite of passage in one sense or another. In this respect, perhaps equally salient as Foucault's (1967) construction of a heterotopia in the interpretation of locker room experiences among marginalized boys is Lyotard's (1989) concept of *scapeland*. Scapeland is a physical space producing where the normal, safety-producing cultural rules of life may not apply. Scapeland is both a zone and state of being existing before description and definition to an individual; it appears as the erasure of an ideological or narrative support (Lyotard, 1989: 216–17). A scapeland is thus characterized by the absence of direction and destination provided by one's preferred cultural scripts, identities or modes of thinking and understanding. With reference to the high school gym setting, a scapeland is a physical zone of "risk-filled play" for some boys where dominant social identities, ideologies and practices of powers are wielded over them by dominant boys. Scapelands produce personal fear in the recognition of one's aloneness in the context of more powerful others.

A collection of important empirical studies of masculinity in sport have pointed to the type of heteronormative work and gender disciplinary that accompanies involvement in gym locker spaces (Burstyn, 1999; Cauldwell, 2006). However, most studies have not examined the context of locker rooms as the focus of research, but rather noted the setting as a place where masculinity is performed in cultural practice. Within traditionally "male" locker rooms, normative sex, race, ethnic, class and national identities with a broader culture are both confirmed and consolidated (Anderson, 2009).

Perhaps more so than any other private social space in which young boys interact, the locker room is a zone of hyper-normative/dominant masculine affirmation. Heterosexual discourses involving the objectification of women, ideal-type male bodies, and coercively organized power differentials between boys are all on display therein.

In drawing upon White & Young's term (1997), the locker room is a place wherein a particularly *"dangerous masculinity"* is reinforced among boys with little monitoring or intervention. The literature on hazing in sport illustrates how teenage boys may find subcultural justification to ritually engage in violence on weaker or more vulnerable boys in the locker room as a statement of dominance (Bryshun & Young, 2007; Johnson & Holman, 2004). Practices and discourses in the locker room are replete with homophobic messages and symbolism. Boys who are deemed too fat, too thin, or generally not as physically capable as the dominant boys are labelled as feminine or their sexuality is questioned. Anderson's (2009) research on masculinity has shown consistently how, at least until recently, the fraternity setting of the locker room often facilitates an intense anti-gay or anti-alternative masculinity environment for young boys who simply do not measure up. For boys who exist on the margins, what they experientially know, prefer and feel as masculine is not a part of the social script in the locker setting, and thus they enter the space with heterotopic fear.

Fusco's human geographical studies of sport, health and physical education settings attest to how the spatial design of the gym as a private field where adults are prohibited partly establishes the heterotopic essence of the arena (2005, 2006a, 2006b). To Fusco, educators and school agents must be attentive to how culturally privatized zones with schools are saturated with a hidden gender curriculum. Heteronormative codes of dominant masculinity are enforced among very young boys with little fear of institutional reprisal. These spaces and the lack of regulation therein create part of the alienating climate in physical education for scores of boys who neither embody nor identify with dominant masculinities. Discourse and praxis regarding the de-gendering of education in Canada aside, then, with the generational turning of a blind eye to the physical layout of gym spaces and their capillaries within the school setting—and the subsequent cultural codes promoted within them—consistent evidence reveals how discriminatory, alienating and abusive codes of masculinity often accompany physical education instruction for young boys.

Given all of the above, Beck's (1992) widely discussed risk-society thesis encourages a sober taking stock of the many anxieties and uncertainties about gendered identities that have become integral features of late modernity. Within traditional industrial society, institutions such as schools succeeded in concentrating debate on the distribution of "social goods" (i.e., knowledge in the case of education). However, in the movement into the risk society the issue of goods distribution becomes overwritten by public concerns about the production of "social bads" (Beck, 1992: 48). In the wake of growing consciousness about the impact of modern institutional forms and practices on social behaviours and identities, greater public discourse has been granted to how modern social institutions spawn a rash of bads along with goods; in the case of schools, for example, given dominant institutional practices, and the deployment of cultural ideologies within unregulated spatial zones, they become breeding grounds for youth problems including racism, sexual abuse, ostracism, class alienation, violence, drugs, and a full spate of others (Beck, 2002: 4). In a risk society, public practice shifts increasingly to developing within institution mechanisms for protecting people from the very bads the institutions, themselves, may promote. Few in the context of sport and health studies have analyzed the locker room as a heterotopic space where "social bads" are systematically produced and distributed to young boys around their identities as young males.

Risk Filled Play: The Locker Room as Heterotopia

The crisis produced within the locker room is deep and pronounced for boys who do not feel comfortable in that physical, social and emotional space. The process of even entering the physical space of the locker room can be the source of great anxiety for young boys; prompting nerves and even nausea at breakfast or on the way to school on days in which gym is on the schedule of classes. These boys dread the experience so strongly they may often lay awake at night before "gym days" worrying about what humiliation or torment they will endure. It is an amazing cultural shift in ludic experiences among boys. For most of the boys who come to hate gym, they do so after years of childhood exuberance for physical activity and play. Play becomes associated Pavlovian-style with physical, emotional, and mental harm. A great portion of the heterotropic crisis begins within the confined locker room setting. Most school locker rooms are physically protected social spaces. Entryways are typically configured in a zigzag or switchback pattern so that people cannot look directly into the room from a hallway. Floor plans within the rooms vary considerably, but the typical layout is one in which three or all four of the main room's walls feature metal lockers, with long, terribly uncomfortable thin wooden benches bolted to floors directly in front of them. Floors are tiled, few, if any windows are found, and a prison-like open showering pen (with normally 3-8 showering points) is found somewhere between the main changing area and the toilets. The distinctive feel to most school locker rooms is one of openness and of vulnerability for boys who struggle with hegemonic masculinity.

The zone of the locker rooms is simply beyond non-dominant boys' habituses; their socially learned tastes, abilities and masculine preferences. Habitus refers to the learned cultural and physical dispositions one carries almost unreflexively (Bourdieu, 1984; Elias, 1978). In this forced space of physical interaction, the dominant male atmosphere, physical rituals, banter and interpersonal judging neither fit nor resonate with their learned bodies or selves. They are fish out of water and come to view the space as a physical cultural zone where they will be, once or several times a week, ritually embarrassed or humiliated with little hope for protection or consolation. It is truly, in Lyotard's (1989) description, a scapeland where none of the cultural scripts they hold true in life apply. As one boy said to our research team:

> Yeah they do and it's just kind of the behind the scenes stuff that teachers don't necessarily know about. But what I've realized in all my years as a student is you can't teach a student to behave a certain way verbally and I'm not saying get physical. I'm not saying smack them across the face and say, don't do that. I'm saying you have to discipline them and show them there are consequences to their actions and that can't always be done, because they can't keep an eye out everywhere. But I'm encouraging people now because I know nobody's probably going to hear, this but if I could I would encourage people. Hopefully they [teachers] won't give you one of those, "well I'll keep an eye on them and if they do it again I'll discipline them," answers like I got in elementary school because then they'd know the teacher's watching them. So behave for a while and as soon as they turn their back, they're back to it again. (Bob, age 15)

Boys who have concerns about their bodies and their physical abilities find little comfort in the daily or weekly ritual of changing in front of other boys and revealing their lack of embodied, dominant masculinity. The norms of the space (e.g., to remove one's everyday, self-determined and culturally inscribed styles; hence one's sense of self-identity) dictate how that which is theirs is summarily taken from the boys. They need to strip and reveal their culturally male bodies in front of others for subcultural inspection. There is, if one ponders the crisis ritual for one instance, few places in social life where boys are as culturally levelled in front of other for adjudication in such a manner. As such, the locker room zone is an in-between, crisis heterotopia space because it exists between the safe confines of the class (where different masculine traits and characteristics like intelligence and leadership) can be celebrated, and the public theatre of gym (where hegemony might rule, but at least a modicum of safety exists). For some boys, it is the locker room and not gym class itself that produces the most fear and self-loathing about one's supposedly insufficient male body.

As a ritually heterotopic scapeland, the locker room becomes a cultural setting of fear in which boys who do not possess particular ideal-type embodiments of masculinity are placed on display, monitored by conforming boys, and critiqued for their deficiencies (Shott, 2009). The locker room is a quintessentially Panoptic place, as in Foucault's (1967) description. Boys who do not see their physical attributes as sufficiently male are forced to publicly confess their deficiencies on a weekly basis and offer themselves up to conforming males as examples of the pathological. From a Durkheimian perspective (Durkheim, 1956), the heterotopic ritual is a social vehicle for reaffirming the masculine normal and pathological. The physically blessed boys often tease, deride, assert dominance over, and even become aggressive to the visibly weaker boys. Schools thus become implicit in the institutionalization of practices that serve to legitimate dominant codes of masculinity—whether such is acknowledged or not in official pedagogic policy and practice. Boys narrate how lockeroom scapeland rituals, in which the outcomes are never neatly known in advance, are akin to being bullied into kissing the ground in front of other boys on a regular basis.

> I didn't like it [gym class], not all the time. As long as they weren't purposely trying to hit me in the head with the dodge ball [in the locker room] which is what they used to do, I was fine. It's disappointing when you suck at a game. Like volleyball nobody likes but dodgeball was the worst for me because they'd purposely try to hit me in the head. They did that with other people too I think. Just it seems I was a target. I don't know why. It's a good thing that I'm going to a different high school that none of the rest have ever heard of really. Like I used to go to a public school in London [Ontario], so they don't know where it is. (Bob, age 15)

Kissing the proverbial ground is a masculine rite of passage in a million different contexts for young boys who fall outside of physical cultural ideals regarding masculinity. Whether one playfully learns to submit to one's father while wrestling on the living room floor, to not speak back to a male teacher, to accept the orders of a sports coach, or to walk down the opposite side of hallway from older boys, part of the learned code of masculinity is deferral to those above you (in some manner) on the hegemonic masculine ladder. Such is the lesson Sutherland (1947) instructed in his theory of *differential association*. Feminist scholars since the 1960s have equally noted how the power mongering, resource gathering, commodity accumulating, and sexual conquesting that comprises everyday life might be categorized as the social practice of (male) *bullying*; of acquiring one's wants, needs, desires, or extending one's will over others through aggressive, exclusionary, domineering, or quasi-exploitive social means. We should expect little difference in masculine practice in the hyper-vulnerable space of the locker room wherein the embodiment of young masculinities is thrust onto the table for cultural dissection. Traditional masculine power and authority is largely earned by the deployment of accepted social, physical, mental and emotional bullying by males. Such is the case of the locker room experience. While not deliberately designed within the educational system as such, the culture of the locker room dictates otherwise. Authoritarian masculinity is won among young boys in small scales through one's ability to bully in a socially accepted or at least tolerated manner. "Healthy" bullying sorts the herd and inspires greatness in others as the physical cultural logic of the locker room goes. Therefore, bullying in culturally protected or ignored spaces like the locker room helps produce the types of men who learn to assert their authority and "get away with it." Farr (1988) argues that male superiority and privilege is often won when men bond with the strong, while avoiding and deriding the so-called weak. Even teachers in most settings are aware of how young boys will attempt to sort out the herds themselves unless the process is disrupted:

> Usually when we're picking teams and stuff, I'm one of the last ones picked but our gym teacher, he puts us, like the last few people into a group because he doesn't want the last person to be picked to feel extremely bad. So he takes the last few people and puts them into the teams himself and so it's not really that bad because you can't really tell if you're the last pick or you could have been the next pick. (John, age 15)

A significant portion of the ritual fear, risk and uncertainty pertains to exposing their bodies in gym or in the locker room to other males. Here, marginalized boys routinely speak about being muscularly deficient in some respect, overweight, or simply too thin. Some may take refuge in toilet stalls and change out of their clothing behind closed doors therein. Few can avoid having to shower, though, in front of others at the end of class. Boys may try to evade the showering process, but physical education teachers often inspect them after class to ensure they have undertaken the ritual. Shower pens are especially unforgiving to boys who do not measure up on the masculine ladder. The open space of the showering pen is a Mecca for those boys who seek to assert minor hegemony through the castigating and emasculation of the socially different male. Boys report patterned histories of teasing and abuse within the shower space. Showering, ostensibly a practice to ensure proper hygiene following the rigors of gym, is transformed into heterotopia; a crisis event in which few if any of the statuses, role sets or achieved identities the boys have outside of the practice count as currency. John said:

> It's weird because they guys get an open shower but the girls don't. I don't know why. Maybe the guys like seeing each other but I don't think so. I don't know why they have open showers for guys. Like I got late for French 2 times in a row [because he waited to shower until the other boys left] and he said next time you go into the office. So and then if I miss my bus then I have to wait 20 minutes for my mom to pick me up, so I don't want to miss my bus. I take too long, so I don't anymore ... I don't shower anymore. I just shower when I get home and again the guy who bugged me [bullied], he's like "why don't you take a shower?" I said because I don't feel like it.

Alarming are stories about physical confrontation, tormenting and outright violence in the locker room. Some boys recount tales of being pushed into lockers, surrounded and teased by several other boys, "snapped" with wet towels, having their clothes or school kit stolen or vandalized, and even punched or kicked on a repeated basis:

> There's [locker room] games where you throw balls at people and they're kind of like go sit down or they kind of go for me and think it's funny … they go for me because they think it's funny or I've thought of another solution it's kind of like back to the animal thing, you know, I don't like comparing it to animals but it's the easiest way. It's kind of like eliminating the weaker ones. Well, I guess they see me as the easier target and besides the fact they think it's funny. They're just going to…it's like, just get rid of the ones that are easier to get rid of first. (Mythic Artist, age 15)

Other boys get off lightly as the recipients of verbal abuse. Quite predictably, they are called "fag," "fat ass," or "pussy" because of their supposed physical disabilities as young boys. These are the insults and jeers, which if promulgated in the classroom or in the cafeteria, might be the source of detention or suspension. But in the control agent free zone of the locker room, this brand of masculine bullying is all too common discourse.

The unregulated, protected, adult-free zone of the locker room is a crisis place for boys who view themselves as on the margins of normative masculinity. The social fishbowl setting is one in which there is little opportunity to escape surveillance and the reminding of how one's male body does not make the grade.

Locker Rooms, Gym and Hegemony

All of the discussion above relates deeply to the idea that the locker room is a cultural space where young male hegemony is established. Gramsci's (1971) now canonized construction of hegemony purports the idea that rulers in a society cannot enforce control over vast groups of people without some ideological convincing or set of ritual practices that engenders consent to rule. To Gramsci (1971), socially legitimate and enduring power like that borne from masculine patriarchy, is established and maintained through diffuse, subtle and surreptitious inter-institutional and cultural means; what he referred to as a process of *hegemony*. Hegemony is political, ideological, social and cultural power that flows from diffuse leadership within a society. A ruling class (including ruling gender formations) maintains its hegemony in civil society by creating and enforcing its norms, values and statuses that are, in turn, promulgated and normalized through political parties, schools, media, the church, and other voluntary associations, what Althusser (1971) describes as a society's "ideological state apparatuses"; the school, as scholars have documented, is a rhizomatic apparatus of hegemonic masculinity (Rich & Evans, 2006).

Gramsci (1971) argues in *Prison Notebooks* that hegemony is ultimately exercised through the promotion of a nested and ubiquitous false consciousness among its targets of power, such that I or you believe the values and life choices we make for ourselves (i.e. to go to school, wear particular clothing, get married, have children, live in a certain area, or to participate in gym class) are indeed our own, and not part of a larger class-based social agenda. Hegemony operates wherein one is convinced to sleep comfortably in a dream world of thickly blurred realities, unaware of the power mechanisms underpinning one's existence. Further still, hegemony is clearly present when people realize or believe in few alternative realities; such that there are, in the case of this paper, alternatively acceptable male bodies, male physical practices, or male identities. Hegemony is ultimately the process to which Gramsci (1971) refers when explaining why people seemingly consent to being ruled (under the rubric of "our common culture") within a relative state of social domination. Many of the boys interviewed, for example, spoke about the natural male order in gym, and the ways in which physical activity is for the naturally gifted boys. When presented with the opportunity to exit from the physical education curriculum in school, they did so, for they simply decoded it as the preserve of the popular, the strong, the social elite, or those favoured by physical education instructors. A boy named Mythic Artist (age 15) said:

> I've noticed that most of the people that are really good in gym aren't as good at English or stuff like that so maybe they feel they can't really do English, and they go and need to do gym and it can also go vice-versa. But in my case I was just already into books and stuff like that and I just didn't like gym but I think for them gym's one of the only things they've got.

Boys who choose to remain in gym class despite constant ridicule and exclusion, do so at their own peril. These boys remain in a constant state of risk from Beck's (1992) perspective, or in Goffman's (1959) terms exist in the social sphere as "discreditable deviants."

Resisting hegemony and shedding off its ideological trappings proves difficult in most social settings. This is especially the case for young boys who possess little social, economic or cultural capital to engage such resistance. The options for boys who wish to partake in physical and health education but who are uncomfortable in the traditionally hegemonic setting of gym class is clear; whether one consents to rule or one withdraws. Indeed, policy changes allowing boys to withdraw from physical education in Grade 10 in Ontario punctuate the point with considerable cultural emphasis. Should we honestly expect that the boys themselves work towards a "revolution" that would truly serve their collective physical education needs in these contexts? Such would be foolish thinking. What is more likely to happen, given what the boys speak about in interviews, is that they will either find physical activity in do-it-yourself fashion outside of school time, forsake physical activity all together, and/or develop more extended anti-jock cultural attitudes which appear to be blossoming in Canada (Wilson, 2006). Consider the following:

> The main reason I quit was because I just don't enjoy football and I was mainly doing it because everybody else wanted me to, not because I wanted to and the other reason is I hate jocks. I don't want to be so direct but that's...they're generally bullies. They're not academic generally and their big and they just...they're really...I just don't like them. They're not...I don't really know the word I'm looking for here. They're just kind of egotistical and they think because they're jocks they're better than everybody else and I was afraid that playing football would turn me into one of those things and I didn't want to become something that I hate. I didn't want to become someone that I'm not because I would much prefer a quiet evening at home reading a good novel than being out on the football field knocking people over. (Spikeshade, age 15)

Gramsci (1971) argued for "wars of position" and "wars of manoeuvre" as mechanisms for combating the tyranny of hegemony. Wars of position are culture battles in which anti-capitalist/authoritarian elements seek to gain a dominant voice in mass media, mass organizations, and educational institutions to heighten class-consciousness, teach revolutionary analysis and theory, and inspire revolutionary organization. Following the success of a war of position, new leaders would be empowered to begin wars of manoeuvre, the actual insurrection against the established power bloc, with mass support. Violent overthrow in the education system is clearly not the answer to problems of masculinity in the locker room / physical education setting! But there is considerable hope and merit in the idea that educators and policy makers on the inside might strive to alter the physical culture of gym in the school setting to make it more inclusive. What is patently obvious is that groups inside of the power blocs in school need to deploy their social capital to help boys on the margins. Stated differently, educators and policy makers in Canada must no longer help, through acquiescence and reluctance to view masculinity as something which matters in the policy and practice of physical education, to help boys "dodge the dodge-ball."

What is specifically required in this case? First and foremost, the young boys teach us how physical educators must seek to recognize and protect multiple masculinities. Anderson (2009) reminds us to challenge the singular construction of a single, legitimate hegemonic masculinity, and argues that there are many men with different kinds of masculinities in any cultural setting. But most do not participate in a universal brand of hegemony, Gramsci (1971) articulates, or in a broader structural-cultural hegemony as Connell (1995) outlines. They have frailties, inadequacies and impure masculine statuses that exclude them from ideal-type categorization. These boys and men can be ruled, dominated, influenced and stigmatized by other boys and men, and sometimes, by women in seemingly innocuous manners.

Important is that unless discourses and practices sensitive to multiple masculinities are revealed to young men as acceptable and normative, the notion of multiple masculinities often escapes young boys who do not see gender in such complex, contradictory, or challengeable terms.

Consider how young boys often view masculinity along flagrantly essentialist (biological) lines. Males are big, strong, fast and authoritarian, while non-hegemonic males tend to be smart, emotive and intuitive. Binaries between established and outsider masculinities are reinforced in the classes, and unless exposed there, such ideologies become embedded in the habitus. An interviewee named Rod said, "*In the change room like they would say well you're not like me and say you're not cool enough and I didn't like how they would say well I'm bigger than you so I have more authority, so you should listen to me.*" To young boys like Rod, masculinity is a world of black and white, right and wrong, and of inclusion and exclusion. Troubling is how physical activity too often is associated with the "right" kind of masculinity and its life-long embodiment. Just as troubling is how they, themselves, learn to label other boys as unintelligent or un-artistic because they excel in gym class. Perhaps as a defence mechanism, marginalized boys condemn "jocks" as stupid and inferior at complex intellectual tasks.

Second, Gramsci's (1971) description of hegemony suggests that any prevailing cultural norms cleaving people into powerful or ruled groups are not immutable. Rather, the ideological roots of status hierarchies and the institutions, practices, beliefs which support them can be critiqued as reversible systems of domination. Norms and cultural ways of life promoting certain young boys as dominant masculine in any social context can be destabilized, and challenged and dissected as exploitive techniques of power. Translation; the normativity and heterotopia of the locker room can be destabilized. Private showers and changing spaces are but small steps in deconstructing the cultural landscape and hegemonic possibilities of the locker room. Fragments of such awareness were exposed through interviews with boys:

> So it [would be] better if there's stalls where people can just have their own shower. I'd have to put up with that. So I usually take my shower at home but if I was really running or doing stuff, then I would have to take it at the gym and I don't really like to do that but just if I'm really sweaty. (Bob, age 15)

Gramsci's (1971) construction of hegemony has been modified and extended by contemporary gender theorists, who read contemporary power struggles in social life as contests over the ability to define reality. In taking steps toward de-emphasizing a particular kind of masculinity (and its corporeal representation) in and through the locker room, we may begin by altering the heterotopic reality of the locker room.

By taking the lead of radical social constructionists and post-structuralists including Foucault (1979, 1980), Pringle (2005) contends that power is more closely linked to a group's access to the production and dissemination of knowledge (or, means of representing social truth) than strict membership in elite status or class positions. What goes on in locker room space is as much, unfortunately, about disseminating what it means to be a dominant young boy as it is about ritually changing one's clothes to prepare for a physical education class. The space is heterotopic for boys as it is defining zone of male reality foreign or inaccessible to them. The reality of their masculinity is pejoratively defined within the space by others, and not by them. Individuals who control processes of ontological framing in a society—Foucault (1979, 1980) refers to those who dictate discourse within particular social formations, and shape cultural *dispotifs*—are hegemonic in contemporary life. From this perspective, young boys themselves are given, in a *carte blanche* sense, the authority to reinforce and shape dominant masculine *dispotifs* in the locker room.

> I have not brought my gym uniform, my gym clothes to school on so many occasions that if I don't pass the exam I'm not going to get the credit for gym and that was a conscious choice on my part because I did not want to participate because I brought it a few times but I would wear it underneath my other clothes and I would just take those off in the change room and have my gym uniform on because I was uncomfortable with my body and I was afraid of what other kids would say to me because in grade 8 I know in the change room I got made fun of a lot. When I would take my shirt off to change into my other shirt people would scream and look away and stuff just to make fun of me. So I had had enough of that and I decided that I was either not going to bring my uniform or just not participate altogether. (John, age 15)

If boys in underprivileged masculine under-classes make social in-roads into these positions, then the historical ideologies that have served to marginalize them as socially inferior can be de-centered and replaced with alternative hegemonies. This must begin, as some boys teach us, by changing the pedagogy of physical education.

The boys interviewed almost universally cited three main problems with what counts as physical education. While most desired more in-class health education, they detest physical education which: is based on power and performance team-based sports; occurs in a context in which the teacher is also a sports coach; and, one in which grades are earned meritocratically through sports performance. For the boys, team-based sports tend to become gang-bullying contexts of dominance bonding (Farr, 1988). Popular, muscular boys are positioned as team captains, stack their teams with their friends, and leave the least physically dominant boys to be selected last. In competition, physical performances only heighten codes about dominant masculinity enforced in the locker rooms. It is no empirical surprise why the boys learn to fear and loathe collective participation in physical education. But surprising is how many boys point to the teacher/coach's pivotal role in the masculinity confirmation process. Several of the boys narrate how coaches laugh at or mock the boys' physical problems with a particular gym task; or, how the teacher serves to legitimate a masculine hierarchy in the class.

> The teacher plays a major role because he's the one who will...they try to follow the curriculum pretty well probably and he's the one who will maybe if it gets out of hand like give them heck and chastise them for it, who will tell them to set a good example and represent Carlisle [school] well when we go out on field trips and stuff. In the gym class the teacher mainly plays the role of the coach and he's not really trying to gear it towards everybody. He's just trying to go, okay this is what we're doing, this is the sport, I'm going to blow the whistle, and you go out there and block. (Rod, age 15)

Boys like Rod find little cultural or structural justice in the system. Because the teacher may actually coach and befriend the dominant boys on a team setting, there is systematic bias and structural inequality in the grading system. Quite interestingly, they are actually punished academically for not living up to dominant gender performance standards. Boys who are on the margins are then presented with a double-bind in gym class, as they are deemed culturally and then academically inferior.

Third and finally, few seem to listen to these boys and how they would relish a different ethos and praxis of physical education. These are not "naturally lazy" or unmotivated boys as discourse often positions them. They are interested in different sorts of physical activities, leisure pursuits and even sports that do not find a way onto the curriculum. Programs of physical education which are co-ed, multi-sport and activity-based, are portioned out in balance between physical activity and health education, and are not overseen by hegemonic male authority figures in the school might go a long way in encouraging different perspectives about the place of masculinity in PE.

> Then maybe put something like that in just because it's interesting or just do other interesting things like archery, just other physical stuff that isn't aggressive or maybe just put more stuff like skiing or walking or running because they focus more on sports. They have a little bit of running at my school but you know, not too much. I'm good at running and maybe if they're more enthusiastic about that. (Mythic Artist, age 15)

> Other ways you could improve gym class would probably be they could make it instead of being geared just towards the jocks or the athletic kids, they could make it maybe even 50/50 time in the gym and the classroom so it's geared towards everybody...the academically driven and the athletically driven and I think that would be better because then nobody feels like, man I can't do this. This isn't like everybody here is better at this than I am. Nobody would feel like that because it focuses on both interests equally and I think that would really help because then you eliminate

these feelings of, I hate gym class. I'm not good at it because you would think I don't care for the athletic part of gym class but that's okay because we're in the classroom also. So just about as much time as we're in the gym, so I can still pass this for my classroom. But the thing here is no matter how much they don't judge based on skill and it's just participation, even if it's that, if you're not academically driven you're not going to want to participate in the gym part and you can't pass for just the classwork. But I think it would be better if you could because then you'd feel better about participating in gym no matter how badly you get because you think hey even if I do badly here, my classwork can save my mark and I think that would be better for the whole image thing and maybe...I don't know having enforcement in the locker room. I don't know how they'd be able to do that, but maybe having just one person who's either a teacher or maybe a student in the class who's to report to the teacher with maybe so and so was being bullied in the change room by whoever and whoever. I think that would help a lot with the acceptance aspect of it. (Spikeshade, age 15)

Conclusion

The social bads produced with the context of physical education instruction for young boys who do not live up to prevailing codes of dominant masculinity are rarely tackled within educational policy settings. Preliminary data reveal disturbing trends about how historically marginalizing codes of masculinity remain overtly and covertly apparent in the gym setting. Lenskyj (2003) describes sport as a place with an institutionally "chilly climate" for young girls. There is ample evidence to indicate that many young boys are "chilled" in physical education and sport settings. Perhaps even more paramount for boys is, however, that the athletic body is heavily tied to the socially acceptable male body. The present data indicate that these boys are slipping through cracks in the physical education program in certain Ontario high schools because their alternative modalities for doing and being masculine are ignored or rejected outright within gym settings. New spaces and opportunities must be created for boys, especially given the considerable empirical documentation of how inactivity and disengagement from athletics in early life leads to sedentary behaviour through adulthood. Of course, such an empirical problem speaks nothing about the self-identity issues and traumas associated within patterned social belittling through adolescence. Several decades worth of research on the problems associated with instructing a singular masculinity through physical education into education policy reform must be further translated in policy settings in order to improve the ways in which physical activity *for all* is delivered as part of public education.

Notes
1. This paper emerges from a large-scale, Social Sciences and Humanities Research Council of Canada project on the social construction of boys'

bodies in gym class, and the problem of attrition in gym. Data reviewed in this paper were gathered as part of the process, and an earlier version of the paper was presented at the 2009 Canadian Society for the Study of Education meetings in Ottawa, Canada.

Bibliography

Althusser, L. (1971). *Lenin and philosophy and other essays.* London: New Left Books.

Anderson, E. (2009). *Inclusive masculinity.* London: Routledge.

Atkinson, M., & Young, K. (2008). *Deviance and social control in sport.* Champaign: Human Kinetics.

Beck, U. (2002). *Power in the global age.* Cambridge: Polity Press.

Beck, U. (1992). *Risk society: Towards a new modernity.* London: Sage.

Bourdieu, P. (1984). *Distinction: A social critique of the judgement of taste.* Cambridge, MA: Harvard University Press.

Bryshun, J., & Young, K. (2007). Sport-related hazing: An inquiry into male and female involvememt. In K. Young & P. White (Eds.), *Sport and gender in Canada* (pp. 267-292). Toronto: Oxford University Press.

Burstyn, V. (1999). *The rites of men: Manhood, politics, and the culture of sport.* Toronto: University of Toronto Press.

Cauldwell, J. (2006). *Sport, sexualities and queer theory.* London: Routledge.

Connell, R. (2000). *The men and the boys.* Berkeley: University of California Press.

Connell, R. (1995). *Masculinities.* Berkeley: University of California Press.

Davison, K., & Frank, B. (2007). Sexualities, gender, and bodies in sport: Changing practices of inequity. In K. Young & P. White (Eds.), *Sport and gender in Canada* (pp. 178-193). Toronto: Oxford University Press.

Durkheim, E. (1956). *The rules of sociological method.* Glencoe: Free Press.

Elias, N. (1978). *The civilizing process.* Oxford: Blackwell.

Farr, K. (1988). Dominance bonding through the good old boys sociability group. *Sex Roles, 18,* 259-77.

Foucault, M. (1967). Of other spaces. Reprinted in *Diacritics* 16 (1986), 22-27.

Foucault, M. (1979). *Power/knowledge: Selected interviews and other writings 1972-1977.* Brighton: Harvester Press.

Foucault, M. (1980). *The history of sexuality, volume 1: An introduction.* London: Allen Lane/Penguin Books.

Fusco, C. (2005). Cultural landscapes of purification: Sports spaces and discourses of whiteness. *Sociology of Sport Journal, 22,* 283-310.

Fusco, C. (2006a). Inscribing healthification: Governance, risk, surveillance and the subjects and spaces of fitness and health. *Journal of Health & Place, 12,* 65-78.

Fusco, C. (2006b). Spatializing the (im)proper subject: The geographies of abjection in sport and physical activity space. *Journal of Sport and Social Issues, 30,* 5-28.

Goffman, E. (1959). *The Presentation of Self in Everyday Life.* London: Penguin.

Gramsci, A. (1971). *Selections from prison notebooks.* London: Lawrence & Wishart.

Kehler, M. (2007). Hallway fears and high school friendships: The complications of young men (re)negotiating heterosexualized identities. *Discourse: Studies in the Cultural Politics of Education, 28,* 259-277.

Kehler, M., Davison, K., & Frank, B. (2005). Contradictions and tensions of the practice of masculinities in school: Interrogating "good buddy talk." *Journal of Curriculum Theorizing*, 21, 59-72.

Kehler, M., & Martino, W. (2007) Questioning masculinities: Interrogating boys' capacities for self-problematization in schools. *Canadian Journal of Education*, 30, 90-112.

Johnson, J., & Holman, M. (2004). *Making the team: Inside the world of sport initiations and hazing*. Halifax: Canadian Scholar's Press.

Lenskyj, H. (2003). *Out on the field: Gender, sport and sexualities*. Toronto: Women's Press

Lyotard, J-F. (1989). Scapeland. In A. Benjamin (ed.), *The Lyotard reader* (pp. 212-219). Oxford: Basil Blackwell.

Pringle, R. (2005). Masculinities, sport, and power: A critical comparison of Gramscian and Foucauldian inspired theoretical tools. *Journal of Sport & Social Issues*, 29, 256-278.

Rich, E., & Evans, J. (2006). Fat ethics: The obesity discourse and body politics. *Social Theory and Health*, 3, 341-358.

Shott, D. (2009). The informal regulation of gender: Fear and loathing in the locker room. *Journal of Gender Studies*, 16, 183-186.

Sutherland, E. (1947). *The professional thief*. Chicago: University of Chicago Press.

White, P., & Young, K. (1997). Masculinity, sport, and the injury process: A review of Canadian and international evidence. *Avante*, 3, 1-30.

Wilson, B. (2006). Ethnography, the internet and youth culture: Strategies for examining social resistance and "online-offline" relationships. *Canadian Journal of Education*, 29, 307-328.

CHAPTER FIVE

Consuming Media, Constructing Masculinities: A Study of Youth Audiences and Physical Education in "Reflexively Modern" Times

Brad Millington and Brian Wilson

T hough it could well be said that adolescence has never been easy, the current moment brings with it a unique set of challenges for young people. In particular, the growing sophistication of technologies, when paired together with late capitalism's emphasis on perpetual and highly personalized consumption, means that media messages increasingly infiltrate the various contexts of daily living (Giddens, 1991; Thrift, 2003). Youth are thus required to make ongoing decisions about what behaviors and modes of self-presentation are "appropriate"—and what behaviors/modes are not. This situation is especially complicated because images of "desirable" male and female body types, styles, and character-types abound in television, film, and other media. Furthermore, a small body of empirical research suggests that the various contexts young people move through on a daily basis also contain differing expectations about how media should be understood. That is to say, certain interpretations of media messages may be appropriate in one location or with certain people (e.g., at school or with peer groups), yet wholly unacceptable elsewhere (e.g., at home or with the family), meaning youth must be carefully reflexive at all times (Miles, 2000).

Despite these manifest complexities in youth culture(s), there is a tendency in mainstream discourses (e.g., in popular media or in governmental debates) to oversimplify young people's relationship to prominent media depictions. Giroux (2001), for example, identifies an ascendant "myth of childhood innocence" whereby young people are seen as passive and impressionable (i.e., void of agency) in their media consumption. Violent imagery in particular is seen to have direct and deleterious consequences for youth consumers, despite the fact that youth themselves are rarely consulted in appraisals of their media literacy or in commentaries about "media impacts" (Wilson, 2006). These developments are made even more troubling by the fact that academic researchers studying media often disregard or discount how young people react to media messages as well.

This chapter is a response to these issues, and specifically to the need for studies that are sensitive to the perceptions and experiences of youth audience members. Our focus in this case is on young males—a group exposed to variable media depictions of "manhood," but typically targeted through portrayals that show strength, aggression, and emphasized heterosexuality as naturally residing in the male figure (Messner, Dunbar & Hunt; 2002). In what follows we report key findings from an ethnographic study that took place over five months at a Secondary School set in the Lower Mainland of Vancouver—a study that was designed to investigate the complex relationship between media consumption, school physical education, and masculinity. In particular, influenced by literature on media consumption in late modernity, as well as by physical education scholars like Kirk (2002), we aimed to better understand: (1) how young males make sense of the now ubiquitous media portrayals of strong, tough, domineering and explicitly heterosexual masculinities; and (2) how such interpretations seem to complement and/or counteract their experiences of masculinity in the constructed physical education environment. In other words, underlying our project was a desire to examine how interpretations of masculinity relate to performances of masculinity, and how the interpretations and performances of young males are influenced by the social contexts they inhabit and their social positioning in relation to others (e.g., within peer hierarchies). We were especially attentive to how the concept of hegemony is useful for explaining the relationship between (youth) agency and social structures in a "reflexively modern" moment. We thus begin by reviewing how hegemony has been influential in scholarship on youth cultures, media consumption in late or reflexive modernity, gender studies, and physical education. We then detail our methodological approach in this research, before turning to our key findings. Finally, our conclusion stresses the need for future studies devoted to strategies and programs for harnessing the critical media literacy of youth.

Literature Review

Youth Consumption and Social/Cultural Context

Building from Gramsci's notion of hegemony, critical scholars have offered updated perspectives on youth consumption in the contemporary moment. Willis' (1990) "symbolic creativity" is a notable contribution because it suitably encapsulates his observation that young people make strategic and critically informed consumption decisions that suit their lifestyle interests. Miles (2000) and Bennett (2000) offer nuance and context to Willis' argument in their suggestions that acts of critical consumption are part of a process whereby youth construct alternative lifestyles that give them a sense of "ontological security" and coherence in a world lacking stability and meaning. Similarly, Furlong & Cartmel (2007) argue that youth consumption is increasingly individualized and tied to identity formation in late modernity (as noted in our introduction), but add that the freedoms and flexibilities associated with enhanced choice are linked with risks and personal responsibilities. Put another way, contemporary youths' subjective understandings of their social worlds—understandings that were once shaped largely by class, gender, ethnicity, and neighborhood relations—can be complicated and obscured because options for consumption-related activities seem endless and almost indistinguishable. This can lead youth to feel increasingly "disembedded" (Giddens, 1991). Of course, this movement toward individualization does not mean that consumption activities take place in isolation from structural constraints that frame and are the basis for consumer-decisions (Sweetman, 2004). Instead, it means that accounting for social and cultural context alongside classical variables associated with social position (i.e., race, class, gender) is necessary when attempting to explain consumption habits and strategies.

Deriving from these critical perspectives is a series of specific theoretical arguments relevant to the experiences of youth in contemporary consumer-driven cultures—arguments that we draw on and assess throughout this research. The first of these is that identities of young people are increasingly neo-tribal and individualized, meaning that youth are more likely than in the past to simultaneously be members of various social and cultural groups (Bennett, 2000; Furlong & Cartmel, 2007). As noted, this is not to discount the lasting impacts of cultural background and economic resources on lifestyle and leisure choices; rather, it is to recognize that young people do not organize in all cases around class, gender, and race/ethnicity-related factors. A second argument is that youths' consumption-related identity performances are context dependent. That is to say, there are sets of social and cultural expectations that are maintained within (and specific to) the various social groups that young people move between, and youth perform a range of context-dependent identities. Often these variable identity performances are directed by the goal of attaining status or "subcultural capital" (Miles, 2000; Thornton, 1995). Finally, and closely related to these first two points, we assess the idea that the relationship between youth agents and social structures is hegemonic. Researchers have claimed that young people's cultural activities, while creative and oftentimes subversive, are seldom the basis for meaningful (i.e., more than symbolic) challenges to pro-consumerism ideologies. Such analyses are not intended to dismiss the role of cultural activity in identity negotiation for youth; they aim instead to identify how certain forms of seemingly resistant activity may in fact reinforce existing relations of power in Western consumer-driven societies (Willis, 1990), or may be confined to the contexts in which they are carried out (Lull, 2000).

Youth, Media, and Consumption

These arguments are further linked with theories that commonly guide analyses of how youth audiences interpret and use media contents. Indeed, there is an historical relationship between audience research and studies of youth consumption practices (Côté & Allahar, 1996; Wilson & Sparks, 1996; 2001). Researchers have long contended that young people's ability to negotiate media messages is related to and limited by their social and cultural experiences, including social background and peer group affiliations. Media researchers have also attempted to discern when (and the extent to which) youth are active/critical audience members, and when they are influenced by and are susceptible to media messages (Alasuutari, 1999; Buckingham, 1993). Miles (2000), for example, argues that youth possess the ability to be critical in their consumption of media, but that reflective, oppositional (Hall, 1980) interpretations are context dependent and rarely influence behavior in other social settings. Although research focused on youth interpretations of media may be helpful in understanding how interpretive communities of young people (whose community membership is defined by, for example, peer group status, gender, ethnicity, and class) make sense of and use media, these communities only exist in social, historical, (sub)cultural contexts. For this reason, views expressed in media-viewing contexts may translate into a range of actions in other settings (Murphy, 2005; Radway, 1996).

Gender, Media, and (Youth) Identities

In a similar way, recent attempts to theorize gender-related identity negotiations acknowledge that understandings of gender are constructed and context dependent. Connell's (1995; 2009; Connell & Messerschmidt, 2005) concept of hegemonic masculinity is commonly employed to explain how gender-based power imbalances are fostered and sustained. For Connell (1995), the promotion of certain masculinities reproduces and reinforces taken-for-granted assumptions regarding the "naturalness" of these gender identities. Certain traits thus come to be informally sanctioned as appropriate, allowing those who embody or express these characteristics significant cultural power. Although hegemonic masculinity is commonly equated to a static masculine form that is reliant upon stereotypical traits (e.g., physical strength and heterosexuality) (Hearn, 2004), Connell's framework allows the possibility for multiple, simultaneous hegemonic masculinities, and for individuals to shift subject positions according to context (Connell & Messerschmidt, 2005).

These theoretical suppositions are especially valuable to media studies. Although diverse masculinities are represented in media, researchers have demonstrated how strength, aggression, and heterosexuality are typically portrayed as "necessary" masculine characteristics (Messner, 2002: White & Gillett, 1994). Media portrayals of this kind are commonly accompanied by limited depictions of femininity and "alternative" masculinities that assign stereotypical traits like passivity and weakness to female and some male characters (Kane & Lenskyj, 1998). Such representations of dominant masculinities can have shifting, contradictory meanings, particularly when they intersect with ethnicity, race, and class (Dworkin & Wachs, 1998; Jefferson, 1998; Jeffords, 1994; Majors & Billson, 1992; Miller, 1998). Nonetheless, for these purposes it is important to emphasize that media portrayals of strong, explicitly heterosexual, and seemingly empowered masculinities potentially normalize these attributes for, among others, young male consumers. For example, research by Messner et al. (2002) indicates that the pervasive "Televised Sports Manhood Formula" offers youth viewers "a remarkably stable and concrete view of masculinity as grounded in bravery, risk taking, violence, bodily strength, and heterosexuality" (p. 392).

Messner et al.'s (2002) research also outlines the gender ideologies that drive the initial production of media. In sports media in particular, "the invisible apparatus of presentation" (e.g., editing, camera angles) (Silk, 1999) has been shown to reiterate dominant themes that privilege men's pursuits and, concomitantly, hegemonic masculinities (MacNeill, 1996). The process of coding popular media is often done with the intention of attracting particular audiences as commodities (Sparks, 1992). In the case of media that promote stereotypical masculine traits, it is generally young males who are the targeted consumers (Messner, 2002). In spite of this, and in spite of the rich tradition of audience studies in the social sciences (Murphy, 2005), there is a scarcity of research into the diverse ways that youth decode media messages about gender (Lines, 2000). As well, the role these messages play in the everyday experiences of youth consumers remains largely unexplored (Alasuutari, 1999).

Physical Education, Media, and Masculinity

Contemporary physical education also offers the possibility for a range of experiences and identity performances. Yet like the media's reliance on stereotypical gender tropes, so too does PE tend to privilege dominant masculinities (Brown & Evans, 2004; Gorely, Holroyd & Kirk., 2003). In particular, gender hierarchies emerge through PE's traditional reliance upon competitive team activities that champion violence and aggression, and that exclude or marginalize some female and male participants. Furthermore, the physical capital garnered by athletic males in sporting competitions has exchange value in social and cultural realms (Gorely *et al.*, 2003; Wilson, 2002), permitting males that have access to and excel in these exclusive sport cultures privileged status. Hierarchies of gender in PE are also influenced by race (as well as class, sexuality, age and other aspects of identity), rendering further power imbalances (Epstein, Kehily, Mac an Ghaill, & Redman, 2001; Keddie, 2005; Parker, 1996). For example, researchers in education contexts have shown how curricula tacitly or overtly assimilate students of various backgrounds into "appropriate" forms of citizenship that favor a narrowly defined set of acceptable behaviors and cultural/physical activities (Fenton, Frisby & Luke, 1999).

PE has thus been identified as a potential site where problematic notions of identity and embodiment are cultivated. Indeed, Kirk (2002) contends that PE in many ways works in reciprocity with contemporary media, as each of these realms contributes to the privileged status of specific "masculine" body types and identities. Yet there remains limited empirically based consideration of how these key sites of physical culture work contiguously as socializing agents. A notable exception is Kirk and Tinning's (1994) ethnographic research into the articulations of schooling and media. They demonstrate how the narrow definitions of gender that circulate in media potentially foster a sense of "disembodiment" for young people (i.e., a sense that personal body aesthetic does not align with "appropriate" corporeality), and can thus impact how young people experience physical education's daily practices. Inspired by these authors, and by the paucity of empirically based studies that explore the potentially complementary and/or contradictory role of media and PE in shaping how young people understand and practice gender, we undertook our study at a school we will call "Vancouver High."

Setting and Methods

Vancouver High is a secondary school located in an area with elevated average levels of family income and education. According to provincial census statistics, there is a relatively high percentage of families from Asian backgrounds in this area, with a large percentage of the population defining their ethnicity as Chinese (British Columbia Statistics, 2001). These demographic figures are reflective of the sample of participants in this research. Most students came from middle-class backgrounds, and slightly less than half self-defined their race/ethnicity as Asian, Chinese, Chinese Canadian, Taiwanese, or Korean. Approximately half of the participants identified as a combination of White, Caucasian, and European Canadian (namely, British, French, Dutch, or Scottish Canadian), and, of the remaining boys, one identified as Serbian, one as Italian/First Nations, and three gave no response.

From February to April of 2006, three complementary qualitative research techniques—focus groups, interviews, and naturalistic observation—were employed to collect data. This multi-method approach was adopted based on our assumption that the use of numerous, complementary research techniques is beneficial for studying the multifaceted ways that gender is understood and experienced in multiple contexts (Richardson, 1998). The University of British Columbia's Behavioural Research Ethics Board provided approval for this study, as did the relevant high school education board and the participating school. The names of students, teachers, and the school have been altered in this document in the interest of confidentiality.

Two sets of focus groups were conducted with male students (n = 36) from one co-ed and two all-male PE classes. Session One focus groups took place at the beginning of the study and were prompted by a five-minute researcher-constructed video montage showing a selection of prominent depictions of masculinity in media. An emphasis was placed in the video on hegemonic masculinities (McKay, Mikosza & Hutchins, 2005) however these portraits were contextualized with gender representations that can be coded as "alternative" in that they clearly deviate from those commonly considered hegemonic and in that they appear in media less frequently. The purpose of this was to "trigger" discussion on the topic of gender in media. Indeed, the focus group discussions that followed were guided by a set of questions designed to explore the students' perceptions of both the video montage and of masculinity and femininity in the media in general. These conversations were facilitated in a relatively structured manner in that they had a definite goal, involved a media-viewing element and questionnaire, and were informed by (but not tied to) a pre-set interview guide (Wilson & Sparks, 1999; 2001). In this first stage of the study participants were also asked to complete a questionnaire regarding their demographic characteristics (e.g., race, parental income and education, age), their perceptions of the video, the frequency with which they consume these and similar images, and the extent to which they witness comparable expressions of masculinity in their everyday lives.

Near the conclusion of the study, and subsequent to the naturalistic observation phase (described below), Session Two focus groups were held. At this time, the participants' general perceptions of masculinity and PE were discussed, as was the manner in which they characterize the relationship between their media and PE experiences. In total, 22 focus groups (11 in Session One, 11 in Session Two) with the 36 study participants were completed.

Between focus group sessions, approximately three months were spent observing the participating PE classes (roughly 55 hours in the field). The primary researcher acted strictly as an observer at this time, and recorded data on events relevant to the research topics (e.g., verbal and physical relationships between students; visible similarities or differences between the students' opinions of masculinity and their perceived gender performances). The length of the observation period was decided upon following previous qualitative research in education (Humbert, 1995) and according to the development of recurring themes and "data saturation" (Morgan, 1997). At this time, informal (i.e., unstructured and unrecorded) and formal interviews with three PE instructors were also taken up as a final data collection method. These conversations were valuable in that the teachers were knowledgeable of both the participating students and of gender relations in PE more generally. Multiple detailed reads of all transcripts and field notes rendered during data collection were completed in the analysis process, with consideration provided to both observer-identified themes (i.e., those identified in consultation with existing literature) as well as inductive themes unanticipated prior to analysis. Ongoing discussions between the researchers took place as part of a reflexive approach to assessing the collected data and identifying emergent themes.

Findings

The research findings show the complex and often contradictory ways the study participants understand and practice gender. The section on gender and media, reported first, reveals how the students had a tendency to criticize popular representations of gender as well as media production processes. The analysis of PE, reported second, reveals that, contrary to the ways they commonly consume media, the boys showed near unwavering support for hegemonic masculinities in PE class, and thus contributed to an environment that normalized aggressive and competitive masculinities. Acknowledging the complexity and diversity of gender, in what follows we employ the terms "hegemonic," "dominant," and "stereotypical" masculinities synonymously to describe masculinities denoted by traits such as strength, aggression, and necessary heterosexuality (McKay et al., 2005; Messner et al., 2002).

Gender and Media Consumption

In every focus group, the Vancouver High boys suggested that dominant masculinities are built on traits like strength and toughness. Occasionally these masculinities were revered, but more often they were disparaged and interpreted as undesirable. Accordingly, it can be said the students had a sophisticated *ability* to be critical of dominant masculinities in the media.

Criticizing Media Representations, "You gotta be sensitive and caring at the same time to impress the ladies, but you have to be this butch like, can bench press 250 pounds ... to impress the guys."

In response to the video montage, the boys were critical of media figures like action heroes for their reliance on stereotypically masculine traits. Aggressive and ostensibly empowered action stars were seen as overconfident or arrogant, as were some professional athletes. The students similarly admonished the exaggerated musculature and physical aesthetic of popular male bodies. Although the unhealthy consequences often accompanying extreme strength and muscularity are usually unspoken in the media, students in virtually every focus group were attuned to the damaging effects of, for example, steroid use. Allan, for instance, provides a critique of "appropriate" male physiques:

Researcher –	Does the media, you find, give you guys real portrayals of men and masculinity?
Allan –	Not often.
R –	No? How so Allan?
A –	Well, you see 'Roid Droids like the Strongman pulling trucks ...
Cal –	Or like Bowflex ads.
A –	... You need the chiselled abs. Yeah it's good to be healthy and workout and stuff like that, but I think that [they're not] healthy [they're strong] ... [It's] excess in the portrayal of masculinity.
R –	What do you mean by excess?
A –	Like you need 500 girlfriends and all these steroids ... and a huge mansion and stuff like that to be a man. (FG Session 1).

This rejection of chiselled bodies was occasionally mitigated by a simultaneous dismissal of "scrawny" frames (described below), but in this instance Allan condemns portrayals of excessive musculature as well as the stereotypical notions that appropriate masculinity is contingent upon heterosexual conquest and material wealth.

Also of significance in this passage (and a common theme in many groups) is the manner in which Allan addresses the unrealistic nature of media masculinities. Allan's classmate Ryan raises this point as well, arguing that movies are "going back to the old stereotypes where the man is the tough guy" (FG Session 1). An even stronger criticism is levied by Chad—a dominant masculine figure himself in PE—and Gavin:

Gavin –   Stereotypically it's like, you gotta be a strong, manly man
           …
Chad –   You gotta be strong, you gotta be courageous …
G –   … but you gotta be sensitive and caring at the same time
           to impress the ladies, but you have to be this butch like,
           can bench press 250 pounds one arm kind of guy to
           impress the guys. So you have to multi-task basically.
C –   That's stereotypically though … That's what everybody
           thinks. That's what you expect of a real …
G –   Manly man (*said in a mocking, grizzled voice*), Arnold
           Schwarzenegger type of guy.
R –   And do you guys agree or disagree with that?
C –   No, no. I think it's stupid.
           (FG Session 1).

Mark and Peter evoke a similar critique, suggesting "the perfect man" is presented as humorous, athletic, and confident all at once, and that media productions are "saying that everybody should strive to be that sort of guy" (Peter, FG Session 1).

Criticism of this kind was not limited to portrayals of masculinity. Students also noted that media images of women are often steeped in derogatory stereotypes. Ryan, for example, expressed admiration for film portrayals that contravene stereotypical notions of "emphasized femininity" (Connell, 1995). Steve condemned music videos that "exploit women in bad ways" (FG Session 1), while his friend Zach criticized "necessary" feminine traits shown in media like thinness and physical weakness (FG Session 1).

Criticizing Media Production: "Most of those music videos or TV shows are just the director living out his dream."

Some participants also provided explanations for the ubiquity of stereotypical gender portrayals in media. Students in a few groups believed that media producers are solely concerned with monetary dividends or with attracting the attention of particular viewing audiences, and construct exaggerated masculinities to achieve these goals. After fervently criticizing hegemonic masculinities, Howie notes, "That's how the producers make them 'cause it makes money, and it's all about making money for them" (FG Session 1). Chad tied the surrealism of TV shows and movies to producers' desire for viewership, asking rhetorically, "everything's overdramatic and stuff just to ... get viewers, right?" (FG Session 1). Perhaps the sharpest critique of media production, however, was offered by Allan and Frank. Noticing the frequency with which men are shown in hegemonic roles in the media, as well as the concomitant subordination of women, these students saw media production as the result of masculine fantasies:

Allan –	Those music videos or TV shows are just the director living out his dream.
Frank –	[They build] a fantasy world.
A –	A fantasy. I'm sure 50 Cent doesn't have 15 girls around him at all times.
F –	Like almost like soft-core porno or something. (FG Session 1).

The participants' two-fold critique of media representations and production is best exemplified by Zach. When asked if there are "necessary" masculine traits, Zach answered, "I don't think there is, but we're just kind of, we're trained ... like being strong or not emotional at all" (FG Session 1). Physical and emotional strength are markers of hegemonic masculinity that Zach sees as undesirable, despite their omnipresence. What's more, the notion that "we're trained" implies a critique of an unseen trainer (i.e., producer) who strategically patterns the representations that are directed at young males.

Hegemonic Media Interpretations: "It just looks pretty funny guys doing design."

Hegemonic Masculinities and Physical Education

Despite the frequency with which the Vancouver High boys actively scrutinized media portrayals of gender, it was evident that dominant masculine traits were not viewed through the same critical lens in PE. Characteristics such as strength, toughness, and the ability to intimidate were in fact valorized in PE, permitting students who most obviously embodied and displayed these traits significant cultural power.

Competitive Sport and Hegemonic Masculinities: "Everyone who competes really wants the number one spot, to be praised."

When discussing their PE experiences, boys in every Session Two focus group mentioned the necessity for a competitive sporting ethic. Certainly, competition is not intrinsically problematic, but the Vancouver High boys valued a specific type of competition imbued with the principles of hegemonic masculinity. That is to say, the students conflated competitiveness with strength, toughness, and aggression, and at times saw these characteristics as belonging exclusively to (certain) male students. Female participants were thus deemed unsuited for PE by some boys, as noted when Clayton says, "[Girls are] wimps. They're afraid of the ball," and when Austin contends, "[Girls] just don't do anything" (FG Session 2). Some male students were also deemed out of place in PE. This is best expressed by Chad, a student who, despite his willingness to critique media masculinities, also appropriated a dominant subject position in PE:

Chad –	Remember that dodgeball game we had [a few times ago] where I was telling you how I killed Tim ... I cracked him in the stomach?
R –	Yeah.
C –	I was so happy.
R –	Why was that so exciting to you?
C –	Because he always annoys me ... he's just a sack of shit! He doesn't do anything. (FG Session 2).

It is notable that Chad and Austin, two popular male figures from different PE classes, have employed the same language–"don't do anything"–to describe those female and male students they consider unsuited for this subject. The views of these boys support the contention of one PE teacher that "To be an athletic male is still to be pretty much top of the heap in high school" (Interview #1).

The coding of "appropriate" and "inappropriate" characteristics for PE participation impacted the actual practice of this subject. The collective sanctioning of strength, physical ability, and competitiveness meant those students who most obviously embodied or displayed these characteristics were celebrated by their classmates. As Steve indicates, "everyone who competes really wants the number one spot, to be praised ... for your abilities" (FG Session 2). Furthermore, students displaying these traits were in a position to influence, control, or demean those who were perceived to be weak or incapable. Of course, the power available to these select boys was not solely a matter of consent: strong and aggressive students could act in violent ways because of the very fact they are strong and aggressive. However, in the constructed PE environment, this behavior was normalized, providing power to a small number of boys not only in that they could intimidate their classmates, but also in that intimidation and aggression were deemed acceptable. The fact that (often violent) team activities based on a win/lose binary were a prominent feature of the PE formal curriculum further supported the competitive orientation of this subject.

The observation period of the research revealed how both male and female students at times experienced social injustice in PE. For example, despite Tim's participation and hard work during class, he was generally ignored by his classmates. When attention was given to this student, it was often in the form of physical or verbal punishment, as when Chad "cracked him in the stomach" in dodgeball or when Lance delivered a firm body-check during (non-contact) indoor soccer. In a separate class, it was Harold who was subjected to this treatment, as noted during a team handball activity:

> As the students set up teams for handball, Allan, Frank, and Cal were physically moving some of the boys so that they could be teammates. It was the quieter, less skilled students who were forced to change teams.

> During the game, Kyle controlled the ball with Harold defending him. As Kyle dribbled and pivoted he teased Harold by asking rhetorically "Where's the ball Harold? Where's the ball?" knowing full well Harold did not have the size nor skill to take the ball from him.
> (Fieldnotes, Apr. 19).

Female students at times faced similar marginalization in co-ed classes. During an activity labelled "Murderball," for instance, many girls refused to participate, and those who did were subjected to powerful throws from their male classmates while rarely acting as throwers/aggressors themselves (Field notes, Mar. 24). At the skating rink, female students slowly circled the rink's perimeter while the skilled boys swerved recklessly between their classmates. Male students were occasionally joined by a male teacher in throwing a football to one another at this time, and only ceased in doing so when disciplined by a female instructor. Even the many girls who were obviously talented skaters remained at the rink's outskirts in this clearly masculinist environment.

Students' experiences in PE were mediated by differences of race, in addition to gender. Given that some students spoke Mandarin, Cantonese, or Korean as their first language, the fact that PE was moderated in English left a section of each class at times at a disadvantage. This was most evident when class instructors gave students the opportunity to choose their daily activity. The loudest and most assertive boys—often those who favored physical games like dodge ball—had the ability to verbally overpower the others and thus select the game of their choosing. More disconcertingly, a small number of Asian students were also subjected to physical and verbal mistreatment from their classmates once these activities began. This was particularly evident in the relationship between the aforementioned Tim and Chad. When asked about the disadvantages of PE, the (self-defined) Caucasian student Chad answered, "All the little Asians who study all the time" (FG Session 2), invoking a long-standing stereotype of Asian men as passive and unfit for physical activity (Chan, 2000; also see Millington, Vertinsky, Boyle & Wilson, 2008). In class, Chad revelled in verbally and physically humiliating Tim (an Asian boy), and as a popular and influential student Chad's bullying behavior was mimicked by others:

> Chad teased and provoked Tim during dodgeball today despite the fact that they were teammates. After Tim made a catch, for example, Chad disparagingly asked, "How did Tim catch that?"

> Indeed, there was a general questioning of Tim's ability across the class. Students did not hesitate to forcefully take the ball from Tim, even if on his team.

> During one dodgeball game, Tim was the only member of his team not to be eliminated. Although he only needed to catch one throw from the opposition to bring another team member back into play (a task he earlier accomplished), Tim's teammates apparently decided his failure was a forgone conclusion and signalled to the opposition for a new game to begin. Notably, this pre-emptive termination of the game did not occur when other students were the "last hope" for their team, and this behavior seemingly contradicts the boys' otherwise competitive logic.
> (Field notes, April 7).

Although race was perceived as a non-issue in PE by one instructor (Interview #3), it clearly impacted the students' experiences in PE, as cultural power could be won in this setting according to gendered and racialized hierarchical relations.

These findings reiterate themes from the PE literature—namely, that this setting sanctions supposedly masculine characteristics like physical strength and aggression and thus favors a small number of boys at the expense of other students (Brown & Evans, 2004; Gorely et al., 2003). Having said this, the physical and verbal injustices described here should not wholly eclipse the broad range of PE experiences conveyed by the students and witnessed during observation. Furthermore, hierarchies of gender and race were flexible in PE. The student George, for example, transferred out of a class in which he felt intimidated by the athletic boys and subsequently took up a dominant position with respect to his new peers (FG Session 2). As another example, in a class with many Asian students, Austin's ability to fluently shift languages (instead of speaking English only) afforded him high status among a number of his classmates (Field notes, Feb. 16).

Conclusion

This research offers insights into the complex ways that young people understand and practice masculinities within and across contexts of physical culture. Our participants certainly had varying perspectives on media portrayals of masculinity, yet they were inclined to offer rather poignant criticisms of supposedly laudable male body types, aggressive and domineering behavior, and/or media production practices that were deemed reflective of hyper-masculine fantasies. These critical reviews, however, were also limited to the contexts of media consumption, as the students aided in the reproduction of gender hierarchies in PE by (somewhat ironically) celebrating "male" traits like strength, aggression, and violence when mobilized in the interests of earnest competition.

We hope that our findings will aid researchers who, in future studies, aim to further excavate the complex ties between media consumption and other components of physical culture. While research that gauges audience interpretations brings many challenges (Plymire, 2005), we think it is extremely valuable given the growing infiltration of media into the spaces of daily living. Indeed, in conclusion we wish to (re-)emphasize the broader significance of our data that suggests that young people are reflexive and often critical in their consumption of media texts. Such a finding can fruitfully be juxtaposed against prevailing assumptions (noted at the outset) that young people are passive and impressionable in the face of contemporary media, and thus are likely to mimic what they see in film and on television. It is true that our participants valued hegemonic masculinities in PE, but it is far too facile to say that this stemmed directly from their relationship to gender portrayals in popular media. In fact, we are inclined to argue that our student participants valued traits like aggression and competitiveness in PE *in spite of* rather than because of their media consumption habits.

Furthermore, we think that this tendency for our participants to criticize media masculinities in informal ways (i.e., in casual conversation) could inspire valuable research into the more formal avenues by which youth take up resistance against prevailing definitions of masculinity. In one sense, this might involve studies that investigate how the constructed environment of physical education can be changed to harness the critical media literacy of youth. Specifically, this could involve linking representations of masculinity with their "real life" impacts (e.g., their ability to normalize certain "male" behaviors). This research would fit well within a cultural studies field that has long taken applied scholarship or praxis as a central tenet (Grossberg, 1997; Howell, Andrews & Jackson, 2002). In another sense, researchers might also focus on and find inspiration from the range of youth advocacy and activism groups already in existence that are dedicated to supplanting traditional definitions of masculinity. For example, The Students Commission is a charitable organization based in Canada that, broadly speaking, is "dedicated to creating and promoting opportunities for young people to learn and grow in a positive and safe environment" (Tiny Giant/The Students Commission, 2008). The organization includes a publishing arm called Tiny Giant and an impressive array of youth-run initiatives around social issues such as anti-violence, poverty and human rights, and environmental protectionism. Another project—one particularly relevant here—is titled The Young Men's Guyde. It is a publication that stems from discussion groups held across the country with a diversity of young males that were designed to create a space for these individuals to share personal narratives around gender, violence, and victimization. Notably, the substantive topics of discussion between young males include disillusionment with common gender portrayals in media. This is summarized in the Guyde:

> Young men are not socialized to group together, to be intimate, to support one another, to talk, express themselves. Overwhelmingly young guys cited images in the media as being unhealthy examples of masculinity. As young men we must overcome many elements of our socialization in order to begin to meet both our needs, and those needs of our communities. There is much anger and frustration among young men as a result of the negative stereotypes and resulting socialization.

> There is no one ideal Man, though popular culture would have you believe otherwise. There are, however, many amazing young men, defined by many things, each with their own voice and each, in their own way, infinitely more complex than common stereotypes suggest (Costen & Hodgson, 2003).

Here the publication draws a correlation between representation and socialization, but stops short of suggesting that youth are *necessarily* swayed by media images. Following this passage, there is an incitement in the Guyde for other young males (i.e., presumed readers) to discuss masculinity in their own right, rather than let the issues with which they are concerned "fester."

We do not intend to suggest that this is the sole manner in which problematic media portrayals can or should be confronted. Certainly any manner of "resistance" will also have limitations. But The Young Men's Guyde (the organization also has a publication on "young womyn's issues") is a grounded approach, the type of which could be of interest to researchers concerned with issues of social justice. What makes this a particularly pressing matter is that not-for-profit, youth-focused organizations of this kind are constantly under threat of erasure, given that they often operate under the retrenchment of neoliberal governmental policy that limits forms of advocacy not based in corporate philanthropy, and (often consequently) that they sometimes lack resources to survive in an increasingly competitive NGO environment (Wilson & Hayhurst, 2009). Researchers might thus investigate not only the messages enacted by advocacy groups, but also the tensions they face (e.g., around funding) due to the contexts in which they operate. In short, the complexity of the current moment requires researchers who study youth to not only debunk damaging myths about youth behavior, but also to promote and harness young people's critical media literacy.

Notes

1. The final, definitive version of this paper has been published in American Behavioral Scientist, Vol/Issue (tbd), Month/Year (tbd) by SAGE Publications Ltd. SAGE Publications, Inc., All rights reserved. © [as appropriate]. Website: http://abs.sagepub.com/.

Bibliography

Alasuutari, P. (Ed).(1999). *Rethinking the media audience: The new agenda.* Thousand Oaks, CA: Sage.

Bennett, A. (2000). *Popular music and youth culture: Music, identity and place.* New York: St. Martin's Press.

British Columbia Statistics. (2001). Census profiles. Retrieved from http://www.bcstats.gov.bc.ca/data/cen01/profiles/csd_txt.asp.

Brown, D., & Evans, J. (2004). Reproducing gender? Intergenerational links and the male PE teacher as a cultural conduit in teaching physical education. *Journal of Teaching in Physical Education, 23,* 48-70.

Buckingham, D. (1993). Children talking television: The making of television literacy. Washington, D.C.: Falmer Press.

Chan, J. (2000). Bruce Lee's fictional models of masculinity. *Men and Masculinities, 2*(4), 371-387.

Connell, R. (1995). *Masculinities.* Cambridge: Polity.

Connell, R. (2009). *Gender.* Cambridge: Polity.

Connell, R., & Messerschmidt, J. (2005). Hegemonic masculinity: Rethinking the concept. *Gender and Society, 19*(6), 829-859.

Côté, J., & Allahar, A. (1996). *Generation on hold: Coming of age in the late twentieth century.* London: NYU Press.

Costen, E., & Hodgson, P. (Eds.) (2003). *The Young Men's Guyde.* Retrieved from http://www.tgmag.ca/guydepr_e/index_e.htm.

Dworkin, S.L., & Wachs, F.L. (1998). "Disciplining the body": HIV-positive male athletes, media surveillance, and the policing of sexuality. *Sociology of Sport Journal, 15*(1), 1-20.

Epstein, D., Kehily, M., Mac an Ghaill, M., & Redman, P. (2001). Boys and girls come out to play: Making masculinities and femininities in school playgrounds. *Men and Masculinities, 4*(2), 158-172.

Fenton, J., Frisby, W., & Luke, M. (1999). Multiple perspectives of organizational culture: A case study of physical education for girls in a low-income multiracial school. *Avante 5*(1), 1-22.

Furlong, A., & Cartmel, F. (2007). *Young people and social change: New perspectives.* Buckingham, UK: Open University Press.

Giddens, A. (1991). *Modernity and self-identity: Self and society in the late modern age.* Stanford, CA: Stanford University Press.

Giroux, H. (2001). *Stealing innocence: Corporate culture's war on children.* New York: Palgrave.

Gorely, T., Holroyd, R., & Kirk, D. (2003). Muscularity, the habitus and the social construction of gender: Towards a gender-relevant physical education. *British Journal of Sociology of Education, 24*(4), 429-448.

Grossberg, L. (1997). *Bringing it all back home: Essays on cultural studies.* Durham, NC: Duke University Press.

Hall, S. (1980). Encoding/decoding. In S. Hall, D. Hobson, A. Lowe, & P. Willis (Eds.), *Culture, media, language: Working papers in cultural studies, 1972-79* (pp. 273-314). Hillsdale, NJ: Erlbaum Associates.

Hearn, J. (2004). From hegemonic masculinity to the hegemony of men. *Feminist Theory, 5*(1), 49-72.

Howell, J.W., Andrews, D.L., & Jackson, S.J. (2002). Cultural studies and sport studies: An interventionist practice. In J. Maguire & K. Young (Eds.), *Theory, sport & society* (pp. 151-177). New York: JAI.

Humbert, L. (1995). On the sidelines: The experiences of young women in physical education classes. *Avante, 1*(2), 58-77.

Jefferson, T. (1998). Muscle, "hard men" and "Iron" Mike Tyson: Reflections on desire, anxiety and the embodiment of masculinity. *Body & Society, 4*(1), 77-98.

Jeffords, S. (1994). *Hard bodies: Hollywood masculinities in the Reagan era.* New Brunswick, NJ: Rutgers University Press.

Kane, M., & Lenskyj, H. (1998). Media treatment of female athletes: Issues of gender and sexualities. In L. Wenner (Ed.), *MediaSport* (pp. 186-201). New York: Routledge.

Keddie, A. (2005). On fighting and football: Gender justices and theories of identity construction. *International Journal of Qualitative Studies in Education, 18*(4), 425-444.

Kirk, D. (2002). The social construction of the body in physical education and sport. In A. Laker (Ed.), *The sociology of sport and physical education: An introductory reader* (pp. 79-91). New York: Routledge.

Kirk, D., & Tinning, R. (1994). Embodied self-identity, healthy lifestyles and school physical education. *Sociology of Health and Illness, 16*(5), 600-625.

Lines, G. (2000). Media sport audiences—young people and the Summer of Sport '96: Revisiting frameworks for analysis. *Media, Culture & Society, 22*(5), 669-680.

Lull, J. (2000). *Media, communication, culture: A global approach.* New York: Columbia University Press.

MacNeill, M. (1996). Networks: Producing Olympic hockey for a national television audience. *Sociology of Sport Journal, 13*(2), 103-124.

Majors, R., & Billson, J.M. (1992). *Cool pose: The dilemmas of black manhood in America.* New York: Lexington Books.

McKay, J., Mikosza, J., Hutchins, B. (2005). "Gentlemen, the lunchbox has landed": Representations of masculinities and men's bodies in the popular media. In M. Kimmel, J. Hearn, & R. Connell (Eds.), *Handbook of studies on men and masculinities* (pp. 270-288). Thousand Oaks, CA: Sage.

Messner, M. (2002). *Taking the field: Women, men and sports.* Minneapolis: University of Minnesota Press.

Messner, M., Dunbar, M., & Hunt, D. (2002). The televised sports manhood formula. *Journal of Sport and Social Issues, 24*(4), 380-394.

Miles, S. (2000). *Youth lifestyles in a changing world.* Buckingham: Open University Press.

Miller, T. (1998). Commodifying the male body, problematizing "hegemonic masculinity?" *Journal of Sport and Social Issues, 22*(4), 431-446.

Millington, B., Vertinsky, P., Boyle, E., & Wilson, B. (2008). Making Chinese-Canadian masculinities in Vancouver's physical education curriculum. *Sport, Education, and Society*, 13(2), 195-214.

Morgan, D. (1997). *Focus groups as qualitative research*: Newbury Park, CA: Sage.

Murphy, P. (2005). Fielding the study of reception: Notes on "negotiation" for global media studies. *Popular Communication*, 3(3), 167-180.

Parker, A. (1996). The construction of masculinity within boys' physical education. *Gender and Education*, 8(2), 141-157.

Plymire, D.C. (2005). Qualitative methods in sport/media analysis. In D. Andrews, D.S. Mason, & M.L. Silk (Eds.), *Qualitative methods in sport studies* (pp. 139-164). New York: Berg.

Radway, J. (1996). The hegemony of "specificity" and the impasse in audience research. In J. Hay, L. Grossberg, & E. Wartella (Eds.), *The audience and its landscape* (pp. 235–245). Boulder, CO: Westview.

Richardson, L. (1998). Writing: A method of inquiry. In N. Denzin & Y. Lincoln (Eds.), *Collecting and interpreting qualitative materials* (pp. 345-371). Thousand Oaks, CA: Sage.

Silk, M. (1999). Local/global flows and altered production practices: Narrative constructions at the 1995 Canada Cup of soccer. *International Review for the Sociology of Sport*, 34(2), 113-123.

Sparks, R. (1992). "Delivering the male": Sports, Canadian television, and the making of TSN. *Canadian Journal of Communication*, 17(3). Retrieved from http://www.cjc-online.ca/viewarticle.php?id=101.

Sweetman, P. (2004). Tourists and travelers?: "Subcultures," reflexive identities and neo-tribal sociality. In A. Bennett & K. Kahn-Harris (Eds.), *After subculture: Critical studies in contemporary youth culture* (pp. 79-93). New York: Palgrave MacMillan.

Thornton, S. (1995). *Club cultures: Music, media and subcultural capital*. Hanover, NH: Wesleyan.

Thrift, N. (2003). Closer to the machine? Intelligent environments, new forms of possession and the rise of the supertoy. *Cultural Geographies*, 10(4), 389-407.

Tiny Giant/The Students Commission. (2008). *About us: Who we are*. Retrieved from http://www.tgmag.ca/index_e.htm.

White, P., & Gillett, J. (1994). Reading the muscular body: A critical decoding of advertisements in *Flex* magazine. *Sociology of Sport Journal*, 11, 18-39.

White, P., Young, K., & Gillett, J. (1995). Bodywork as a moral imperative: Some critical notes on health and fitness. *Leisure and Society*, 18(1), 159-182.

Willis, P. (1990). *Common culture: Symbolic work at play in the everyday cultures of the young*. San Francisco: Westview.

Willis, P. (2000). *The ethnographic imagination*. Cambridge: Polity.

Wilson, B. (2002). The "anti-jock" movement: Reconsidering youth resistance, masculinity and sport culture in the age of the Internet. *Sociology of Sport Journal*, 19(2), 207-234.

Wilson, B. (2006). *Fight, flight, or chill: Subcultures, youth, and rave into the 21st Century*. Montreal & Kingston, London, Ithaca: McGill-Queen's University Press.

Wilson, B., & Hayhurst, L. (2009). Digital activism: Neoliberalism, the Internet, and sport for youth development. *Sociology of Sport Journal*, 26(1), 155-181.

Wilson, B., & Sparks, R. (1996). "It's gotta be the shoes": Youth, race, and sneaker commercials. *Sociology of Sport Journal*, 13(4), 398-427.

Wilson, B., & Sparks, R. (1999). Impacts of black athlete media portrayals on Canadian youth. *Canadian Journal of Communication*, 24(4), 589-627.

Wilson, B., & Sparks, R. (2001). Michael Jordan, sneaker commercials, and Canadian youth cultures. In D. Andrews (Ed.), *Michael Jordan Inc.: Corporate sport, media culture, and late modern America* (pp. 217-255). Albany: State University of New York Press.

CHAPTER SIX

The Struggle for Recognition: Embodied Masculinity and the Victim-Violence Cycle of Bullying in Secondary Schools*

James W. Messerschmidt

A *bully*, quite simply, is one who unilaterally engages in harmful, offensive, and/or intimidating conduct against another who is physically, mentally, and/or socially weaker than s/he. Bullying, unfortunately, remains endemic among secondary school students in the United States. For example, approximately 30 percent of 12- to 18-year-old students report being bullied at school during the previous six months (National Center for Education Statistics, 2008). Of these students, 53 percent report being bullied once or twice during that period, 25 percent once or twice a month, 11 percent once or twice a week, and 8 percent daily (p. 3). Furthermore, there exist three major types of bullying in secondary schools: *verbal* bullying (name-calling, humiliation, mocking, insulting), *social* bullying (exclusion from peer groups, gossiping, rumor-mongering), and *physical* bullying (hitting, shoving, kicking, beating up).

Studies across North America and Europe reveal that the two most-common reasons students are bullied at school are *bodily appearance* (perceived by others as skinny, obese, and/or ugly) and *bodily practice* (perceived by others as acting in a shy, insecure, or gender non-normative manner) (Erling & Hwang, 2004; Perry, Hodges, & Egan, 2001; Rigby, 2002; Sweeting & West, 2001). Indeed, the most frequent responses in a recent study of 119 secondary-school students asked, "Who gets bullied?" reported that 40 percent answered because of their bodily appearance and 36 percent because of their bodily practice (Frisen, Jonsson, & Persson, 2007).

In addition to the importance of the body to bullying, being bullied has been found to be strongly associated with reactive bullying and violent behavior at school by those frequently victimized. For example, a predominant pattern in school shootings (by students) is that nearly all of the "school shooters" since the 1990s (at both secondary school and college levels) had themselves been consistently bullied at school. What the case studies of school shooters and other research reveal, then, is that bullying in school often has devastating effects on the initial victims of bullying, and possibly leads to those victims engaging in severe forms of interpersonal violence at school (Klein, 2006). Yet, the school shooting cases not only signal the close association between being bullied and reactive in-school violent behavior, they also beg the question, Why? That is, why the relationship between being bullied and reactive (future) in-school violence?

Although there is increasing interest in why individuals who are bullied themselves engage in in-school *shootings* (Kimmel & Mahler, 2003; Klein, 2006, 2007), *no* research has yet examined the actual "micro-level" in-school *embodied masculine* social processes and dynamics leading from being bullied to engaging specifically in *assaultive violence*—that is, how *embodied* interaction in a particular local in-school gendered milieu may be related to the victim-violence cycle of bullying. Not surprisingly, examination of the relationship among prior bullying victimization, the body, masculinity, and subsequent engagement in in-school violence remains a pressing and crucial area of study. My work seeks to fill this gap by scrutinizing the victim-violence cycle of bullying, or moving from being bullied to engaging specifically in in-school assaultive violence, and how this social process is related specifically to embodied masculinity.

Methodology

The research reported here is part of a larger study based on life-history interviews of thirty white working-class violent (assault and sexual violence) and non-violent teenage (15-18 years old) boys and girls. Through life-history interviews, I have uncovered detailed accounts of embodied gender interaction in three distinct "sites": the family, the school, and the peer group. In this paper, I concentrate exclusively on the second site—the school.

The vast majority of the boys and girls I interviewed grew up in the same environment (they often lived in the same neighborhood and attended the same school). *Data collection* involved tape-recorded life-history interviews of at least two three-hour meetings, and the *data analysis* involved the preparation of individual case studies as well as comparison of the individual life histories to define the similarities and differences among the pathways to violence and non-violence.

These life histories reveal specific types of gendered in-school interaction and practice in the lives of the interviewees. Sampling continued until no new themes or patterns emerged; over thirty interviews, "data saturation" occurred as soon as particular themes and patterns showed up with regularity. And these saturated data provide interesting and compelling information on the reactive movement from being bullied to engaging in interpersonal assaultive violence at school; in other words, the victim-violence cycle of bullying.[1]

During the interviews, I specifically sought detailed descriptions of choices, practices (what a boy or girl did, not solely how he or she felt), and accounts of interactions in families, schools, and peer/leisure groups. And during the interviews each boy and girl consistently expressed a deep concern about the role of "the body" in his or her everyday life, its relation to gender interaction and, ultimately, its relation to the victim-violence cycle of bullying. Interestingly, initially I did not plan to include "the body" as a topic of conversation—it was not part of the interview schedule—yet *each* of the thirty interviewees intensely expressed its importance in her or his daily life. In other words, the *body* was a salient saturated *theme* throughout the data. Moreover, a saturated *pattern* of moving from being bullied to engaging in reactive assaultive violence occurred in three stages—what I call 1) victimization, 2) self-reflection, and 3) recognition—each of which is related to the body, sex category, and gender.[2] In what follows, I illustrate how the above theme (the body) and pattern (the three-stage social process) are related to masculinity through a discussion of two of the individual case studies: an assaultive boy, Lenny, and an assaultive girl, Kelly.[3]

Victimization

The first stage of the victim-violence cycle of bullying is *victimization*, which refers simply to being the victim of consistent bullying in school. I begin this stage of the cycle by discussing Lenny's experiences of being bullied; I then turn to Kelly, and her encounter with this form of violence.

Lenny:
Lenny is a short, obese and shy teenager with short dark hair. To each interview he wore blue jeans, a sweatshirt, tennis shoes, and a sports cap emblazoned with, "Give Blood, Play Hockey." Lenny spoke in a somewhat

skittish and soft-spoken manner. At the time of the interview, Lenny was involved in private counseling for assaulting neighborhood boys.

Lenny did reasonably well in elementary and junior-high school. For the most part he liked his teachers and earned average grades. However, he did not like his classmates. At school Lenny was the victim of constant (every day, throughout the day) verbal bullying because of his physical size and shape (he is much shorter and heavier than the other boys and girls), often being referred to as a "fat pig," "tubby," and a "fat ass." Moreover, the "jocks" consistently called him a "nerd," a "wimp," a "punk," and a "fag." Because of this constant bullying victimization, Lenny developed an intense dislike of school: "I hated to go to school."

I asked Lenny about the structure of cliques at his school, and he mentioned a variety of boys' groups—the "jocks" (the popular "cool tough guys"), the "nerds," the "smart kids" (both boys and girls), the "freaks," the "earthies," the "skaters," and the "losers." Girls' groups consisted of "preps" (the popular "cool girls"), "jocks," "badasses" (the "tough girls"), "freaks," "earthies," "skaters," and "losers."

Although Lenny felt he belonged to none of these groups, he believed that some of the "jocks" considered him a fat "nerd" and a "wimp" because they continually verbally bullied him—not only for his size and shape but also because he did not "fight back" and did not participate in any sport: "The jocks always teased the nerds, and make fun of them for not playing sports." According to the "jocks," those (including Lenny) who did not play sports (especially football) and who did not retaliate in kind when bullied were "wimps," "punks," "fags," and "nerds." In fact, Lenny stated that "jocks" often called him these names because he did not play football and because he was not tough; for example: "The jocks called me a wimp because they said I was afraid of gettin' tackled and afraid of fighting."

Kelly:

Kelly is a short, stocky, teenager who met me at each interview without makeup, with her shoulder-length blonde hair pulled back in a pony tail, and wearing the same worker boots, baggy jeans, and a loose-fitting sweatshirt with a hood. At the time of the interview, Kelly was on probation for an assault conviction. Kelly attended the same school as Lenny, and described a similar structure of school cliques for both boys and girls. Initially Kelly became a "jock." The "jocks" were not organized into a specific group; they "just played sports together." As Kelly notes, "Us jocks hung out with all kinds of people."

Kelly stated that the above-described attire was her usual gender display at school, explaining that she wore "boys clothes" because "it was easier to do "boy stuff" (e.g., wrestling and playing sports with boys). Moreover, she did not "want to look like a girl." Eventually, Kelly shaved the back of her head and wore a duck-bill sports cap to further enhance her effort to avoid "looking like a girl." Nevertheless, and despite these efforts, Kelly was identified and accepted at school as a girl who engaged in situationally defined masculine display and practices.

In the seventh grade, however, Kelly became a loner because her "jock" friends had suddenly rejected her. Henceforth, she was the victim of daily verbal and social bullying:

> I would get bullied, mostly by the jocks, for the clothes I would wear and because I shaved the back of my head. My clothes weren't up to fashion, and they started to call me names 'cause I looked like a boy, you know, and acted like a boy. So I'd get picked on about that. And my old friends would always be talking behind my back.

Although Kelly's girl "jock" friends had no problem with her overall "boyish" embodiment, when she shaved the back of her head they began to engage in social bullying: rejecting her and talking behind her back. "They'd stare at me and then whisper stuff to each other. Then they'd walk by me and call me a 'dyke,' and then they'd all laugh. And once someone drew a picture of me looking like a guy with a 'big dick,' and they put it on my gym locker."

Kelly was primarily subjected to verbal bullying by boys who daily and throughout each day called her a "wimp," told her that she simply "was a fucking girl," and bellowed at her to "stop acting like a guy 'cause you can't do guy stuff." Accordingly, Kelly experienced peer interaction that accentuated the impropriety of her embodied display and practices *as a girl* and *as a boy*. In short, Kelly was deemed doubly deviant at school.

Analysis of Stage I

Both Lenny and Kelly experienced peer interaction that oppressively accentuated a very specific type of verbal and social bullying that centered on the body and featured a perceived imbalance between sex category and gender behavior. What these interview data show is that the meaning assigned by the bullies to Lenny's and Kelly's *gender behavior* is influenced through their *perceived sex category*. In other words, in this first stage of the cycle for both Lenny and Kelly, because their sex category was judged to be incongruent with their gender behavior, they subsequently became victims of consistent bullying.

For Lenny, there was an imbalance between his perceived male category and his alleged unmanly behavior and body (e.g., he did not "fight back"; he did not play sports; and he had a pudgy, soft, and smooth "feminine" body). In other words, Lenny's body size and shape and his bodily behavior were viewed by the bullies as controverting his perceived sex category. According to the bullies, Lenny "failed" to accomplish masculinity in terms of bodily display and practice. Yet, because he was identified as a "male," he was consistently victimized.

For Kelly, both the girls and the boys attempted through their bullying to invalidate her masculine display and practice because of her female sex category. Kelly's sex category was viewed by the bullies to disparage her gender display (e.g., calling her a "dyke") and her gender behavior (e.g., she allegedly cannot do "guy stuff" because she is "a girl"). According to the bullies, because Kelly "failed" in terms of sex category rather than in bodily practice, she was consistently victimized.

For both Lenny and Kelly, then, their *body* and their *bodily behavior* conveyed a sex/gender combined image at school that the bullies viewed as an imbalance between sex category and gender behavior. And it was this situationally recognized bodily imbalance by the bullies—as conveyed through their verbal and social bullying—that *motivated* Lenny and Kelly to engage in the second stage of the cycle, self-reflection, to which we now turn.

Self-Reflection

The second stage of the victim-violence cycle of bullying, *self-reflection*, refers to serious thinking about one's social experiences, and then subjectively deciding how to respond appropriately. Again, I begin the discussion with Lenny, and then turn to Kelly.

Lenny:

Lenny reported that he felt embarrassed at school because of his physical size and shape, and also stated that because he was smaller than the kids who verbally bullied him, he felt insecure about responding as the culture of the school dictated—to physically fight back. In the interviews, Lenny stressed that the people who verbally bullied him were the "tough guys" in the school: "They was the popular tough guys, and everyone laughed when I didn't do nothin'. I couldn't. I felt really small in front of everybody." Consequently, because of his embodied emasculation at school, Lenny became a loner and decided to avoid the "tough guys" and the school as much as possible (e.g., he would immediately run home after school). In other words, through self-reflection Lenny decided to conceal from others—through this embodied practice of running home after school—his inability to "do" masculinity according to the in-school criteria. Lenny rationalized that by avoiding school and the bullies as much as possible, he would not be publicly defined as a "wimp."

Although Lenny also indicated that through self-reflection he actually considered himself to be a "wimp," he nevertheless "wanted to be tough like them." I then asked Lenny:

Q. Are these tough kids looked up to in your school?
A. Oh, yeah. They are the neat kids. Everybody wanted to be tough like them.
Q. You wanted to be tough like them, too?
A. Yeah, I wanted to be like them.

Lenny wanted to "do" masculinity like the other boys. However, through self-reflection he recognized that because of his shape and size in relation to the bullies that he would be beaten up if he physically fought back. He also indicated that this inability to "fight back" really bothered him because it made him feel small in front of others. Lenny told me that kids would laugh at him when he did not respond as the culture of the school dictated—that is, fight back when bullied—and that this encouraged him to think seriously about how he might actually overcome his "wimpish" character.

Because Lenny wanted to be like the "tough guys" at school and longed to gain acceptance from the "cool guys," he decided to talk to his father about the situation. His father recommended the following:

> My dad said that if somebody punches me, then I get the right to punch him back. If I'm being teased, I tease him right back. Call him names back. If they [sic] teasing me always, then my dad tells me that I should punch 'em back.

In addition, Lenny's father advised him to "pick the battles you can win."

Kelly:

Through self-reflection, Kelly concluded she was the sole female "jock" who dressed in a "boyish" manner, and in particular she attributed her head-shaving rejection as "going too far for them." I asked Kelly how she had decided to respond to the ongoing bullying victimization:

> It really bothered me for awhile that my old girl friends turned against me. I felt confused and didn't know what to do. So I stopped playing sports 'cause I didn't want to be around them; I didn't want to be called names, you know. But after a while I knew that they just wanted to be popular, you know. And I hated the popular preppy girls. All they care about is their faces, their ass, and boys. They're wimps and they just do all this boring stuff. My old girl friends just wanted to be like them, and I didn't.

What especially and continually concerned Kelly, though, was verbal bullying by the boys, particularly being told she was a "wimp," allegedly unfit to do "guy stuff." As Kelly stated: "That really bothered me the most, 'cause I didn't like being hassled, but I couldn't fight like guys do. I kinda felt like a wimp when guys would like hassle me, you know, about that." Kelly understood that the *only* appropriate response to this form of verbal bullying in school was to "fight back" physically. Yet because of her physical size—Kelly was shorter than most of the boys who verbally bullied her—she lacked confidence in "fighting back" as the masculine culture of the school dictated. Consequently, Kelly—like Lenny—decided to talk with her stepfather about the bullying at school. "And he said I needed to threaten the boys, you know. To go after the boys, not the girls, so everyone can see me, you know. To do it so kids could see. Like, 'You keep it up and I'll take you down.'"

However, Kelly explained to her stepfather that she felt ill-prepared physically to threaten the boys who verbally abused her. And so Kelly's stepfather taught her specifically how to, as Kelly put it, "fight like a guy": "He taught me that being short made me faster, you know. He said the lower you are to the ground the faster you are. He taught me how I had that advantage, you know." Kelly and her stepfather would "play fight," and he taught her to "scrooch down when he'd swing a punch at me. And then I'd just swipe his feet out from under him or tackle him. My stepfather taught me that. And then he told me to punch them in the face." Kelly eventually "perfected" this method of fighting and used it in response to peer abuse by boys at school.

Analysis of Stage II

Through self-reflection, then, both Lenny and Kelly realized initially that their bodies *restrained* their agency: they could not live up to the in-school masculine expectations of physically fighting back when verbally bullied. This was extremely distressing to both of them, as they felt small and subordinated in front of peers; accordingly, they both concluded they must be "wimps." In other words, Lenny's and Kelly's bodies were actually participating in their agency by suggesting possible courses of social action. Although Lenny and Kelly wanted to respond "appropriately" to the verbal bullying, they realized through self-reflection the limits of their embodied action. So Lenny, initially, would run home immediately after school; Kelly, simply "put up" with the bullying. Frustrated, and given the continual distressing situation, both turned to their father/stepfather for help. And both learned when and how to use their bodies in an accountably masculine fashion. For both Lenny and Kelly, then, their bodies became objects of their social action. Lenny, given specific directions when to use his body, in particular was advised to "pick the battles you can win." And Kelly's body became the object of her social action as she attempted to transform it into a masculine force "appropriate" to her specific school setting.

During self-reflection, then, both Lenny and Kelly came to conceptualize themselves in the way that others perceived them—they reified the images communicated by others. Much of this conceptualization was arrived at by way of interaction and communication with others. Through such interaction and communication, both Lenny and Kelly took an "external" view of themselves, thus becoming the objects of their own self-reflection (Crossley, 2006). Because of the shame and mortification they suffered from bullying victimization, an assault upon their self-definition and social identification emerged. This assault drove them to move from a tacit relationship with their bodies to a more conscious and self-reflective one. In other words, they internalized the "external" by engaging in self-reflection; in the process, they both subjectively determined their courses of action in relation to their bodies and to their social circumstances.[4]

So the second stage of the victim-violence cycle of bullying found Lenny and Kelly internally deliberating about their individual social circumstances at school and, in particular, subjectively reflecting on their bodies to determine what they could and could not "do" in the school setting to overcome their subordinating social situations. Accordingly, their bodies became participants in the generating and shaping of their social practices.

Consider now the third and final stage of this social process, recognition.

Recognition

Recognition involves extending one's self-reflection by consciously engaging in social action(s) that creates circumstances whereby one can be recognized as an "acceptable" gender conformist. As with the first two stages, I begin with Lenny, and follow with Kelly.

Lenny:
During self-reflection, Lenny concluded that he could legitimately target smaller boys, confident in doing so because of "dad's" encouragement to "pick the battles you can win" and to physically fight back against those who consistently verbally bullied him. And so in time, an event at school provided Lenny with the opportunity to practice and demonstrate in-school masculinity. A classmate Lenny referred to as a "high water," who he described as "skinny and ugly," would frequently verbally bully Lenny. At one point—in the middle of a school hallway—Lenny enticed "high water" to make derogatory comments about him. Lenny seized this opportunity, first to retaliate by verbally bullying him and second to beat him up in the hallway in front of a large group of kids. The actual dialogue follows:

> Q. Tell me about that.
> A. There was this nerd of a kid that even I made fun of. He would wear high-waters.
> Q. What are high-waters?
> A. Kids that wear high pants.
> Q. Okay, go on.

A. This high-water is real skinny and ugly. I'm bigger than him. So I go: "You look funny in those pants," and stuff like that. I called him a "nerd," and he said the same back to me. There was all these kids around, and so I beat him up in the hallway 'cause he called me a "nerd" and nobody liked him.

Q. Why did you hit him?

A. 'Cause he called me a name that I didn't like, and I wasn't afraid of him.

Although Lenny actually "beat-up" the "high water," the audience responded in an unpredictable way, saying, "You should pick on kids your own size." So that was Lenny's only fight at school inasmuch as "high water" was the only individual he could "beat up."

Kelly:

As a result of her self-reflection and eventual bodily practice with her stepfather, Kelly now felt confident to use the learned method of fighting in response to verbal bullying by in-school boys who were even a little bigger. The following is a representative example:

> One day a kid [a boy] walked by me in the hall at school and called me a "wimp." He said I was just a "girl," like that. Just a "girl," you know. He'd been hasslin' me like that, sayin' stuff like that, that I couldn't fight, you know. So I was tired of him, you know what I mean? So I decided to fight him right there in the hall. I wanted kids to see what I could do, you know. I ended up breaking his jaw. And I got excused for one day, and then I got to come back the next day.

I asked Kelly if this boy was physically larger or smaller:

> He was a little bigger but I knew I could take him. I felt I could take care of myself—I was shorter but stronger than a lot of kids. I thought about what my stepfather told me, and kids kept sayin' "You're not gonna take any shit, are ya?" And so I did it to him. There were lotsa kids around, so I ran up to him and just liked tackled him, you know. I mean I real fast-like got down on him and just grabbed his legs and pulled him down. He didn't even try to hit me. He just laid right there and let me pound on his face. He kinda seemed afraid to fight back, you know.

I then asked Kelly if she was involved in other fights at school:

> Oh, yeah. After that anyone who called me names like "wimp" or "fucking girl." They thought they were bigger and better than I was. So I proved them wrong. I'd take them down and pound on them with my fists, and slam their head on the floor and tell them to shut the fuck up. And they would.

Kelly never fought girls at school, only boys: "about three dozen fights at school and I'd always win the fights with guys. Because of that I didn't need to fight girls. They saw what I could do and so they just left me alone. I was someone not to mess with, you know."   Moreover, Kelly's old "jock" girlfriends stopped verbally abusing her, and she continued to carefully choose her battles with boys:

> There are a lot of guys that are bigger than me and I wouldn't fight them, you know. Just guys kinda my size. Lotsa times I'd just beat the shit out of guys before they'd say anything. Just go up to them and smash them in the face, and say "You better keep your mouth shut," you know, like that. But the big jocks and stuff, and the preppies, the popular guys, I just left them alone 'cause they didn't want anything to do with me anyway. So it was just other guys my size that I took down. So they wouldn't try to give me shit.

Despite her assaultive violence, at school Kelly remained marginalized as "Other" by both boys and girls. Although Kelly continued to be a loner, she did gain some masculine confidence and respect at school. She "handled" each conflictual situation in a personal and individual way, specifically targeting boys her "size" prior to any verbal bullying—and it worked. To a certain extent, Kelly was accorded the deference she felt she deserved. That is, through her masculine (albeit subordinate) presence at school, the boys who verbally abused her (or might do so) eventually stopped because Kelly either "took them down" or threatened to do so.

Analysis of Stage III

Extending his self-reflection into social action, Lenny responded to "being bullied" by creating an opportunity in which he could be a "bully"—he attempted to use what little physical power he possessed to harm someone less powerful and weaker. Shame and inadequacy threatened Lenny's masculine self as revealed in his self-reflection. Verbal bullying and physical violence against the "high water" was an attempt to validate some type of masculine self for his audience and for himself—compensatory in the sense of attempting to reduce/offset the emasculating interactions and feelings produced at school. Lenny sought compensation—rather than social power—by going after the "high water" rather than the bullies, seeking to define himself as normally masculine in the eyes of others. He hoped his body would facilitate masculine agency and eradicate the "wimp" label. But his audience failed him. Predictably, he remained somewhat emasculated at school because of a socially identified imbalance between sex category and gender behavior. He was subjected continually to derogatory verbal bullying, all of which reinforced his feelings of masculine inadequacy. Indeed, his body continued to *restrain* his masculine agency.

Kelly's newly developed bodily skills allowed her to respond to oppressive verbal bullying by attempting to make use of opportunities where physical domination of boys would be viewed by others—targeting boys she knew she could "take down." Kelly used physically violent power to intimidate others, likewise seeking compensation rather than social power. She too, sought to eradicate any "wimp" label so as to avoid being bullied. And Kelly succeeded—to a point.

Kelly's body now *facilitated* masculine agency, an agency that constructed a more confident sense of self, a new way of interacting with and through her body in the school setting. Despite her actual and successful accomplishment of masculine practices, however, and because of the continued imbalance between her sex appearance and gender behavior, Kelly (as Lenny) remained considerably marginalized at school. And because Kelly's perceived sex category continued to influence the meaning assigned to her bodily display and behavior, she was conceptualized at school (as was Lenny) as a gender deviant. Because she had no friends, Kelly became a loner.

Conclusion

The interview data comprising the three-stage process of the victim-violence cycle of bullying and its relation to embodied masculinity yield certain compelling findings. Let me discuss five salient conclusions.

First, Lenny's and Kelly's actions were shaped by those around them in school. In particular, it is the social embodied practices of boys within the school milieu that are their source of knowledge and information about the "appropriate" bodily behavior for responding to bullying. Lenny and Kelly engaged in embodied interaction or the social process involving both a sex and gender presentation, and a reading of that presentation by co-present interactants. And in seeking acceptance from co-present interactants, Lenny and Kelly were involved in a "struggle for recognition" (Mead, 1967), engaged as they were in embodied practices that were shaped by the practices and opinions of (in particular) the boys at school, hoping that these very same boys would recognize and accept their sex/gender presentation. Lenny and Kelly entered into self-reflection by internalizing and deliberating about their embodied social experiences in the school setting. They mulled over the problem at school, its relation to their bodies, considered how this made them feel, planned and decided what to do, prioritized what mattered most, and assessed how others would respond (Archer, 2007). Finally, they decided to end the bullying by turning to bullying and physical violence, each seeking to eradicate their gender deviance and to be recognized as gender conformists. Both Lenny and Kelly attempted to present the masculine self they wanted others to believe them to be, to actively manage the impressions that others had of them in order to secure recognition as gender conformists, and thereby to reduce or offset the distressing effects of bully victimization.

Second, what we learn from the work of Harold Garfinkel (1967), Erving Goffman (1979), Suzanne Kessler and Wendy McKenna (1978), Candace West and Don Zimmerman (1987), and from the recent outpouring of research on transsexuals and transgenderists, is that our recognition of another's "sex" is dependent upon the presentation of visible bodily characteristics (facial hair, musculature, breast development) together with clothing and hairstyle, makeup, demeanor, gait, speech, and other aspects of personal front. "Sex" then is categorized socially through interpretations placed on the visible body during social interaction; "sex" is achieved through the application of culturally accepted characteristics that proclaim one as "male" or as "female." The conclusion of these sociologists is that recognition of both "sex" and "gender" is a social act that occurs simultaneously. During most interactions "sex" and "gender" are indistinguishable from one another because we recognize their congruence. However, people who present ambiguous bodily emblems of sex, such as transsexuals in transition, produce hesitation in an otherwise smooth process of sex categorization. As a result, they bring the social construction of sex to light. Notwithstanding, the stories of Lenny and Kelly (and of others in my study) add a new twist to this perspective. Arguably, they both presented an easily recognized sex category but simultaneously constructed ambiguous gender behavior; that is, the meaning assigned to their gender behavior was influenced by their perceived sex category (also see Dozier, 2005). What the data reveal, then, is that the perception of "male" or "female" is salient to the interpretation of behavior as masculine.

In particular, the case of Lenny demonstrates that in the school setting, although he was perceived as a member of the "male" category, he "failed" to engage in appropriate masculine behavior—the gendered meaning assigned to his behavior thus influenced by his perceived sex category. Because Lenny "failed" to engage in gender behavior perceived appropriate to his assigned sex, his masculinity was invalidated: Lenny did not exhibit displays/practices perceived "appropriate" to his categorized sex. Lenny "failed" to satisfy the criteria by which masculinity for boys is judged in the school setting. The bullying of Lenny was based on the social perception by other in-school boys of an incongruence between sex and gender that constructed Lenny as a "feminine boy."

Turning now to Kelly, her case specifically demonstrates that in the school setting her masculine behavior was not valued because it was not performed with a socially perceived male body: her sex category did not align with her gender behavior. Thus, the meaning assigned to Kelly's gender behavior was influenced by her perceived sex category. Because Kelly was unfeminine but not unfemale, she was constructed as a "masculine girl."

What these two case studies clearly signal is that a balance between sex category and gender behavior is essential to validating masculinity. During social interaction we see "sex" and "gender" as an inseparable, seamless whole. It is this very incongruency that produces a cognitive dissonance in us, by which people like Lenny and Kelly are subordinated and publicly punished through verbal and social bullying.

Third, the human body is an inextricable component of "doing" sex and gender for several reasons. To begin with, Lenny's and Kelly's bodies were sites on which gender difference was inscribed. Specifically, both bodily displays were constructed to symbolize gender opposition to femininity. For example, both wore boyish clothing, as demonstrated by Lenny's cap emblazoned with "give blood, play hockey" and Kelly's deemphasizing of her breasts, waist, and legs (through loose fitting clothes) and shaving the back of her head. Although both Lenny and Kelly communicated opposition to femininity and the embrace of masculinity, Kelly was different from Lenny in a critical way: she actually attempted to nullify her femaleness—she never wanted to look like or act like a girl. Kelly's body being the primary site on which to inscribe the negation of femaleness, she quite literally attempted to erase any notion of femininity by concealing socially defined female attributes (also see Ekins & King, 2006). And a situationally constructed masculine bodily display was the *only* possibility with which to facilitate such an erasure.

In addition, Lenny's and Kelly's bodies were not neutral in their social action but rather were agents of their social practice in that they constrained and eventually enabled particular forms of gendered social action: their bodies mediated and influenced future social practices. Given the context of school, their bodies would do certain things but not do others. Both Lenny's and Kelly's bodies were "lived" in terms of what they could "do." Yet their bodies were a necessary and mediate component of their social action. Thus, third, gender was experienced in and through their bodies. Both Lenny and Kelly attempted to construct a new gendered self through their embodied practices at school, but only Kelly was successful, as force and power were to a certain extent now embodied in her practices. Kelly literally possessed a different body and a new gendered self (e.g., a don't mess-with-me demeanor). Kelly not only practiced a new and specific kind of bodily skill, she also embodied a new moral and emotional universe—exhibiting particular bodily talent as well as appropriating proper emotional attitudes to accompany and foster embodied masculine success; body and mind—skill and attitude—were indivisible here (see Wacquant, 2004). Kelly literally created a particular way of incarnating masculinity in and through her body. Lenny, however, failed to similarly embody masculinity.

What these two case studies clearly reveal is that the body is the medium by which individuals become active participants in social life. And moderately fulfilling participation in social life depends largely upon the successful presenting and monitoring of one's body. And if a body is interpreted as "failed," then a spoiled gender self-concept may result—especially within specific social contexts. In addition, and not inconsequentially, the two case studies further demonstrate that the body participates in the shaping and generating of social practice—herein most especially including assaultive violence.

Fourth, these two personal stories clearly confirm how secondary schools maintain a "culture of cruelty" whereby boys and girls face many types of bullying (verbal, physical, and social) exacted for failure to conform to certain sex/gender displays/behaviors, and that this bullying helps maintain unequal structured gender relations within the school. Considerable research shows that the tallest and strongest boys in junior high and high school usually are the most popular—admired by peers (and parents and teachers) for their size and athletic prowess—and set the standard for masculine sex category and masculine behavior. For boys and girls who do not display the "appropriate" body in terms of shape, size, and sex, and who do not use, or have no interest in using, their bodies in a particular way (such as sports), they frequently experience distress and frustration due largely to verbal/social/physical bullying. These boys and girls represent subordinated forms of masculinity and femininity, in that they are the inferior Others because their "sex" is defined as not aligning with their "gender." For example, boys and girls perceived as female who construct bodily practices defined as masculine, such as expressing sexual desire for girls (often subordinated and labeled "dyke"), acting sexually promiscuous (slut), presenting as authoritarian, physically aggressive, or take charge (bitch), are viewed as contaminating "normal" gender relations, and thus are verbally/physically/socially bullied. Similarly, individuals perceived as male but who construct practices defined as feminine, such as sexually desiring boys or simply practicing celibacy (often subordinated and labeled "fag"), being passive, compliant, or shy (sissy), and/or being physically weak or unadventurous (wimp), likewise are seen as contaminating "normal" gender relations and are "treated" to verbal, physical, and social bullying (Schippers, 2007).

Arguably, then, the *culture of cruelty* constructs a hierarchy among boys, among girls, and between boys and girls, based on incongruency between "sex" and "gender." The culture of cruelty at school constructs and enforces the gender practices available for "proper" sex/gender embodiment, and its precisely this culture that figured significantly in Lenny's and Kelly's narratives as the major site for gender confrontation, embodied social action, and structured gender relations.

Fifth, in particular Kelly's story weakens any notion that sex category is a natural foundation of gender. Kelly muddies the sex/gender binary: she is not male but masculine; she is female but not feminine. Moreover, Kelly constructed a gendered path that differed from the one assigned her sex, whereby she challenged the validity of any binary conception of gender. Indeed, Kelly can be seen as having transcended both "masculine" and "feminine" categories as she steered an intermediate course constituting a gender blend: a social boy with a vagina—possibly a "third gender." In essence, then, what the case of Kelly demonstrates is that *embodied gender* exists on a continuum rather than in opposition—and that bullying her is in part an attempt to sustain the binary that equates sex with gender.

In closing, let me briefly suggest several salient social policies for curbing the victim-violence cycle of bullying in secondary schools. First, a critical policy concern of the immediate future is managing the culture of cruelty and the widespread bullying that it produces. Such a policy must concentrate on the relationship among bullying, violence, and embodied masculinity. Secondary schools should publish and widely distribute to students, parents, teachers, and town officials a "school policy statement" which emphasizes that the entire community will not tolerate the bullying of one student by another and that the school endorses an "alternative ethos" based on caring and valuing, thereby "critically challenging masculinity and power within the school" (Salisbury & Jackson, 1996: 109). One approach to highlight the policy statement would involve developing school time periods in which students and teachers explore situations when students do not act in accordance with a bullying masculinity. This opens space for students to discuss how and when they act in a courageous, caring, and valuing way to challenge the gender dominant messages in the school. As David Denborough (1996) puts it, "This is particularly empowering when young men articulate that it takes courage, guts, and strength to move away from 'being tough,' as these are words and attributes deemed so necessary to traditional manhood. It is taking the old language and using it against itself" (p. 105). Second, the school curriculum should be scrutinized to create both gender-specific and gender-relevant strategies, such as making gender relations a core subject matter in public schools (gender relevant) and creating personal development programs that are specifically designed for boys and for girls (gender specific). Such a curriculum will help address gender hierarchies and bullying by including topics such as developing communication skills; interpersonal violence; conflict resolution; sex/gender awareness; valuing "feminine" qualities; health, fitness, and sexuality; and life-relationship goals (Connell, 1996). Finally, schools should pursue an explicit goal of social justice because many masculine practices in schools perpetuate injustice—such as bullying—and therefore pursuing justice requires addressing gender patterns that support these practices (p. 223-224).

Arguably, developing programs in schools that challenge division and emphasize empathy are essential. Building empathy into the curriculum enables a school to begin challenging the notion of "other" and to organize knowledge based on inclusion of the least advantaged in terms of gender and sexuality, such as gay, lesbian, bisexual, and transgendered youth. Such a policy reconfigures knowledge to open up the possibilities that current social inequalities conceal, demanding a capacity for empathy and thus taking the viewpoint of the other (Connell, 1995).

These suggested policies—school policy statements, gender-relevant and gender-specific curriculum, and emphasis on empathy and pluralism in schools—obviously neither exhaustive nor comprehensive—argue persuasively that the topic of embodied gender is highly relevant to debates on the victim-violence cycle of bullying. What these policies essentially aim to do is "re-embody" youth by allowing them to recognize alternative and different ways of acting in and through their body, thereby helping to develop embodied capacities other than those associated with bullying and interpersonal violence.

Notes

1. I also used an "open coding" methodology, or a line-by-line examination of each life history that identified themes and patterns (see Strauss and Corbin, 1998).
2. I follow West and Zimmerman's (1987) conception of *sex category* as social identification as "male" or "female," and *gender* as the corroboration of that identification through embodied social interaction.
3. I have, of course, used pseudonyms for both interviewees.
4. For my conceptualization of "self-reflection," I am indebted to the discussions of "internal conversation" and "reflexive deliberation" outlined in Archer (2007) and Crossley (2006).
5. Earlier drafts of this paper were presented to seminars at the following: the Sociology Department at the University of Akron; the Childhood Studies Department at Linkoping University, Sweden; the Childhood Studies Department at the University of Stockholm, Sweden; the Law and Criminology Department at the University of Oslo; the Race & Gender Project at William Paterson University; and the Childhood Studies Department at Rutgers University. For valuable comments and suggestions I thank the participants at the above seminars.

Bibliography

Archer, M. (2007). *Making our way through the world: Human reflexivity and social mobility*. New York: Cambridge University Press.

Connell, R. (1995). *Masculinities*. Berkeley, CA: University of California Press.

Connell, R. (1996). Teaching the boys: New research on masculinity and gender strategies for schools. *Teachers College Record 98*(2), 206-235.

Crossley, N. (2006). *Reflexive embodiment in contemporary society*. New York: Open University Press.

Denborough, D. (1996). Step by step: Developing respectful and effective ways of working with young men to reduce violence. In C. McLean, M. Carey, and C. White (Eds.), *Men's ways of being* (pp. 91-115). Boulder, CO: Westview.

Dozier, R. (2005). Beards, breasts, and bodies: Doing sex in a gendered world. *Gender & Society, 19*, 297-316.

Ekins, R., & King, D. (2006). *The transgender phenomenon*. Thousand Oaks, CA: Sage.

Erling, A., & Hwang, P. (2004). Swedish 10-year-old children's perceptions and experiences of bullying. *Journal of School Violence, 3*, 33-43.

Frison, A., Jonsson, A., & Persson, C. (2007). Adolescents' perception of bullying: Who is the victim? Who is the bully? What can be done to stop bullying? *Adolescence, 42*, 749-761.

Garfinkel, H. (1967). *Studies in ethnomethodology*. Englewood Cliffs, NJ: Prentice-Hall.

Goffman, E. (1979). *Gender advertisements*. New York: Harper & Row.

Kessler, S., & McKenna, W. (1978). *Gender: An ethnomethodological approach*. New York: John Wiley.

Kimmel, M., & Mahler, M. (2003). Adolescent masculinity, homophobia, and violence: Random school shootings, 1982-2001. *American Behavioral Scientist, 46*, 1439-1458.

Klein, J. (2006). Cultural capital and high school bullies: How social inequality impacts school violence. *Men and Masculinities, 9*, 53-75.

Klein, J. (2007). Punking and bullying: Strategies in middle school, high school, and beyond. *Journal of Interpersonal Violence, 22*, 158-178.

Mead, G.H. (1967). *Mind, self and society*. Chicago: University of Chicago Press.

National Center for Education Statistics. (2008). *Indicators of school crime and safety, 2007*. Washington, DC: National Center for Education Statistics.

Perry, D., Hodges, E., & Egan, S. (2001). Determinants of chronic victimization by peers: A review and new model of family influence. In J. Juvonan and S. Graham (Eds.), *Peer harassment in school: The plight of the vulnerable and victimized* (pp. 73-104). New York: Guildford.

Rigby, K. (2002). *New perspectives on bullying*. Philadelphia: Jessica Kingsley.

Salisbury, J., & Jackson, D. (1996). *Challenging macho values: Practical ways of working with adolescent boys*. London: Falmer Press.

Schippers, M. (2007). Recovering the feminine other: Masculinity, femininity, and gender hegemony. *Theory & Society, 36*(1), 85-102.

Straus, A. & Corbin, J. (1998). *Basics of qualitative research*. Thousand Oaks, CA: Sage.

Sweeting, H., & West, P. (2001). Being different: Correlates of the experience of teasing and bullying at age 11. *Research Papers in Education, 16,* 225-246.

Wacquant, L. (2004). *Body and soul: Notebooks on an apprentice boxer.* New York: Oxford University Press.

West, C., & Zimmerman, D. (1987). Doing Gender. *Gender and Society, 1,* 125-151.

CHAPTER SEVEN

Soft Pedagogy for a Hard Sport: Disrupting Hegemonic Masculinity in High School Rugby through Feminist-Informed Pedagogy

Richard Light and Jeanne Adèle Kentel

R eal men don't eat quiche
Real men don't cry
Real men don't apologise
Real men don't say splendid

The aforementioned clichés infused with tongue-in-cheek intentions speak to the pervading socially-coded norms for males to be "real men." Real men display power, aggression, and strength in games such as rugby, Australian football and ice hockey. Heavy contact sports have been identified as practices through which exemplary hegemonic masculinity is promoted as *the* way of being a man that all boys should aspire to (Grunneau & Whitson, 1993; Hickey, Fitzclarence & Mathews, 1998; Light & Kirk, 2000; Wedgwood, 2003). Being *manly* typically involves the explicit expression and execution of power and force to dominate others, and the celebration of violence, and values being tough, detached, and putting one's body on line for the team (Connell, 1995; McKay 1991; McKay & Middlemiss, 1995; Messner, 1992). This reproduction occurs through discourses within media-sport participation and through processes of social practice embodied through particular regimes of intensive physical training (Light, 1999; Wacquant, 1995). We, the authors (one male and one female), argue that this is a pedagogical concern. Moreover, we suggest that the notion that masculine is male and feminine is somehow female adopts a one-dimensional view of the ways in which gender is constructed (Connell & Messerschmidt, 2005) and this vantage point is problematic within multiple and multifaceted social, cultural and biological ways of being.

Despite significant pedagogical evidence developed through feminist perspectives (hooks, 1994; Thompson, 1997) the influence of sport and physical education pedagogy in the construction of gender is in infant stages of examination (for an example of this work see, Light & Georgakis, 2005). In order to further the pedagogical discourse on gender construction this chapter draws upon an incident from a study of high school rugby in Australia as a pathway to a conversation about the ways in which pedagogy, in particular critical pedagogy, might influence the masculinities developed by young men through long-term participation in sport. It further examines one incident from this study where the 1st XV (top rugby team in an elite independent school) challenged tradition by attempting to play a less structured, more intuitive and creative style of rugby. This is extended to a discussion on the significance of pedagogy for the social construction of masculinities in sport whereby the possibilities of coaching approaches comprised of feminist perspectives, which disrupt the influence of hegemonic masculinity on young men involved in heavy contact sports are considered. At the core of this argument is a view of the concepts of *hard* and *soft* being complementary in relation to both the nature of heavy contact sports and the coaching pedagogy required to accommodate this relationship. Hence, we underscore the significance of pedagogy for the social construction of masculinities in sport more broadly and explore the possibilities of "non-genderist pedagogy" (Kentel, 2009) that is informed by feminist theory for coaching young men in contact sports. Whilst this inquiry focuses upon the development of masculinities in *males*, we enter this discussion cognizant that the construction of gender is the interplay of masculinities and femininities across a spectrum of orientations that cannot be fully addressed within this chapter.

Learning, Gender, and Sport

What children and young people learn through participation in sport extends well beyond the mastery of skills such as how to catch, throw a pass, or kick a ball. Their participation in sport can benefit their social, moral and personal development and contribute to the notion of learning as a lifelong, ongoing process (Light, 2008a). This idea of learning as a lifelong process is distinct from the notion of lifelong learning that forms a key feature of formal educational policy in many developed countries. Blackmore (2006), for example, suggests that lifelong learning refers to all learning *activities* in formal and informal settings across the lifespan. While this presents a broad conception of learning, the conception of learning we engage with for this chapter is more broadly construed, in that we view learning as an inescapable dimension of social life expressed in the idea that living = learning (Begg, 2001). This perspective of learning offers a useful means of examining the social construction of gender as a process of learning shaped by other biological and social dynamics such as sex, culture and class, thereby forming a significant aspect of what Dewey (1916/97) refers to as the "human growth" of young people. From this perspective learning gender arises from participation in social life within particular socio-cultural contexts (Light, 2008c). These contexts are numerous, varied, and multi-faceted yet sport emerges as a significant site shaping the forms of masculinities and femininities developed as part of young people's identity formations (Kentel, 2009). Henceforth, we examine one case whereby sport and, in particular, sport pedagogy serves as a context for young men learning gender.

Pedagogy, Game Style and the Construction of Masculinities in an Australian School

Rugby in Australian Schools

It is in the schools of the ruling classes (Connell, Ashenden, Kessler & Dowsett, 1982) where sport is most explicitly used to develop a class-specific form of hegemonic masculinity in Australia. For well over a century rugby has been used in Australian independent schools as a mechanism for turning boys into particular types of men (Connell, et al.; Light & Kirk, 2000). In the late nineteenth century independent schools serving the Australian middle classes adopted the practice of educating boys through team games. Despite massive social, economic and cultural change in Australia since then team sports continue to form a central element in the education of the sons and daughters of the social elite (Connell et al.; Light & Kirk, 2000). Indeed, these schools serve as masculinizing institutions (Connell et al.) for the ruling classes whereby rugby forms a pivotal physical practice for the reproduction of a hegemonic form of masculinity. It is within this context that rugby has formed a central practice for what Kirk (1998) refers to as schooling the body in processes through which class and a class-specific form of masculinity is embedded into the bodies of young men.

The Study

This inquiry revisits a case drawn from a four-month ethnographic study of the 1st XV rugby team in an Australian elite independent school referred to in this chapter under the pseudonym of the GPS School (for a more detailed account of the research see Light & Kirk, 2000). The study focused on the ways in which the practices of GPS rugby acted to embody a class and culture-specific form of masculinity in young men. Data were generated through extended, conversational interviews using open-ended questions and observational notes. Analysis was conducted using a grounded theory approach (Glaser & Strauss, 1968) that, rather than posing a theoretical framework prior to data collection, involved theory emerging through a process of coding, conceptualizing, and categorizing.

Traditional Coaching at the GPS School

As a heavy contact sport, rugby requires power and force in addition to skill, tactical understanding, decision-making, anticipation and communication. The coaching and the related training practices traditionally adopted at the GPS school emphasised physical force and domination over skill and tactical knowledge. Some of the boys in the 1st XV at the time of this study (1997) described the school's traditional approach to playing rugby as "no mistakes" rugby. They indicated that it was highly structured, conservative, predictable, and heavy. The coaching approach employed for this style of play required particular practices that combined with a dominant discourse of manliness at the school, over time embodied a particular form of hegemonic masculinity. Messner (1992) suggests that this typically encourages an instrumental, detached and objective view of bodies whereby bodies become objects used as weapons to dominate, or even injure, other young men.

The coaching at the school limited choice and player independence to emphasise heavy, powerful and purposeful physical contact focused on the generation and use of bodily force to overcome the opposition, to take over opposition territory, and get the team moving forward. While getting the team moving forward in order to facilitate attacking plays is a fundamental strategy in rugby play, the training at the school often encouraged players to seek out heavy contact for the sake of establishing and demonstrating a dominant position. This was invariably given preference over tactical play that involved creating and using space to gain an advantage. In the words of one of the forwards, the team had to get on top and "show them who's boss." The forwards were encouraged by their coaches in particular to put their "bodies on the line" for the team.

On rugby teams the eight players in the forwards are typically more

involved in direct physical confrontations where power, aggression and size are of prime importance than the backs (the other 7 players). However, not all the boys in the forwards on this team were inclined to disregard their physical welfare. For example, Tom's (a pseudonym) parents were medical professionals and his father was what could be referred to as an "Old Boy" (a graduate of the school). Tom played in the forwards and "talked up" the need for aggression and the need to intimidate the opposition but was reluctant to take the risks that one or two other boys (who were constantly injured) were. Early in the study, players in the backs had supported the school's emphasis on power, intimidation and heavy physical domination during interviews. For example, in an interview in the lead up to the first game of the season one of the wingers, Tony made this clear:

> It's a hard game and at this level you've got to get on top of them from the start. You've got to be skilful as well but especially in the forwards you've got to show them who's boss to build a platform for the backs.

While all the players in the firsts initially appeared to embrace the school's traditional approach to rugby, interviews conducted over the study suggested that it was not so straightforward. Each of the boys had complied with its demands to varying degrees and interpreted it in different ways but had not been completely comfortable with it or convinced of the need to put their bodies on the line. While complying with the pattern of hegemonic masculinity operating at the school they had also resisted it in significant ways which was expressed in the style of rugby they aspired to playing that differed from this traditional approach.

The Challenge of a New Game Style

There was a two-week break in the GPS rugby competition during which the 1st XV played in a schools rugby carnival that involved teams from Victoria, NSW, Queensland, New Zealand and some Asian countries. The carnival was conducted over a week during which the team stayed in a hotel together and played rugby every day. The rules of the competition were modified to accommodate the large number of teams competing, specifically, there were shorter games that were freer flowing than GPS games typically were. The transformation in the style of play adopted for the carnival also involved very significant changes in the interaction and relationships between the players as well as the coach and the players. The boys were excited by the way in which they played and enjoyed being empowered to make decisions about how they played and the tactics they used. As they progressed through the carnival their communication improved, shouting and calling to each other during games.

They took more risks and were more supportive of each other when things went wrong. In the euphoria and back slapping following one game, one of the players captured the excitement of the team: "This is awesome. Everybody's having a good time. We are just throwing it (the ball) around, trying lots of stuff and really enjoying it." Far more communication and interaction between them off the field was also observed.

Released from the restraints of must-win rugby the team played a game style that was more open than usual. This required better communication and understanding between players, more decision-making, more anticipation and more risk taking than GPS rugby. This intuitive game style requires a different set of skills to the heavily structured "no mistakes" fashion normally played at the school and whilst the team was not initially up to the demands of playing more creative rugby, this developed as the tournament progressed. The players' enthusiasm for the open rugby they were engaging with grew when they dared to experiment and take risks. This allowed a previously restrained sense of dissatisfaction with the traditional "no mistakes" rugby to emerge during conversations with the players. After a game during the carnival Tony expressed frustration with the team's normal training approach:

> The (GPS) training is too structured and we need to play more open rugby like we are here. Look at how we are playing down here. We're moving the ball, trying new stuff and its all coming off. I reckon the way we train at school restricts us. Training should allow us to try more things and be more creative than we are in GPS games.

After being introduced to a different style of play Tony began to shift his way of thinking about rugby and to disrupt the pedagogical approach. The GPS School team had a successful carnival and after such a positive experience of playing a more open style of rugby the coach, Gordon, decided to experiment with applying the same approach in the remaining two games of the GPS competition. Just as the players had been prepared to take risks in their games, Gordon was prepared to take the risk of trying to play GPS rugby in a very different way. The enthusiasm for open rugby by the players and the coach was triggered by their experiences of the carnival but was situated within the growing influence of professional rugby and its development into a valuable form of entertainment on a global scale (Ryan, 2008). During the carnival and immediately after it there was more response to open, entertaining rugby shaped by the emergence of the professional Super 12 (now Super 14) rugby tournament played between provincial teams from Australia, New Zealand and South Africa and financed by media tycoon Rupert Murdoch. Minor rule changes and a strong emphasis on entertaining rugby had produced a far faster and more open version of the game that the boys in the 1st XV aspired to, as the team captain, "Hicksey" explained:

You go to a Super 12 game and see the incredible pace of play and it blows you away. They're just throwing the ball around and playing amazing running rugby and you compare it to how we have usually played rugby here and its boring and predictable.

The players and the coach had taken a considerable risk in adopting the new playing style in the first GPS game after the carnival and were elated with a good win. The risks involved in departing from traditional "no mistakes" rugby provided more to cheer about after the victory. The players seemed happier and more animated after this game than they had been for the entire study and they expressed both joy and relief in the post-game euphoria during which Lurch, the big front row forward, confirms in a brief interview:

Oh how good was that? That was just the best game. Unbelievable. We all just played so well and this is the best feeling to win like this. This game was so good. Awesome. We played how we wanted to and it all came off. Unbelievable. This is how we should be playing all the time.

After the enjoyment of the rugby carnival and the elation of the victory in the first test of the new game style in a GPS game the fairytale came to an abrupt end. In the last game of the season a stronger opposition team did not provide the GPS School with the time and space that it needed to play its new style of rugby and the team finished its season with a disappointing loss. The approach adopted by the GPS School 1st XV requires very well developed skills and understandings that take more time to develop than the few weeks that the team had. A particular way of playing rugby developed over five years at the school was difficult to change in such a short time.

As Bourdieu (2005) might suggest, while the *habitus* (in a collective sense) is not fixed, neither is it easily changed. It seems that it takes longer than this team had to successfully challenge a style of play reproduced by generations of boys at the school. The coach has also struggled to let go in his coaching and empower his players in the way that the new game style required. His coaching habitus was also difficult to change. This was a task made more difficult by the sense of surveillance within the school and the GPS rugby community that he felt he was often under. Furthermore, the notion of success measured by winning alone is problematic. The complexity of success is rarely played out in sport which is deliberated through wins and losses and on occasion draws which are perceived as shared celebrations or shared disappointments. Is winning itself subjected to the dominant way of being in sport? Etymologically "win," derived from the Old English term *winnan* means to strive, to struggle for, to work at. In sport winning means to dominate, to be victorious. Is winning aligned with masculine domination? If the primary goal of sport is to "win" does this mean that sport itself perpetuates a hegemonic masculinity? And where are we pedagogically if we introduce less dominant forms of play when, in the end, the ultimate goal is one of domination?

Game Style and the Embodiment of Masculinities

Connell (1983) suggests that different forms of masculinity are developed around combinations of power and skill in sport. In rugby, Australian football, ice hockey and American football the nature of combinations of force/power and skill vary according to the position played and to the tactics and strategies adopted. Analysis of the different emphases placed on force (including skill and tactical and strategic understanding) offers a useful means of identifying the significance that particular ways of coaching and styles of play have for the embodiment of masculine identity. As the aforementioned example suggests, playing rugby in ways that place more emphasis on communication, anticipation and tactical understanding would be likely to contribute to the learning of forms of masculinity that vary from those reproduced through an emphasis on power and aggression.

The collective joy, excitement, enthusiasm and increased interaction between the boys evident at the carnival carried on into training for, and playing, the final two GPS games of the season suggests a different experience of rugby for the boys in the firsts. Much of this enjoyment and motivation arose from the experience of playing a new style of rugby, the different training practices employed to develop it, and the ways in which this seemed to free the boys from the shackles of tightly structured rugby. In this approach there was room for more intuitive responses, creativity, anticipation and communication between players than had been the case with "no mistakes rugby" at the school. It required a change in coaching from a highly structured approach to an approach that relied more on the capacities of the players to respond to what is going on around them and to make instant decisions. Such an approach also inherently involved a change in power relations between the coach and the players providing more player autonomy, more decision-making power and taking more responsibility both at training and on the field. The new style required more dialogue between coach and players, and between players, during training and in games.

The Significance of Sport Pedagogy in the Construction of Developing Masculinities

In this examination of the experiment at the GPS school 1st XV, a transformed game style pedagogy emerges as a factor shaping the influence this might have in the formation of masculinities. Learning to successfully play rugby in the new style previously described involves more than the coach providing particular drills and activities. It also requires a shift in pedagogical

philosophy. The difficulties involved in such a change in theoretical orientation and practice could have been a limiting factor for the coach and team adjusting their style of play over a short period of time. The communication, anticipation and creativity that such a style of play requires cannot be learned through the direct instruction that the coach initially relied upon. Instead, it requires training that provides an appropriate environment in which players learn to communicate, react and make decisions within contexts that are similar to matches. The pedagogy of Game Sense, for example, provides a strong case for such an approach. It aims to provide an environment in which players learn through experience in modified games, reflection on play, collaboration, and the collective development and debate of ideas whereby the coach facilitates learning rather than directs it (Light, 2004). This approach to coaching necessarily involves empowering players to take responsibility for their learning, increased dialogue between players as well as between coaches and players, and relationships that are more reciprocal and collegial. Characteristics of such player-centred coaching approaches provide an effective means of developing a particular style of play that is more open and creative. They also provide learning experiences that can contribute toward enriching the schooling experience of young men. For example, the emphasis on interaction and higher-order thinking that such pedagogy stimulates might also be seen as a positive aspect of learning in other settings such as in a mathematics lesson.

Approaches taken to coaching the "hard rugby" traditionally practised in the GPS School are invariably top-down, authoritative, and directive. They typically involve unbalanced power relations between coaches and players and dictated monologues rather than the dialogue that is possible in approaches such as Teaching Games for Understanding (TGfU - Bunker & Thorpe, 1982) and Game Sense (Evans, 2006; Light & Fawns, 2003; Light, 2004). Traditional hard approaches to rugby coaching reduce player autonomy and emphasise the development of superior physical capacities to win games. With these approaches decision-making in training is primarily the responsibility of the coach. At the outset the coach in the study sample took full responsibility for training and for the team's fortunes in games. He led all practice sessions and, with a little input from the captain, he planned and drilled the set attacking moves. He did enjoy a good relationship with the boys; that is, he did not shout at them, intimidate them or ridicule any of them in any way. He was almost always calm and approachable. There was, however, little player autonomy, independence, or room for creativity and risk-taking. While he suggested that he gave the captain autonomy in training, this was noted to be comparatively limited. Early in the study there was little evidence of any player dissatisfaction with traditional regimes of training and game style and players seemed to accept that this was the way in which the GPS School played and trained. It was not until after the team's participation in a school rugby carnival that dissatisfaction with traditional rugby emerged as a dilemma.

The experimentation with open rugby involved more debate and discussion between the players and between them and the coach than the traditional approach did as they took on more responsibility for their learning. This approach empowers players due to the way in which it provides opportunities for them to experiment by developing ideas and strategies, testing them and reflecting upon the results in a process that is central to a constructivist approach to learning (Fosnot, 1996). It has been used to inform the development of student-centred pedagogies such as Teaching Games for Understanding (TGfU) (for examples see Griffin & Butler, 2005; Light, 2004). Such an approach offers learners/players opportunities to collectively develop and "carry through" ideas that Dewey (1916/97) suggests are central to learning. For players to develop the intuition, anticipation, communication and flexible skills required to play creative rugby, they also need to be provided with a socio-moral environment in which "mistakes" are seen as a positive aspect of the learning process (DeVries & Zan, 1996). This sort of environment is supportive, collaborative, empowering and can be liberating when compared to traditional directive coaching and teaching (Light, 2002; Light & Georgakis, 2005).

Developing the intuitive and creative style of rugby the players in the firsts aspired to entails a particular pedagogical approach that sanctions learner autonomy. It requires pedagogy that encourages players to collaboratively solve problems through talking, discussion, and negotiation. These are areas in which boys are typically seen to need encouragement, with academic and popular writing on boys' education suggesting that such coaching pedagogy would contribute toward positive learning for males (Imms, 2001). Moreover, an emphasis on the "academic" curriculum in schools and the subsequent marginalization of subject areas such as creative arts, music, and drama that can provide for emotional education are aspects of boys' schooling that are currently often lacking.

Had the 1st XV won their last game of the season with the new game style the experiment would likely have been seen as being more successful in terms of their performance and because of this we continue to question the ways in which a "must win" ideology figures into masculine domination. Reconceived pedagogies employed over a longer period of time and the nature of the social interaction arising from these might contribute toward the construction of masculinities that depart from or even challenge the hegemonic pattern traditionally reproduced at the school. This suggests that pedagogy in sport coaching is molded by particular discourses of masculinity (or femininity) and that, in turn, it plays a significant role in shaping the construction of gender. An authoritative "command" style approach conceived as a process of the expert passing on objective knowledge coupled with the notion of mastery perpetuate a model of knowledge transmission whereby there is little interaction and a marked power imbalance between coach and players. Conversely, player-centred approaches involve more interaction between players and between coaches and players as well as equitable power relations.

The Significance of Sport Pedagogy in the Construction of Developing Masculinities

Viewed from the perspective of Mosston and Ashworth's (1986) notion of a spectrum of teaching styles, the two approaches of traditional coach-centred "hard" coaching and player-centred "soft" coaching can be seen as sitting at opposite ends of the spectrum ranging from the coach-centred "command style" to the player-centred problem-solving teaching style. We suggest that these opposing styles can also be seen as gendered constructs situated at the extremes of a spectrum of pedagogies with hard coaching being a masculine approach and soft coaching being feminine. We recognise the danger here at a practical level. Many males are likely not to engage with feminist theory and pedagogy at the same level as do females due to their perception of feminism promoting femininity or that which is female. Yet according to Leathwood (2006) "critical" feminist pedagogy aims to challenge competitive individualism and the culture of educational institutions with an emphasis on liberatory education and the provision of opportunities for life-changing learning through ordinary activities of daily life and in social and political activities. Embedded within the ideal of feminist theory there is no subverted binary in the masculine/feminine construction of gender. Research, which has focused on process instead of product and the implicit social learning that can arise from it, suggests that this is not so removed from the possibilities offered by TGfU and Game Sense pedagogy (Light, 2002; Light & Georgakis, 2005). Francis and Leathwood (2006) suggest an even stronger affinity between feminist pedagogy and the sport pedagogies we argue for here by suggesting that: "Feminist pedagogy emphasises intellectual, emotional, practical, pleasurable and political possibilities of learning as opposed to reducing learning to targets, standards and skills" (p. 182). They further suggest that feminist pedagogy "interrogates" the social construction of knowledge and notions of what counts as being expert or valued.

The suggestion of a sport pedagogy consistent with feminist pedagogy advocated here may, at first, seem at odds with the nature of rugby as a heavy contact sport requiring the generation and execution of force. This, we propose, would be a misreading arising from a narrow view of the nature of rugby (and other contact sports), which is heavily influenced by the discourse of hegemonic masculinity. Exemplary hegemonic masculinity, promoted as the only way of being a man in contact sports, tends to focus on the hard, heavy, and deliberate aspects of matches that characterise masculine domination (Carrigan, Connell & Lee, 1985) and overlooks the other aspects of what are typically complex sports that involve both hard and soft aspects of play. In doing so the nature of rugby and similar team sports are misrepresented by emphasising the hard, heavy and deliberate while marginalising the "soft" aspects. Connell's (1983) ideas about the balance between force and skill in the construction of masculinities provides one way of beginning to draw attention to this complexity and its significance for the construction of young men's identities. Rugby requires the use of superior force and a degree of aggression, or legalised, "instrumental" violence (Elias, 1986) in particular areas of the game such as tackling, rucks and mauls, and the scrum, as perhaps the most explicit contest of power and controlled belligerence in the game (Light, 1999). However, it also requires guile, anticipation, communication, evasion and tactical understanding. Although there are times in matches for head-on heavy contact and the execution of enhanced force, there are also many, if not more, occasions when it is more prudent to evade contact in order to gain advantages over opponents. Similarly, as much as rugby play requires the hardness of physical power and aggression, it also requires intelligence and tactically informed decision-making.

Effective individual and team play needs to develop both the hard and the soft aspects of play, and coaches require evidenced-based approaches that can assist in this. This is not so much a case of compromising between opposites as it is a case of realising the complementary relationships between them, such as those evident in Eastern philosophical traditions. Eastern philosophy emphasises the balance and complementary relationships in life between apparent opposites (for example, soft/hard, male/female) that characterise the practice of traditional martial arts. While the diverse forms of martial arts categorised as kung fu in China, and judo, kendo and karate in Japan have undergone significant change in meaning and practice as they have been Westernised or "sportified" (Inoue, 1997), they remain underpinned by Eastern philosophic traditions of balance between opposites captured in the Chinese notion of yin/yang. Eastern martial arts such as karate and judo demonstrate and require a dynamic balance between hard and soft in both defence and attack. From a Western perspective one has only to think of the frustrations of trying too "hard" to drive a golf ball to provide insight into the complementary relationship between soft and hard in sport.

Accepting that there is a complementary relationship between hard and soft aspects of rugby strongly suggests that the use of feminist pedagogy such as introduced in Game Sense would assist in both improving play and experience in "masculine" sports "on the pitch" and in shaping young peoples' social learning and identity formation "off the ball." For example, utilising game sense pedagogy in contact sports could help develop balanced, independent players with tactical knowledge and an ability to adapt to the demands of changes in play without detracting from their ability to play hard when required. At junior club levels, and in schools in particular, it could also provide a means of making rugby (and other sports) a more valuable part of young men's experiences of schooling and contribute positively, in a small yet significant way, toward their social and moral development while helping address concerns with the negative influence of hegemonic masculinity on young men that is so pronounced in heavy contact sports. Yet, in suggesting a feminist pedagogy, we are aware of the challenges men might encounter in taking it up (Kaufman, 1999). We further concede that whilst masculine domination (Bourdieu, 2001) is problematic, discrimination of any sort, including that against men is not our intent. Instead, we offer the notion of non-genderist pedagogy as a basis from which to reconceive the complexities encountered by all persons in the construction of gender-infused identities.

Towards a Non-Genderist Pedagogy

While a student/player centred pedagogy can be and has been enacted within physical education this is more difficult to achieve in sport, especially in the more "masculine" sports. We therefore propose a non-genderist pedagogy as one means of furthering the conversation around this difficulty. Non-genderist pedagogy comprises both feminist and masculinist discourse, disrupts dominant masculinity, and is open to multiple theoretical orientations (e.g., queer theory, transgender theory, etc.). It recognises that all humans have masculine and feminine traits inhabited by both sexist and non-sexist tendencies. It further acknowledges that there may exist an innate predisposition for some males to be masculine and some females to be feminine and vice versa. It is a critical pedagogy that disrupts all forms of ascendency and marginalisation and provokes learners to critically appraise the ways in which representations of dominance figure into and do not figure into their own identities. Non-genderist pedagogy asserts that our ways of thinking and being are biologically, socially, and culturally contrived, which can and should be interrogated via critical inquiry and furthering and deepening understanding of the complex nature of gender construction. In putting forward non-genderist pedagogy as a way of thinking and speaking about gender construction we acknowledge that its major tenets are nothing novel. Rather, its guiding principles are worked out in detail by gender theorists elsewhere (see for example, Connell, 1982; 2005) and as such we look upon it as an impetus for the potential merger of these contributing theories. Non-genderist pedagogy values the *hard* and the *soft* as well as a full complement of combinations and fusions along a continuum of identities.

Conclusion

Regardless of what pedagogical approach is employed, the negative influences that elite and highly competitive contact sport encompasses will continue to present a problem for the physical, social and personal growth of young men (see for example, Messner, 1992; Messner & Sabo, 1990; Mills, 1997). However, we suggest that non-genderist pedagogy focused upon engaging learners in working towards understanding of the complex nature of the masculine/feminine continuum might begin to address this problem. Team games such as rugby can offer opportunities for valuable social learning when this is made an explicitly articulated learning objective linked to larger school curricula and policy and appropriate pedagogy is utilised. Despite the raft of difficulties involved with boys' (and girls') participation in heavy contact sports they can provide positive social learning such as working as a member of a team, setting and striving to achieve collective and individual goals, and subjugating individual needs to the needs of the group (Light, 2008c). They also provide potential media for developing some of the skills such as problem solving, weighing up risk against the possible benefits of achieving a particular goal, and resilience, which are needed in the work place and daily living. This is not, however, achieved at the expense of performance because, as we have argued here, such approaches can meet the complex demands of rugby and other contact team sports through education informed by a vision of the complementary relationships between binary constructs.

Writing on TGfU during the 1990s was dominated by a "technique verses tactics" debate that failed to see the inextricable relationship between the two. More sophisticated analyses over the past decade recognise the interrelationships between technique, skill and tactical understanding and the need for them to be developed together in context. In a similar vein we argue for a more holistic and complex conception of contact games such as rugby that recognise the complementary relationships between what are otherwise considered as binaries. We wonder if non-genderist pedagogy could be used as one way of improving the experience of playing rugby and providing a locale for the development of masculinities that challenge the restrictions and the host of worrying influences of hegemonic forms.

Although there is a range of positive social learning that can occur through participation in sport and team sport, in particular, we do not assume this an automatic outcome of playing rugby. The learning that arises from involvement in sport, including the implicit construction of gender, is shaped profoundly by the interwoven discourses of hegemonic masculinity, elite level commercial sport, and of sport as a form of moral education originating from the nineteenth century schools of the English middle classes (Mangan, 1981). When viewed as being part of the extended school curriculum structured to achieve desired learning outcomes and objectives, sport can offer a valuable medium for social and moral learning in schools. Pedagogies for teaching games and coaching sport that have emerged over the past two decades, such as TGfU and Game Sense, hold considerable potential for beginning to actively address what has been seen as sport and physical education's role in the "problem" of masculinity (Messner, 1992; Tomsen & Donaldson, 2003). Enacting non-genderist pedagogy may offer one means of beginning to realise the potential that team sports hold as educational media for promoting positive social learning in the education of young men and, though not discussed here, young women as well. This potential, we contend, might be what real men of the future regard as *splendid*.

Bibliography

Begg, A. (2001). Why more than constructivism is needed. In S. Gunn & A. Begg (Eds.), *Mind, body and society: Emerging understandings of knowing and learning* (pp. 13-20). Melbourne: Dept of Mathematics and Statistics, University of Melbourne.

Blackmore, J. (2006). Unprotected participation in lifelong learning and the politics of hope: A feminist reality check of discourses around flexibility, seamlessness and learner earners. In C. Leathwood & B. Francis (Eds.), *Gender and lifelong learning: A critical feminist perspective* (pp. 9-26). London & New York: Routledge.

Bourdieu, P. (2001). *Masculine domination.* Stanford, CA: Stanford University Press.

Bourdieu, P. (2005). Habitus. In J. Hillier & E. Rooksby (Eds.), *Habitus: A sense of place* (2nd ed., pp. 43-52). Aldershot, UK: Ashgate.

Bunker, D., & Thorpe, R. (1982). A model for the teaching of games in secondary schools. *Bulletin of Physical Education, 18*(2) 5-8.

Carrigan, T., Connell, B., & Lee, J. (1985). Toward a new sociology of masculinity. *Theory and Society, 14*(5), 551-604.

Connell, R. W. (1983). *Which way is up? Essays on sex, class and culture.* Sydney: Allen & Unwin.

Connell, R. W. (1995). *Masculinities.* Sydney: Allen & Unwin.

Connell, R. W., Ashenden, D. J., Kessler, S., & Dowsett, G. W. (1982). *Making the difference: Schools, families and social division.* Sydney: Allen & Unwin.

Connell, R. W., & Messerschmidt, J. W. (2005). Hegemonic masculinity: Rethinking the concept, *Gender & Society, 19*(6), 829-859.

DeVries, R., & Zan, B. (1996). A constructivist perspective on the role of the sociomoral atmosphere in promoting children's development. In C. T. Fosnot (Ed.), *Constructivism: Theory, perspectives and practice.* New York & London: Teachers College, Columbia University.

Dewey, J. (1916/97). *Democracy and education.* New York: Free Press.

Elias, N. (1986). An essay on sport and violence. In N. Elias & E. Dunning (Eds.), *Quest for excitement* (pp. 150-174). New York: Basil Blackwell.

Evans, J. (2006). Elite level rugby coaches interpretation of Game Sense. *Asian Journal of Exercise and Sport Science, 3*(1), 17-24.

Fosnot, C. T. (1996). Constructivism: A psychological theory of learning. In C. T. Fosnot (Ed.), *Constructivism: Theory, perspectives and practice.* New York & London: Teachers College, Columbia University.

Francis, B., & Leathwood, C. (2006). Conclusion. In C. Leathwood, & B. Francis (Eds.), *Gender and lifelong learning: A critical feminist perspective.* London & New York: Routledge

Glaser, B., & Strauss, A. (1967). *The discovery of grounded theory: Strategies for qualitative research.* Chicago, IL: Aldine.

Griffin, L. L., & Butler J. (2005). *Teaching games for understanding: Theory, practice and research.* Champaign, IL: Human Kinetics.

Grunneau, R., & Whitson, D. (1993). *Hockey night in Canada: Sport, identities and cultural politics.* Toronto, ON: Garamond Press.

Hickey, C., Fitzclarence, L., & Mathews, R. (1998). *Where the boys are: Masculinity, sport and education.* Geelong: Deakin Centre for Education and Change.

hooks, b. (1994). *Teaching to transgress.* London: Routledge.

Imms, W. (2001). Multiple masculinities and the schooling of boys. *Canadian Journal of Education, 25*(2), 152-166.

Inoue, S. (1997). Sports and the martial arts in the making of modern Japan. Paper presented to the International Conference for the Sociology of Sport, Kyoto, Japan, March 27-29.

Kaufman, M. (1999). Men, feminism, and men's contradictory experiences of power. In J. Kuypers (Ed.), *Men and power* (pp. 59-83). Halifax: Fernwood Books.

Kidman, L. (2005). *Athlete-centred coaching: Developing inspired and inspiring people.* Christchurch, New Zealand: Innovative Print Communications.

Kentel, J. A. (2009). Pretty boys and butch girls: Examining the development of masculinities in physical education. Paper presented at the *Council of University Professors and Researchers (CUPR)* Annual Meeting, April-May 2009, Banff, Alberta, Canada.

Kirk, D. (1998). *Schooling bodies: School practice and public discourse 1880-1950.* London & Washington DC: Leicester University Press.

Leathwood, C., & Francis, B. (Eds.). (2006). *Gender and lifelong learning: A critical feminist perspective.* London & New York: Routledge

Light, R. (1999). Regimes of training and the construction of masculinity in Japanese university rugby. *International Sports Studies, 21*(2), 39-54.

Light, R. (2002). The social nature of games: Pre-service primary teachers' first experiences of TGfU, *European Physical Education Review, 8*(3), 291-310.

Light, R. (2004). Coaches' experiences of Game Sense: Opportunities and challenges. *Physical Education and Sport Pedagogy, 9*(2), 115-132.

Light, R., & Georgakis, S. (2005). Integrating theory and practice in teacher education: The impact of a Games Sense unit on female pre-service primary teachers' attitudes toward teaching physical education. *Journal of Physical Education New Zealand, 38*(1), 67-80.

Light, R. (2008a). *Sport in the lives of young Australians.* Sydney: Sydney University Press.

Light, R. (2008b). "Complex" learning theory in physical education: An examination of its epistemology and assumptions about how we learn. *Journal of Teaching in Physical Education, 27*(1), 21-37.

Light, R. (2008c). Learning masculinities in a Japanese high school rugby club. In R. Light (Ed.), special issue, Boys, the body, school and sport, *Sport, Education and Society, 13*(2), 163-180.

Light, R., & Fawns, R. (2003). Knowing the game: Integrating speech and action in games through TGfU. *Quest, 55*(2), 161-176.

Light, R., & Kirk, D. (2000). High school rugby, the body and the reproduction of masculinity. *Sport, Education and Society, 5*(2), 163-176.

Mangan, J. A. (1981). *Athleticism in the Victorian and Edwardian public school, The emergence and consolidation of an educational ideology.* Cambridge, UK: Cambridge University Press.

McKay, J. (1991). *No pain no gain? Sport and Australian culture.* Sydney: Prentice Hill.

McKay, J., & Middlemiss, I. (1995). "Mate against mate, state against state": A case study of media constructions of hegemonic masculinity in Australian sport. *Masculinities, 3*(3), 28-34.

Messner, M. (1992). *Power at play: Sports and the problem of masculinity.* Boston: Beacon Press.

Messner, M., & Sabo, D. (Eds.), (1990). *Sport, men and the gender order:* Critical feminist perspectives. Champaign, IL: Human Kinetics.

Mills, M. (1997). Football, desire and the social organization of masculinity. *Social Alternatives, 16*(1), 10-13.

Mosston, M., & Ashworth, S. (1986). *Teaching physical education* (3rd ed.). Columbus: Merrill.

Ryan, G. (Ed.). (2008). *Professionalism and tensions in Japanese rugby. The changing face of rugby: The union game and professionalism since 1995.* Cambridge, UK: Cambridge Scholars Press.

Thompson, J. (1997). "Really useful knowledge": Linking theory and practice. In J. Thompson (Ed.), *Words in edgeways: Radical learning for social change.* Leicester, UK: NIACE.

Tomsen, S., & Donaldson, M. (2003). *Male trouble: Looking at Australian masculinities.* Melbourne: Pluto Press.

Wacquant, L. (1995). Pugs at work: Bodily capital and bodily labour among professional boxers. *Body & Society, 1*(1), 65-89.

Wedgwood, N. (2003). Aussie rules! Schoolboy football and masculine embodiment. In S. Tomsen & M. Donaldson (Eds.), *Male trouble: Looking at Australian masculinities.* Melbourne: Pluto Free Press.

PART THREE

Emerging/Contesting Masculinities

Negotiating Masculinities in PE Classrooms: Boys, Body Image and "Want[ing] to Be in Good Shape"

Michael Kehler

This chapter draws from a subset of data taken from a national study aimed at examining why some adolescent males are reluctant to participate in mandatory grade-nine health and physical education classes in Canada. The purpose of the study was to provide a more nuanced understanding of how fourteen-fifteen-year-old boys negotiate masculinities among other boys in the context of secondary school gym classes. Prompted by a growing concern for inactivity among youth (Active Healthy Kids Canada, 2008) and a noticeable absence of attention to body image and adolescent boys, this research explores the intersection between masculinities, body image and education. I raise questions in this context specifically because of the increased hyper-visibility of masculine bodies in schools and the un-examined body image issues among adolescent boys that remain largely invisible from current health and fitness debates in education. In short, concern for inactivity among youth has moved some boys, literally found on the sidelines of the gym, into the foreground. It has become virtually impossible to be a wallflower when physical health, read physical activity, has become mandatory in schools across Canada. The discussion in this chapter centres on an initial reading of data gained through semi-structured interviews, weblog entries, and field observations of the participants during five consecutive days they were in PE class. The data analysis and interpretation I provide in this chapter is not intended to be conclusive, as the study is ongoing.

Media Hype or Is Body Image *Really* a Problem among Boys?

Local, national and international headlines provide but a glimpse into growing concerns about rising inactivity among youth. Significantly contributing to a burgeoning rhetoric connecting youth, inactivity, increased obesity rates and education, media outlets offer a picture of who is to blame, how the issues are defined and public perceptions. Consider for example, a recent survey of Canadian online newsprint dailies. The headlines read: Ontario investing millions to promote healthy living, (CP, 2006), Single-parent kids more likely to be fat (CP, 2003), Childhood obesity: a growing epidemic, (Sun Media, 2004), Overweight children find fast food too tempting (AP, 2003). By far not exhaustive but rather suggestive of the range of media coverage across Canada, as well as the language to name and define concerns for youth inactivity, health, and obesity, the media contributes in powerful ways to both how and what is understood about particular news worthy issues such as inactivity among youth. At the same time, much of this coverage has remained silent on the complexity of factors such as social class, gender and ethnicity that influence levels of sport participation. (see AHKC, 2008)

The public perception and construction of social issues through the media is particularly useful. In his analysis of US news print media, for example, Titus' (2004) keyword search of archives and electronic databases illustrates how "rhetoric is used to assert the existence of some condition, define it as problematic, publicize a version of the problem, persuade audiences, and mobilize support for ratifying the claim" (p. 147). The simplified accounts of obesity and inactivity among youth are captured by the media and generate a wide range of public perceptions about, for example, teens, fast food, eating habits, preventive strategies and physical education. As with the *moral panic* about boy's underachievement in schools examined by Titus, he reminds us that the success of the media to convey a sense of moral panic or in the case of obesity, an "epidemic" of crisis proportions, "relies not on its ability to reflect complicated nuanced effects but its ability to oversimplify highly complex situations, forecast danger, and attribute blame" (p. 158). In education for example, decreasing underachievement levels have been defined as a boy problem and as such, a gender problem. Obesity and youth inactivity among "teens" is framed in the public eye with an awareness of the already present perceptions of healthy bodies and body image. The media spin on this issue however has not begun to acknowledge the underlying damaging culture of body image issues related to youth, both boys and girls. Azzarito (2009) describes the impact that pre-existing understandings and emerging ideas of the body have in a "world of images, a world of bodily visibility through which cultural messages about the body are constantly produced" (p. 19).

Particularly striking in the context of the evolving debate about inactivity among youth is a study in which Frost (2003) explains that boys, not dissimilar to girls, were found to be obsessed with aspects of physicality. She reminds us that desirable attributes associating boys with their bodies are intimately connected to

> physicality and physical strength, the ability to play sport, win fights and "stand up for yourself." The body, for boys, is a crucial factor in identification, and some groups and some individuals are almost automatically excluded and outcast as a result. (Frost, 2003, p. 65)

Sound-bite news accounts of a complex issue such as obesity are narratively produced and reduced to issues of youth inactivity, health and schooling minus any complex intersections linking masculinity, body image, and schooling. From financial efforts aimed at developing healthy living and reducing the tax burden on a health care system to linking single parenting to an inability to buy healthy food, Canadian media accounts and responses to *explain* "the battle of the bulge" are reduced to a series of name-blame reports. In their examination of obesity reports and an emerging health discourse, Evans, Davies & Rich (2008) critique the current health *crisis* named "obesity" and examine "a panic discourse used to either establish new or reinstate fragile social norms of 'discordant,' 'damaged' and 'unhealthy' lives" (p. 120).

The news accounts mentioned above and elsewhere (Gard & Wright, 2005; Evans et al., 2008) are increasingly common on an international scale. In the United States, for example, reporting in *Time* magazine (2006, March 19) not dissimilar to Canadian coverage, connected obesity with costs to the health care system. In a feature article titled, "the politics of fat," Karen Tumulty describes the extent of the concern for obesity, quoting the Surgeon General as saying "obesity is a greater threat than terrorism" (p. 41). The *USA Today* (2005, July 31) a popular American daily, draws from a study cited in *Pediatrics*, reporting that a nationwide survey of 10,000 adolescents reveals that "as Americans overall become fatter and further away from the thin toned body that society considers ideal, teens are increasingly turning to extreme behaviours to achieve what's often unachievable" (Weise, 2005). Highlighting the gravity of the situation and suggesting a concern for body image, the reporter explains that "almost 5% of teenage boys and 2% of girls use potentially unhealthy products" (Weise, 2005). Interestingly, though not routinely addressed in the media, previous studies have already established the fact that "body image is integral to a boy's self-concept and to the construction of his masculinity, therefore those who fail to live up to these expectations face guilt, self-consciousness and poor body image" (Drummond, 2001). The connection between masculine identity, body image, and inactivity has remained relatively silent in the media portrayal of the "battle of the blubber."

Early indicators point to body image dissatisfaction among adolescent males but as of yet, the actual experiences of adolescent males have not been well examined particularly in the school context. (Grogan, 2006) In fact in a literature review of 17 studies on body image in boys, Cohane & Pope (2001) found that there are sufficient and troubling patterns of concern expressed through poor self-concept and a focus on "bigness" and "muscularity" among boys in these first-generation studies. Gill, Henwood & McLean (2005) draw attention to a changing visual landscape once dominated by women and girls to the exclusion of masculine bodies. More recently however the canvas and public billboards include both the masculine and feminine body. The singularity of the body as either or, masculine or feminine and as an "idealized and eroticized" vision has not changed. But, as Gill et al. (2005) argue, what has changed is the way "the male (body) has become an object of the gaze rather than simply the bearer of the look" (p. 39). There has been a noticeable shift in which "men's bodies as *bodies* have gone from near invisibility to hypervisibility," contributing to an emerging and alarming context in which males may increasingly be defining themselves through their bodies (p. 39). Concerns such as these give rise to further studies and clearly warrant a great investment in both practical and theoretical terms to better understanding what percolates beneath the rising public debate.

Body image research of adolescent boys has gone under-examined and under-theorized, leaving much of the concerns for boys and their bodies as taboo or a gay issue. (Connell, 1995; Davison, 2000; Drummond, 2001; Pope, Phillips, & Olivardia, 2000) Not dissimilar to research examining body issues among women and girls, Hargreaves & Tiggemann (2006) report that societal beauty ideals and media images of lean, muscular men contribute to body dissatisfaction among men and boys, but it remains under-reported and as such, a "hidden problem" (Labre, 2002). They note that the invisibility of the concerns of body image and links to mass media may be explained by "the existence of a social prohibition among boys admitting to body dissatisfaction" (p. 569). Grogan (2006) explains that "body image is implicated in a number of unhealthy behaviours" and "can affect the likelihood that we will engage in, or avoid exercise" (p. 525). The link between adolescent male concerns for body image and investment in physical activity in the context of school PE classes however requires ongoing in-depth research. And while the weakness and vulnerability often associated with body image and femininity partially explains the invisibility of issues intersecting masculinity, health and body image, it nonetheless leaves a considerable gap in current official responses at the provincial and federal levels to address inactivity among youth and specifically adolescent males struggling with body image issues in schools.

Masculinities and the Dis-placement of Adolescent Male Bodies in School

Physical education classes are important sites for understanding, seeing, and hearing how gender is negotiated and renegotiated through the bodily practices of high school young men (Azzarito, 2009). The school context is particularly powerful and informative because it is here where, according to Mills (2001), "those boys who do not measure up, the effeminate, the overweight, and the underweight and who do not compensate for this by engaging in other masculine activities, often related to alcohol, motor bikes, or cars, are usually made to suffer the consequences of their lack of 'masculinity'" (p. 26). As such current efforts at the provincial and federal level to increase physical activity and produce healthy bodies requires a careful reconsideration of both the gendered assumptions about the levels of student engagement as well as the impact on healthy bodies. The conceptualization and re-conceptualization of the body as a site of negotiated meanings that diverge or converge with dominant notions of masculinity and femininity is a powerful location for understanding the degree of participation of youth in health and physical education classes. (For a thorough discussion of the centrality of the body in the sporting arena, see Wellard, 2009.) Be they curricular or community health initiatives, attempts to promote healthy life practices raise concerns surrounding the unexamined and unquestioned circumstances of student (dis)engagement from authorized healthy body practices typically promoted through health and physical education (Adams, 2005; Boyce, Roche & Davies, 2009; Drummond, 2003, 2001; Field, 2000; Light & Kirk, 2000; Martino & Beckett, 2004; Messner, 1997, Prain, 2000).

Building on theories of gender and gender identity in feminist and masculinities research, I argue that masculinity is actively and routinely constructed through interactions. From within masculinities research I argue that the ways the boys enact, display, or produce masculine identities as boys reveals the degree to which boys purposefully respond to and understand codes of masculinity. Boys routinely organize and reorganize ways of being boys according to what is deemed as appropriately masculine behaviour. "Gender is not fixed in advance of social interaction, but is constructed in interaction" (Connell, 1995, p. 35). Practices of masculinity are layered, characterized by instability and constant flux. They are neither static nor unitary but rather "represent compromise formations between contradictory desires or emotions, or the results of uncertain calculations about the costs and benefits of different gender strategies" (Connell & Messerschmidt, 2005, p. 852). As such, boys experience and project displays of masculinity differently, and accordingly, not all boys experience the same kind or degree of power by virtue of being a boy (Kaufman, 1994). Connell (1995) explains that we must go beyond recognizing a diversity in masculinities to recognizing

> the relations between the different kinds of masculinity: relations of alliance, dominance and subordination. These relationships are constructed through practices that exclude and include, that intimidate, exploit, and so on. There is a gender politics within masculinity" (p. 37).

I build on his argument in this chapter, taking up the position that power and privilege are intricately woven to the body and the ultimate performativity of masculinities is contingently located in space and time in such places as classrooms and health and physical education classes. In a recent study, Wellard (2009) explores the sporting experiences of adult men. His study raises significant questions about the taken-for-grantedness of the bodily practices of men in a sporting context. Interestingly his study looks at the ways the masculine body is used, directed and engaged within sport. This chapter diverges from his study in several ways. First, the participants whose voices and experiences appear in this chapter are adolescent boys who are currently in school. As such, their experiences are in the present and not a reflection or memoir of their past. These young men are telling their stories now as a reflection on the present context of issues intersecting masculinities, health, and schooling. Second, Wellard concentrates on how the masculine body is expressly utilized or engaged to display a sporting masculine identity. Though this is certainly significant, I shift the attention to the body as a textual representation of masculine identities in a health and education context. The focus, then, is on the understandings adolescent boys have of their bodies as bodies and the interplay between what they know of and about their bodies and how that contributes to participating in healthy life practices, particularly in school. In short this research diverges from Wellard in its more nuanced examination of the ways boys *read* their bodies, how other boys read and misread the masculine body, and the implications this may have for long-term health practices among adolescent males.

Earlier feminist deliberations on how bodies are socially defined through outward markers of masculinity and femininity provide a useful foundation for moving forward in explorations of masculine subjectivities. Theoretically informed by the work of Butler (1999), I acknowledge the fluidity of gender as well as its unstable and uncertain location and as such, reject essentialist arguments that limit masculinity as static and unchanging. I agree with Butler (1999), who further argues that gender is "the repeated stylization of the body, a set of repeated acts within a highly rigid regulatory frame that congeal over time to produce the appearance of substance, a natural sort of being" (p. 33). This research also builds on past work on the sociology of the body (Atkinson, 2003; Gorely, Holroyd & Kirk, 2003; Hickey et al, 2000; Hickey &

Fitzclarence, 1999; Light & Kirk, 2000; Shilling, 2004; Sparkes & Silvennoinen, 1999; Wiegers, 1998; Wienke, 1998; Wright, 2000, 2001) which argues for re-envisioning masculinity as socially constructed through corporeal engagement in social and cultural practices of masculinities.

Although Canadian curriculum documents presently support additional variety in content and in pedagogical practices, school-based physical education continues to reinforce and reify traditional masculine values associated with competitive team sport. As Connell (1995) explains, the significance of the body becomes emblematic of valued and undervalued masculinities from much theorizing in which "true masculinity is almost always thought to proceed from men's bodies—to be inherent in a male body or to express something about a male body" (p. 45). Boys' decisions to engage or disengage with physical education within secondary schools are underscored by the socio-cultural understandings they have of their bodies and specifically, how these understandings relate to the masculine identities. In her discussion of the criteria of young male group acceptability, Frost (2003) notes the masculine body as "physically strong, sporty and tough," as a central medium through which exclusion, derogation may be the (damaging) outcomes for some young men" (p. 66).

Schools are not neutral sites but are actively involved in a process that either perpetuates or challenges the reproduction of normative masculinities. And despite the best efforts and intentions of recent provincial directives to encourage and promote healthy living and healthy bodies among youth, I agree with Connell (1995) arguing that, "bodies cannot be understood as a neutral medium of social practice. Their materiality matters. They will do certain things and not others" (p. 58). Bodies are a part of the social arrangement into which they are invited. At the same time, bodies and the maintenance of them in relation to developing positive body images, remain unspoken and unacknowledged among boys and men. These concerns and talk of body image is reportedly a feminine or gay issue. (Hargreaves & Tiggeman, 2006)

Particularly salient, then, is the degree to which bodily practices are encumbered with gendered knowledge related to masculine identities. McLaren's (1991) discussion of the body within schools argues that schools "undervalue language and representation as constitutive factors in the shaping of the body/subject as the bearer of meaning, history, race and gender" (p. 156). He continues, arguing that "we have bodies not just because we are born *into* bodies but because we *learn* our bodies, that is, we are taught how to think about our bodies and how to experience our bodies" (McLaren, 1991, p. 156). In his examination of male bodybuilding, Wieger's (1998) notes the import the male body has as a vehicle for asserting self-identities. Muscularity and the sculpting of the body is a means by which men negotiate between expected masculine traits and the realities of men's lives. Masculinities scholar Connell (1995) argues that through bodily reflexive practice, ideas of masculinity shape and inform how boys use their bodies. This, then, is connected to the expectations among boys for what it means to be a "real man." Seidler (1997) explains that "our bodies are things that we *do* things with in order to prove both to ourselves and to others that our masculinity is intact" (p. 187). Kehler, Davison and Frank, (2005), among others (Adams, 2005; Drummond, 2003; Gard & Meyenn, 2000; Kehily, 2002, 2001; Kehler, 2007; Kehler & Greig, 2005; Mac An Ghaill, 1994; Martino & Pallota-Chiarolli, 2003; 2005), have shown how degrees of gender movement are monitored in situations where boys and young men face constant surveillance and policing by other boys. Equally surprising however, as Ricciardelli, McCabe & Rita (2006) explain, is the dearth of studies exploring masculine body image concerns in the context of sport or physical activity. In the next section I look more closely specifically at an ongoing national study that in part, explores adolescent masculine body image issues in Canada.

The Study: The (In)visibility of Boy's Bodies in Grade Nine PE Classes

The data from this study provide initial readings offering a narrative insight and critical sociological perspective of how masculinities, understandings of body image, and health intersect in the structured setting of secondary school grade nine health and physical education classes. The recruitment of participants for this study was a formidable task in and of itself. Interestingly and perhaps not surprisingly, the difficulty of conducting such research was met by a sense of trepidation from some teachers. Why should I be concerned about adolescent body image? My foray into this research stems from past masculinities research in which I found the body and its navigation among boys to be a powerful textual representation of various masculinities. (Kehler, 2007) After some reassurances and clarification about my own investment in youth adolescent body image research and concerns for inactivity among youth, I was soon given greater support from secondary school teachers. There was however another concern expressed from a teacher, namely the potential for students to "teacher bash." This concern was set aside by most teachers. In the pilot project leading up to the national study, seventeen schools were contacted and invited to participate. I visited each school and provided a brief explanation of the study. Teachers were asked to identify students who demonstrated a reluctance to participate in class. Evidence of "reluctance to participate" included, but was not limited to: repeatedly missing class, ill-prepared to participate, lacks initiative in class, and signs of discomfort with activities in class.

Particular to this study is the salience of the data that was captured "in the moment." That is to say that the accounts and events of these boys are not recollections but rather immediate and presently occurring. Whereas previous studies have called upon adult males to recollect their experiences of high school health and physical education, this study aimed at examining the experiences and understandings of boys who were currently participating but reluctantly so in health and physical education classes. The research project was designed to capture the stories and experiences of being an adolescent boy struggling to participate and engage in a setting that has historically been neither inviting nor welcoming, especially to young men who are uncomfortable in an arena in which men are supposed and expected to be competent. Drummond (2001) building on Connell (1995), explains that participation in sport and physical activity is culturally significant both as a masculinising domain as well as the broader meaning it has as a rite of passage for adolescent men. As such, our aim was to discuss the experiences of being in a mandatory health and physical education class when in actual fact these young men were reluctant to be there. According to many of these boys, the primary reason expressed for being in class was "to get the credit." The underlying questions in this study explore the ways adolescent males navigate masculine identities in an arena regarded as a masculinised domain. In short, our study focus was on the understandings and impression these young men have of the physical body as a signifier and marker of masculinity, what Adams refers to as a "promotional device" wherein "ideas about men's bodies and what they should or should not do give shape, quite literally, to the bodies in which men live" (2005, p. 65).

We purposefully designed semi-structured in-depth interviews for this project. And although Hargreaves & Tiggemann (2006), for example, argue that focus groups might "encourage participants to discuss the questions primarily with each other, providing access to participants' own language" (p. 570), we saw the possibility of greater risk and vulnerability for an already very vulnerable group of young men. Another concern with a focus group setting was the potential this context had for young men to display particular forms of masculinity. As much as possible we wanted to avoid "boys doing boy" (Kehler 2007) and instead, we wanted to allow for open disclosure between the participants and researcher. Our research draws from ethnographic traditions wherein we opted for individual interviews and unobtrusive field observations. A primary concern driving the research protocol was the hidden issue of body image among adolescent boys and the accompanying sensitivity and vulnerability adolescent boys associate with this topic. In light of these concerns, we followed the prescriptions of interview strategies outlined by Lofland & Lofland (1995) which support the participant's ability to negotiate the direction of the conversation. The interview strategy was intended to empower participants and elicit highly descriptive responses.

The interviews were audio-taped while the field observations were hand written. During our interviews we were interested in opening up a dialogue that would allow these boys to explain and describe how their physical bodies were implicated in a health and physical education context. The research team was interested, for example, in learning how the physicality of boy's bodies factored into conversations and interactions among boys. We asked questions such as "What are some of the difficulties you have experienced in gym class?" and "Describe for me when you feel most anxious. Uncomfortable? Or feel out of place during the gym class?" In addition to the interviews, we invited the participants to visit a secure weblog site designed for this project. This site gave strict access to participants and did so in a manner that no participant knew or saw any other entries. This was an online journal log intended to allow the participants to access and recount experiences from PE class after the researchers had left the school site. As we eventually found, web blogging was not a well-used venue at this time for this particular population. For the purpose of this paper I am drawing primarily on interview data.

Our initial analysis of the data revealed patterns and consistent themes emerging across the experiences of these young men. Our aim was not to provide findings that generalize to all adolescent boys reluctantly participating in health and physical education classes. Our primary aim was to provide a forum through which a particular group of adolescent boys might be heard and better understood not because they have been misunderstood, though this may also be the case, but rather because they have been largely absent or missing from any discussion of body image research to this point. The richness of their voices and the complex and troubling stories they share reveal the need to continue this research but also to extend the spaces in which these young men and other young men are able to name and identify their own bodies without the threat of homophobia that potentially silences and denies the realities of the locker room fears and jeers they endure in school. In the following section I provide accounts to illustrate how some adolescent boys understand their bodies in relation to other boys, to describe how they see masculinity embodied by the physical body and to share how their feelings of inadequacy contribute to a painful and enduring set of ways for being a boy among boys that may potentially affect attitudes and behaviours toward life-long practices of healthy living.

"I want to be in good shape": The Desire and Appeal

According to many of the boys in this study they did not have a dislike for being in shape or fit but rather a discomfort about *participating* and being *accepted* in the current climate that characterizes their PE classes. In varying degrees each of them "liked" physical activity. Mythic explains:

> I'm concerned. I want to stay, I want to be in good shape. It's just a lot of the ways people stay in good shape doesn't really appeal to me, like team sports and competitiveness. I'm not really into that. . . . A lot of them play hockey, basketball. During the summer they play mostly baseball and soccer but it's pretty much hockey for them.

In Rod's case he explains that he needs to improve and develop skill. For Rod there is a disconnect between "being in good shape" and the ways boys participate in typically aggressive and competitive sports such as hockey and other teams sports. The tension he expresses is one between a highly valued sporty masculinity and a less valued and oft ridiculed weaker masculinity. He is not adverse to the idea of being active, but interestingly, he equates developing skill with a form of defence or strategy to protect him from ridicule. He suggests that having specific skills to play games is one way to avoid being teased. He states:

> Well I need to improve more on lifting weights but other than that, I have good skills. I like basketball or soccer. You just have to know how the game goes and you have to know what strategies you can do to take the ball away from the other person. . . . Because I don't want, I don't want anybody to really embarrass me at all. Like say they called me fat, whatever. I wouldn't like that at all. . . .

He acknowledges that knowing how to play sports and games is important but remains concerned about the perception of his body as "fat." He continues:

> They mostly get picked on if they're not doing so well in gym, like at running. I'm kind of an average runner. I've become more active doing more running.

As our interview progresses, he mentions weight lifting.

> Michael: But the weights, is that a big thing here?
> Rod: Well you just seem more healthier and more muscular. I don't know, I guess it just impresses their friends.

His impression of being healthy is equated with being muscular. Interestingly Rod connects health, muscularity and a kind of currency exchange value which translates into garnering popularity among peers through the production of normative masculinity. In the next excerpt, Bob, like Rod, explains that weight lifting serves a specific purpose among adolescent boys. The value of being bigger and more muscular allows these boys to "show off" and in some ways mark their space separate from those who are less athletic. Bob states:

They might also like it just because they can lift heavier weights. They can show off. Like running faster than the other guys, it's an achievement so...

The ways in which boys are positioned among boys and by boys in PE class significantly underscores the kinds of experience and impressions these boys develop about the masculine body. Each of these boys repeatedly makes connections between sport, health and muscularity and popular masculinity suggesting that the production of one's body is intimately if not inextricably representative of one's expression of manliness (Robertson, 2003). The emergence of a discourse of the muscular male ideal among men and adolescent males is troubling and, as Labre (2002) argues, is "neither achievable by most men nor required for optimum health" (p. 235).

Dalley-Trim (2007) explains that the active and purposeful physical positioning of the masculine adolescent body, in what she refers to as "body work" is part of "an outward encoding of masculinity beyond the level of spoken language—a "macho posturing" (Measor & Woods, 1984 in Dalley-Trim, 2007, p. 203). In the next excerpt Joey explains the tension between a desire to participate and the power other boys have to keep some boys on the sidelines.

> It's pretty important because I want to know that I'm at least doing good and not just okay and I try and participate as much as possible but it's hard to do when nobody passes you the ball in games and stuff, so it kind of brings down my participation mark a little bit.

The physical space and physically subjective self is ever present in the ways these boys locate themselves in the class and alongside their peers. As Spike explains in the following, he is not "built' for athletics. The physical body is understood by these young men as largely inadequate, requiring training and skill development not for the sake of health but rather for the purpose of defending and navigating other forms of more highly valued muscular, sporty masculinities that tend to dominate PE classes. These young men see the ways bodies operate around them. It is however, less clear whether or not they understand the athletic body not as natural but as "the product of social practice" (Messner, 1997, p.149)

> I mean I'm not built for athletics. Like I said before, I'm not built for gym class and I don't excel at sports because I can't run fast or I can't play basketball and the other people will be faster than me and stuff like that and I'll just be a bench warmer basically and I'll be last picked for everything.

Spike sees where specific students "fit" in this class. The strengths and weaknesses of students in PE class continue to be dichotomized by students who see the relationship between the physical and intellectual as being diametrically opposed. Spike explains:

> The ones who are doing worse are the little or big academic guys who would much rather probably be writing an essay than doing gym and the guys who maybe have a better vocabulary, a better understanding of the academic portion of school, they're not doing as well in gym because that's not who it's geared towards. It's geared towards the jocks whose vocabulary mainly consists of, "yo man what's up, how ya doing?" stuff like that.

There is a tension for some adolescent boys who suggest a divide between the physical and the intellectual. Spike explains that gym is not "geared towards" people like him who are "big academic guys."

"Boys will be boys": Acting Tough and "Showing Off"

For many of these boys, health and physical education remains an arena not for developing or nurturing confidence and enthusiasm for physical and healthy practices, but rather a place to showcase and display the muscled and fit among boys. Martino & Beckett (2004) describe practices that differentiate and categorize boys as part of a process "of surveillance and regulation of the gendered body or rather the disciplining of the gendered body inscribed with certain hegemonic traits of masculinity" (p. 245). Rod describes how teasing, similar to earlier mentioned forms of harassment, occurs in relation to being "tougher," "bigger" and acting "cool" at the expense of those who are "not good in gym class." The "cool pose" among boys is well documented as an active masculinising process by which boys marginalize other boys thereby valorizing hegemonic masculinity. (Connell, 1989; Martino & Pallota-Chiarolli, 2005, Kehler, 2007) Rod explains:

> People sometimes like to tease you because people try and tend to act tougher when they're older and they're bigger and they want to kind of just pick on the other person... They just do that to show, I don't know, that they're cool... They'd say rude stuff about other people that are not good in gym class

Across their experiences these young men repeatedly mention "strength," "show[ing] up others" and locating the dominant masculine boys as actively striving to position themselves as more powerful than other young men. Mythic describes the process:

> I think it's to show people what they can do, like show up their physical strength and they can't think of any other ways to do that so the only way would be gym and that's one noticeable way . . . so I think that's why they really enjoy gym just so they can use their strength and physical stuff so people will notice . . . and I think the only reason they like gym is because they get more out of their physical strength than when they're doing something else. . .

He elaborates, defining how masculinity and the performance he sees is constructed through "showing off," He understands "showing off" as a form of masquerade that hides vulnerabilities and weaknesses lurking in "parts of them that aren't strong." Kehler & Martino (2007) identify the ways boys routinely problematize and interrogate masculinizing practices. The difficulty for many boys, particularly boys marginalized by these practices, we argue, is the "institutionalization of hegemonic heterosexual masculinity in schools that denies and silences such critical discourses in the first place" (p. 92). In a safe, supportive interview, Mythic is able to explain with clarity and insight:

> I think they're showing off . . . probably showing off for some people like probably their friends or you know, girls that they have feelings for but maybe actually they're showing off for themselves because there's parts of them that aren't strong so they're showing off their physical strength kind of blocking out the other things.

The value of performing masculine and performing a tough, hard, and cool masculinity is understood. Kaufman (1994) explains that it is in locker rooms and by extension PE classrooms that boys find ways to affirm themselves, find common ground with other men and collectively exercise their power" (p. 151). Mythic continues:

> I think it's because generally as a rule people do get noticed more for their physical strength. It's like actually kind of like animals. Most animals, we only notice the larger more aggressive ones and it's just like as a rule the larger more aggressive ones get more attention. So I think not being one of the larger more aggressive ones, it's kind of annoying. It's not that I don't want to be one of them. It's just that there's so many of them.

An interesting tension exists between the ways some boys "show off" and parade the body as an expression and demonstration of masculinity and the purposeful development of bodies to hide weakness or vulnerabilities. In her study Azzarito (2009) describes an awareness among adolescents, boys and girls, of the ideal body. Her participants spoke of perceptions, popularity and the ways that muscularity and body size intersect in daily configurations of masculinities in schools.

In the following excerpt Spike suggests there is a shared understanding in high school that "boys will be boys." The acceptance of this attitude feeds the climate previously noted above in which "guys are guys" and they are expected to "get over it." Spike explains:

> I mean, in high school they've really got the boys will be boys attitude and what that means is they expect guys to be loud and rude and making fun of each other and stuff and I don't think that's fair because not all guys are like that.

In his further elaboration he makes a distinction about his broader view of masculinity but acknowledges that his view is relatively uncommon especially in gym class. According to Spike:

> What it means to be a boy in grade 9 is you're definitely going to be picked on or discriminated against if you're not this image of a man that society has. And really, thinking back on it, I think my view of a man is somebody who's just. It's a male human being really, when it comes down to it and it's a guy who's not afraid to be himself and doesn't care what other people think of him. That's a real man and I think in grade 9 gym, not a lot of people think that. They have more the "you're guys, get over it" point of view.

Dissenting voices such as that expressed by Spike are indeed rare. The relative absence of these views in addition to the prevailing dominance of hegemonic masculinity is reason for concern. (Connell, 2008; Hickey, 2008; Light & Kirk, 2000; Martino & Beckett, 2004) The ways that adolescent boys negotiate masculine identities are intimately connected to perceptions of being boys and expressions of masculinity. The masculine body for boys is one means by which boys actively, intentionally and purposefully display evidence of heteronormative masculinity in differing arenas. In considering dance as a physical activity, for example, Gard (2008) argues that the issue that appears to be at stake here. . . is what people *think* and *feel* to be a good and (not insignificantly) gender appropriate way to use their body (p. 186).   His suggestion that the body is imbued with feelings and understandings about gendered behaviour is useful in considering why the young men in our study persisted in their attempts, against considerable odds, to "perform" like the other boys. Borrowing from Frost (2003), boys do bodies differently and as such are subject to a set of evaluative standards based in masculinizing practices designed and intended to prove and convince others that you are not feminine. "The approval of and respect from other men, which is the ultimate accolade of masculinity, may be withheld if the boy cannot produce a body worked to a lean and muscular form" (Frost, 2003, p. 67). In this initial read of the data of some boys' responses and experiences in this study, attaining the sculpted or lean body was unachievable and most importantly undesirable, though well understood. Through forms of humiliation and isolation these young men are marginalized and stigmatized even in situations where they attempt to be active and "healthy" among the boys.

"Now that they know their body can do more..."

On one level the impressions adolescent boys have of their bodies as masculine subjects is influenced and informed by media constructions of masculinity. Labre (2002) for example reports that "there is evidence that the male body ideal disseminated by the media is becoming more muscular and that body dissatisfaction and related problems are increasing among males" (p. 233) On another level, peer relations and social peer interactions provide yet another context where the masculine body operates as signifier of masculinity. Connell (2008, 1995) describes the lessons boys learn in health and physical education as both instantiated through typical relationships and practices in PE but also limited by such practices. He elaborates, arguing that "to understand embodiment and hegemony, we need to understand that bodies are both objects of social practice and agents in social practice" (Connell & Messerchmidt, 2005, p. 851). Each of the boys talked about their bodies by identifying a series of traits typically associated with normative masculinity. Mythic states:

> I think it's because they've gone into puberty and so their bodies are developing and becoming stronger and they've been physical for a long time but I think, now that they know their body can do more, that they're starting to take it even more seriously because I think they just want to show what they can do.

Each boy explains that there is an emerging awareness among boys about what they "*know* their body *can do.*" This knowledge about the body as a symbolic signifier of masculinity is captured in the connections they make to more public displays and expressions of physical dominance.

The unchecked domination and regulation of boys sporting practices in PE contributes to a form of "hyper-masculinity characterized by the preparedness to expunge weakness and exploit vulnerability" (Hickey, 2008, p. 155). There emerges among and across these boys lines of demarcation where the insiders and outsiders literally operate on different playing fields. The comments from these boys demonstrate that even though they appeared to be on the gym floor and "participating," observations of the boys revealed a field within a field. In short, though each of these boys was suited and positioned, they remained relatively docile and, for all intents and purposes, disengaged from play. As mentioned above, these boys participated but they did so with the threat of harassment and ridicule. Both Joey and Bob explain how adolescent males display and impose their bodily dominance in physical education classes.

> I have seen a few people flex their muscles in class and stuff and then ask one of the senior people to flex their muscles and then say that they're doing really good but you can kind of sense some sarcasm in their voice. (Joey)

> Maybe they look at other people and say "oh I'm better than them. I have bigger muscles" or something like that. "I can run faster than them." The way they perform in certain activities make them surpass other people. So it's kind of like comparing themselves to other people because if everybody's the same, you can't really say you're better than them. (Bob)

The notion of "comparing" and "perform[ing]" in order to assert dominance over others is striking. The negotiation of bodily practices again fuses with sporty athleticism in which bodies are looked upon and judged or evaluated. Spike explains the impact the surveillance of the body has on him.

> I know what the experiences are that stand out for me . . . probably when somebody would make a rude comment to me about my weight and I just wouldn't retaliate because there's just no point. I'm not sinking to their level. They can say whatever they want. It doesn't really affect me but well, evidently it does because years of it has led to my poor body image but at the moment it doesn't affect me and there have been a few times where, I'm just going to come right out and say this, where I've been like people have smacked my fat and laughed at it because it jiggled and I've been smacked right across, well my man boobs. . . (Spike)

Spike acknowledges the long-term impact this context is having on how he knows and accepts his body. He further explains the importance of body image and the fear he harbours about his body weight.

> Roughly last time I weighed myself I was around 260. I hope I'm not really anymore than that now because I wasn't comfortable with that weight and so my weight has always been a big concern, not just because of the health problems. It can be associated with it because I'm afraid of what I look like and how other people perceive me and I know. It's kind of a grey area because I'm not sure what a healthy body weight for my height would be yet . . . So what I'm really trying to do is lose the fat and build muscle. So I may weigh the same. I may end up weighing more but weight isn't really as important to me as physique.

Spike's fears run deep and extend outward to how other people "perceive" him. His confusion about a healthy body weight is complicated with a desire for "build[ing] muscle." There is a toxic discourse permeating the locker room and PE classes for adolescent males like Spike who desperately want to "lose the fat and build muscle" so they achieve a "physique" that is more acceptable and more valuable.

Conclusion

The World Health Organization (2000) has identified gender and masculinity in particular, as a significant factor shaping men's expectations, behaviours, and health, yet there has been very little done to address this relationship in physical health education classes. This chapter has argued for a closer look and ongoing examination of the intersection of masculinity, health, and physical education in high schools. I acknowledge and agree with what Evans, Davies and Rich (2008) argue is a problematic and disturbing trend reducing health to a singular measure of one's body mass index. I also agree that to accept one dominant narrative that appears to have been "storied into existence" is extremely dangerous and misguided. This chapter has not engaged with deconstructing the debate of the current obesity discourse, but rather has argued for a critical response to the calls for action that transform into pedagogical practice and curricular initiatives while ignoring the deeper more complex issues. An awareness of "regulative and instructional aspects of obesity discourse [that] constitute the health pedagogies that now feature in communities and schools" (Evans, Davies, & Rich, 2008, p. 120) allows researchers to begin examining and interrogating the realities of the lives of youth in whose name these policies are being implemented.

Bodies are entities upon which gender is inscribed and through which gender is constructed. (Neverson & White, 2002) For men and women, boys and girls, choices are made either to affirm and thus support or resist and thus reject dominant codes of masculinity and femininity expressed through performative acts of gender. This chapter extends previous work in the sociology of sport, by shifting the focus to the experiences of adolescent young men disenfranchised through health and physical education practices and health initiatives aimed at nurturing and supporting particular models of masculinity. In this round of interviews the research team has been struck by an emerging set of themes, several of which are discussed in this chapter. The experiences and impressions of these boys in grade nine PE classes highlight a) tensions that arise as students participate to be healthy and, at the same time, negotiate their identities according to normative and restrictive models of masculinity b) struggles to identify the body as capable but not "naturally" "built to be athletic" or "physically strong," and c) the persistent regulative and performative practices that routinely implicate the body in all, too, often stigmatizing and marginalizing processes that alienate and marginalize adolescent males. As such, this research contributes to a deepening knowledge of the interactions of boys among boys in a context where "it is expected that young males will learn how to practice and embrace dominant cultural understandings of masculinity" (Hickey & Fitzclarence, 1999, p. 53).

Concerns for obesity among children and particularly among adolescent boys prompts a relatively unexplored set of questions about the relationship between the masculine body, gender identities, healthy lifestyle practices, and schooling. The practices of masculinity demonstrated through the beliefs, attitudes, and understandings of what it means to "be a man" and the link to health and physical education (dis)engagement is not well understood. This chapter contributes to the theorizing of education, masculinities, and physical education to more fully examine a culture of masculinity, health and harassment in schools that contributes to the suppression and silencing of anxieties about body image among adolescent males.

The centrality of the male body and ongoing negotiation of masculine identities among youth can no longer remain silent. Drummond (2001) found that "the development of poor body image and self identity may occur due to increasing despondence towards the non-physical body" (p. 62). It is the responsibility of teachers and teacher educators as well as health care professionals to begin a discussion and to begin to acknowledge male body image concerns. I agree with Connell (1995) who argues that men need to develop diverse senses of the body so that males learn different ways for "using, feeling and showing (their) bodies" (p. 233). Only by initiating a dialogue among boys and addressing their fears and body perceptions not as something unusual or rare, can we begin to address what we have long known. We need to alleviate, eradicate and eliminate the feelings of intimidation and inadequacy often heard from young men reluctant to participate in PE so that their high school experiences are not allowed to contribute in damaging and enduring ways to poor self-concepts and body image issues among adolescent males.

Educators and teachers need to remember that bodies matter in the ongoing management and expression of gender identities and as such require closer examination because of the routine ways young men are "physically positioned within a repertoire of masculine codes that are read off and enacted by the body" (Kehler, et al, 2005, p. 64) To suggest that the complex aspects of physicality located in bodies, boys, and locker room banter are not interrelated is to displace the masculinised bodies of boys from a gendering process already manifest in social institutions such as schools.

Notes

1. This chapter emerges from a nationally funded research project supported by the Social Sciences and Humanities Research Council of Canada. The author acknowledges the ongoing support for this three-year study to examine why some adolescent young men are reluctant to participate in grade nine health and physical education classes. Data included in this chapter is taken from the larger ongoing study and as such is preliminary though suggestive of early analysis, and was part of an earlier version of a paper presented at the 2009 American Education Research Association conference in San Diego, California, U.S.A.

2. Psuedonyms, chosen by the participants, have been used to protect participant anonymity.

Bibliography

Active Healthy Kids Canada [AHKC] (2008). Canada's report card on physical activity for children and youth – 2006. Toronto, ON: The author.

Adams, M. L. (2005). "Death to the prancing prince": Effeminacy, sport discourses and the salvation of men's dancing. *Body & Society, 11*(4), 63-86.

Associated Press. Overweight children find fast food too tempting. (2003, October 16). Retrieved from http://www.ctv.ca/servlet/ArticleNews/story/CTVNews/1066307816015_100?s_name= &no_ads

Atkinson, M. (2003). *Tattooed: The sociogenesis of a body art.* Toronto, ON: University of Toronto Press.

Azzartio, L. (2009). The penopticon of physical education: pretty, active and ideally white. *Physical Education and Sport Pedagogy, 14*(1), 19-39.

Boyce, W., Roche, J., & Davies, D. (Eds.). (2009). *Adolescent health: Policy, science and human rights.* Montreal, PQ: McGill-Queen's University Press.

Butler, J. (1999). *Gender trouble.* New York: Routledge.

Canadian Press. Ontario invests millions to promote healthy living. (2006, June 20). Retrieved from http://www.ctv.ca/servlet/ArticleNews/story/CTVNews/20060620/health_program_060 620?s_name=&no_ads=

Canadian Press. Single-parent kids more likely to be fat: study shows. (2003, August 13).

Cohane, G. H., & Pope, H. (2001). Body image in boys: A review of the literature. *International Journal of Eating Disorders, 29*(4), 373-379.

Connell, R. W. (1989). Cool guys, swots and wimps: The interplay of masculinity and education. *Oxford Review of Education, 15*(3), 291-303.

Connell, R.W. (1995). *Masculinities.* Berkeley, CA: University of California Press.

Connell, R.W. (2008). Masculinity construction and sports in boys' education: A framework for thinking about the issue. *Sport, Education and Society. 13*(2), 131-146

Connell, R.W., & Messerschmidt, J.W., (2005). Hegemonic masculinity: Rethinking the concept. *Gender & Society, 19*(6), 829-859.

Dalley-Trim, L. (2007). 'The boys' present...hegemonic masculinity: A performance of multiple acts. *Gender and Education. 19*(2), 199-217.

Davison, K. (2000). Boys' bodies in school: Physical education. *The Journal of Men's Studies, 8*(2), 255-266.

Drummond, M. J. N. (2003). The meaning of boys' bodies in physical education. *The Journal of Men's Studies, 11*(2), 131-138.

Drummond, M. (2001). Body image and health: Emerging issues for boys and young men. *Virtually Healthy Newsletter, 19.*

Evans, J., Davies, B., & Rich, E. (2008). The class and cultural functions of obesity discourse: our latter day children saving movement. *International studies in Sociology of Education, 18*(2), 117-132.

Field, C. (2000) Boys, education and sp[ort: The Darfield high school model. *Journal of Physical Education New Zealand, 33*(3), 37-42.

Frost, L. (2003). Doing bodies different? Gender, youth, appearance and damage. *Journal of Youth Studies, 6*(1), 53-70.

Gard, M. (2008). When a boy's gotta dance: new masculinities, old pleasures. *Sport, Education and Society, 13*(2), 181-193.

Gard, M., & Wright, J. (2005) *The obesity epidemic: Science, morality, and ideology.* London: Routledge.

Gard, M., & Meyenn, R. (2000). Boys, bodies, pleasure and pain: Interrogating contact sports in schools. *Sport, Education and Society, 5*(1), 19-34.

Gill, R., Henwood, K., & McLean, C. (2005). Body projects and the regulation of normative masculinity. *Body and Society 11*, 37-62.

Gorley, T., Holroyd, R., & Kirk, D. (2003). Muscularity, the habitus and the social construction of gender: Towards a gender-relevant physical education. *British Journal of Sociology of Education, 24*(4), 429-448.

Grogan, S. (2006). Body image and health: Contemporary perspectives. *Journal of Health Psychology, 11*(4), 523-530.

Hargreaves, D. A., & Tiggemann, M. (2006). "Body image is for girls": A qualitative study of boys' body image. *Journal of Health Psychology, 11*(4), 567-57.

Hickey, C. (2008). Physical education, sport and hyper-masculinity in schools. *Sport, Education and Society. 13*(2), 147-161.

Hickey, C., Fitzclarence, L., & Matthews, R. (2000). *Where the boys are: Masculinity, sport and education.* Geelong, Victoria: Deakin University Press.

Hickey, C., & Fitzclarence, L. (1999). Educating boys in sport and physical education: Using narrative methods to develop pedagogies of responsibility. *Sport, Education and Society, 4*(1), 51-62.

Kaufman, M. (1994). Men, feminism, and men's contradictory experience of power. In H. Brod & M. Kaufman (Eds.), *Theorizing Masculinities* (pp. 142-163). Thousand Oaks, CA: Sage Publications.

Kehily, M. (2002). *Sexuality, gender and schooling: Shifting agenda in social learning.* New York: RoutledgeFalmer.

Kehily, M. (2001). Bodies in school: Young men embodiment and heterosexual masculinities. *Men and Masculinities, 4*(2), 173-185.

Kehler, M.D. (2007) Hallway fears and high school friendships: The complications of young men (re)negotiating heterosexualized identities. *Discourse: Studies in the cultural politics of education, 28*(2), 259-277.

Kehler, M.D., & Martino, W. (2007). Questioning masculinities: Interrogating boys' capacities for self-problematization in schools. *Canadian Journal of Education, 30*(1), 90-112.

Kehler, M.D., & Greig, C. (2005). Boys can read: exploring the socially literate practices of high school young men. *International Journal of Inclusive Education, 9*(4), 351-370.

Kehler, M.D., Davison, K., & Frank, B. (2005). Contradictions and tensions of the practice of masculinities in school: Interrogating "good buddy talk." *Journal of Curriculum Theorizing, 21*(4), 59-72.

Labre, M. (2002). Adolescent boys and the muscular male body ideal. *Journal of Adolescent Health, 30,* 233-242.

Light, R., & Kirk, D. (2000). High school rugby, the body and the reproduction of hegemonic masculinity. *Sport, Education and Society, 5*(2), 163-176.

Lofland, J., & Lofland, L. (1995). *Analyzing social settings: A guide to qualitative observation and analysis.* Belmont, CA: Wadsworth.

Mac an Ghaill, M. (1994). *The making of men: Masculinities, sexualities and schooling.* Bristol, PA: Open University Press.

Martino, W., & Beckett, L. (2004). Schooling the gendered body in health and physical education: Interrogating teachers' perspectives. *Sport, Education and Society, 9*(2), 239-251.

Martino, W., & Pallotta-Chiarolli, M. (2003). *So what's a boy?: Addressing issues of masculinity and schooling.* Maidenhead, Philadelphia, PA: Open University Press.

Martino, W., & Pallotta-Chiarolli, M. (2005). *Being normal is the only way to be: Adolescent perspectives on gender and school.* Sydney, NSW: University of New South Wales Press Ltd.

McLaren, P. (1991). Schooling the postmodern body: Critical pedagogy and the politics of enfleshment. In H. Giroux (Ed.), *Postmodernism, Feminism and Cultural Politics* (pp. 144-173). Albany, NY: State University of New York Press.

Measor, L., & Woods, P. (1984) *Changing schools: Pupil's perspectives on transfer to a comprehensive.* Milton Keynes: University Press.

Messner, M.A. (1997). *Politics of masculinities: Men in movements.* Thousand Oaks, CA: Sage Publications.

Mills, M. (2001). *Challenging violence in schools: An issue of masculinities.* Philadelphia, PA: Open University Press.

Neverson, N., & White, P. (2002). Muscular, bruised and sweaty bodies...:This is not Barbie territory. *Canadian Woman Studies, 21*(3), 44-50.

Labre, M. (2002). Adolescent boys and the muscular male body ideal. *Journal of Adolescent Health, 30,* 233-242.

Pope, H.G., Jr., Philips, K.A., & Olivardia, R. (2000). *The Adonis complex: The secret crisis of male body obsession.* NY: Free Press.

Prain, V. (2000). Playing the man and changing masculinities. In C. Hickey, L. Fitzclarence, & R. Matthews (Eds.), *Where the boys are: Masculinity, sport and education* (pp.55-66). Geelong, Victoria: Deakin University Press.

Robertson, S. (2003). "If I let a goal in, I'll get beat up": Contradictions in masculinity, sport and health. *Health Education Research, 18*(6), 706-716.

Ricciardelli, L. A., McCabe, M. P., & Ridge, D. (2006). The construction of the adolescent male body through sport. *Journal of Health Psychology, 11*(4), 577-587.

Seidler, V. (1997). *Man enough: Embodying masculinities.* London: Sage Publications.

Shilling, C. (2004). Physical capital and situated action: A new direction for corporeal sociology. *British Journal of Sociology of Education, 25*(4), 473-487.

Sparkes, A., & Silvennoinen, M. (1999). *Talking bodies: Men's narratives of the body and sport.* Finland: University of Jyvaskyla.

Sun Media, (2004, January 12). Childhood obesity a growing epidemic. Retrieved from http://chealth.canoe.ca/channel_health_news_details.asp?news_id=9373&news_channel_id=40&channel_id=40&relation_id=1237

Titus, J.J. (2004). Boy trouble: Rhetorical framing of boys' underachievement. *Discourse: Studies in the Cultural Politics of Education, 25*(2), 145-169.

Tumulty, K. (2006, March 19). The politics of fat. *Time,* 40-43. Retrieved from http://www.time.com/time/magazine/article/0,9171,1174679-1,00.html

Weise, E. (2005, July 31). Adolescents bulk up their bodies. *USA Today.* Retrieved from http://www.usatoday.com/news/health/2005-07-31-teens-bodies_x.htm

Wellard, I. (2009). *Sport, masculinities and the body.* Routledge. New York, N.Y.

Wiegers, Y. (1998). Male bodybuilding: The social construction of a masculine identity. *The Journal of Popular Culture, 32*(2), 147-161.

Wienke, C. (1998). Negotiating the male body: Men, masculinity and cultural ideals. *The Journal of Men's Studies, 6*(3), 255-282.

World Health Organization (2000). *What about boys?: A literature review on the health and development of adolescent boys.* Department of Child and Adolescent Health and Development.

Wright, J. (2001). Gender reform in physical education: A poststructuralist perspective. *Journal of Physical Education New Zealand, 34*(1), 15-25.

Wright, J. (2000). Bodies, meanings and movement: A comparison of the language of a physical education lesson and a feldenkrais movement class. *Sport, Education and Society, 5*(1), 35-49.

CHAPTER NINE

Marginalized Boys Speak Out: Insights from School Physical Education for the Obesity Crisis

Nate McCaughtry and Amy Tischler

As the other chapters in this text suggest, the issue of youth obesity has reached worldwide panic, with the notion that it has emerged as a "global pandemic." Although this obesity discourse is not without its critics (e.g., Gard & Wright, 2001, 2005; Oliver, 2006), those within the conservative mainstream health and biomedical fields readily accept the reality of an obesity crisis and have subsequently, as with any pandemic of global proportions, turned their attention to ameliorating it. As a result, school physical education has been advocated for on a variety of fronts as a primary site of intervention (e.g., Irwin, Symons & Kerr, 2003; NASPE, 2002; Thomas, 2004; U.S. Department of Health and Human Services, 2001). While the fact that all school children attend physical education classes (most for every year of their education often until high school) combined with the obvious fact that healthy bodies is the core of that subject area might sound alluring to policy makers and social epidemiologists searching for solutions to the rising obesity crisis, the question still remains whether school physical education, in its current configuration, is well suited to assume such a quest. The focus of this chapter lies not in arguing whether an obesity crisis exists, how pervasive it has become, or whether it's necessarily a good or bad thing. Rather, for argument sake, this chapter hypothetically (albeit begrudgingly) entertains the existence of a crisis and instead takes issue with whether school physical education has any role to play in rectifying it. Our central argument, in fact, is that masculinity configurations endemic to most worldwide physical education programs fundamentally prevent them from helping a wide swath of children, especially boys, learn to love and gain skillfulness in movement—presumably physical education's foremost asset in reducing obesity. As our case study illustrates, the reality too often is that school physical education privileges and supports boys who are already fit and skilled, while marginalizing boys who would seem to be in the most need of the kinds of services that school PE could ideally provide. Our argument concludes by suggesting that without widespread curricular reform with a specific focus on unraveling and altering traditional masculinity configurations, as well as other gender-based practices (McCaughtry, 2004, 2006), the potential for physical education to play any significant role in addressing youth obesity will forever remain unrealized.

Masculinity Theory and Research

Over the last 25 years, there has been a veritable explosion in the sociological study of men and boys, which has resulted in a complicated and nuanced understanding of the concept of hegemonic masculinity (Connell & Messerschmidt, 2005). Drawing on the pioneering work of Connell and others (Atkinson & Wilson, 2002; Connell, 1995, 1998, 2003; Davison, 2004, 2007; Demetriou, 2001; Edley & Wetherell, 1997; Frank, Kehler, Lovell & Davison, 2003; Jandt & Hundley, 2007; Kane, 2006; Kehler, 2004; Kehler, Davison & Frank, 2005; Kehler & Martino, 2007; Kimmel, 1990; Mac an Ghaill, 1994; Martino, 2000, 2003; Messner & Sabo, 1990; Nilan, 2000; Swain, 2005; Young, 2000), we now have a more sophisticated understanding of many of the key features of the male experience. For example, we have learned that masculinity is not a stable trait that someone either has or does not have, or increases or decreases; rather, multiple masculinities operate within any social setting and any one individual embodies multiple masculinities. We have also learned that masculinities operate in hierarchical configurations and some achieve dominance, even hegemonic status, over others. However, those configurations shift and change over time in response to differing cultural conditions. We know that both men and women play significant roles in masculine configurations, and that, from a relational perspective, broader macro social movements heavily influence local practices.

For the purposes of this chapter, three additional features of masculinity theory are worth mentioning as they will prove essential in understanding the current case study and the light it might shed on disrupting physical education's place in popular obesity discourse. First, masculinity must be seen as an embodied experience, where the body plays a central role in becoming, enacting, and managing the self. Studies of masculinity must attend to the multiplicity of roles that bodies play in masculinity processes. As Connell and Messerschmidt (2005) contend, embodiment must become much more central in studies of social practice such as masculinities,

> The common social scientific reading of bodies as objects of a process of social construction is now widely considered to be inadequate. Bodies are involved more actively, more intimately, and more intricately in social processes than theory has usually allowed. Bodies participate in social action by delineating courses of social conduct; the body is a participant in generating social practice. It is important not only that masculinities be understood as embodied but also that the interweaving of embodiment and social context be addressed (p. 851).

Second, masculine configurations often differ across social settings, even settings that are highly similar. As a result, cross contextual analyses have the upside of informing efforts toward equity, social justice and transformation. Third, because masculine configurations have the possibility to change over time, it is important to specifically examine the agency and resistance that boys and men whose masculinities are marginalized in particular social settings muster against dominant, hegemonic forms that wield oppressive conditions. In doing so, we can bring light to this resistance, which can disrupt or unsettle the hegemonic, taken-for-grantedness of deeply ingrained patterns of social stratification.

Two social settings that have undergone intense masculinity analysis recently are elite youth sport and school physical education. Most researchers have examined how masculinities operate within these settings, more specifically, showing how they simultaneously support and privilege certain forms of similar hegemonic masculinities while marginalizing others (Bramham, 2003; Connell, 2008; Davison, 2000; Drummond, 2003; Gard & Meyenn, 2000; Hickey, 2008; Larsson, Fagrell, & Redelius, 2009; Light, 2008; Millington, Vertinsky, Boyle, & Wilson, 2008; Parker, 1996; Pringle, 2008). For example, in elite youth sport settings such as intermurals, intramurals, and club sport, masculinities that almost uniformly achieve hegemonic status include those that embody strength, speed, power, muscularity, fitness, athleticism, acceptance of injury risk, warrior mentalities, and lack of empathy for other participants (Bramham, 2003; Davison, 2000; Drummond, 2003; Gard & Meyenn, 2000; Hickey, 2008; Light, 2008; Parker, 1996; Pringle, 2008). Elite sport settings have been shown to not only support and privilege those forms of hegemonic masculinities, but also to tolerate cultures that often exclude and abuse boys who embody alternative masculinities (Gard & Meyenn, 2000; Hickey, 2008; Pringle, 2008; Millington, et al., 2008). For example, Hickey (2008) demonstrated how, through the differentiation of "insiders" and "outsiders," individuals who embodied alternative masculinities were subjected to oppression and violence by those who embodied hegemonic masculinities. Similarly, Millington, et al., (2008) showed how boys who embodied "Chinese masculinities" (small, effeminate, and weak bodies) were victims of obvious as well as concealed forms of domination that normalized and supported "White" hegemonic masculinities, which also extended to the broader school environment and community. Additionally, through the collective stories of eight men's experiences with rugby union, Pringle (2008) demonstrated how "sporty boys" embodying common, sport-based hegemonic masculinities were privileged, while boys performing alternative masculinities were bullied. Due to their non-aggressive modes of participation in rugby, these men recalled humiliating and violent experiences such as being pushed, tripped, laughed at, hung on coat hangers in locker rooms, and having their heads submerged in toilets. Gard and Meyenn (2000) reported the physical activity preferences of 23 Australian boys from secondary schools that strongly supported and valued elite male contact sports while revealing various tactics boys and institutions used to normalize the violent nature of sport. Without fail, these boys reported that the risk of injury (receiving and giving pain) through physical contact played a major role in their choices of physical activities. They believed that a major part of "becoming a man" was engaging in contact sports where the risk of injury was high and also by tolerating pain when injuries occurred.

In a similar vein, researchers have also noted that sports, in particular team sports, continue to dominate worldwide physical education curriculum and function as locations where similar hegemonic masculinities commonly found in elite youth sport settings are privileged and supported over others (Bramham, 2003; Davison, 2000; Drummond, 2003; Larsson, et al, 2009; Parker, 1996). For example, using Connell's (1995) concept of hegemonic masculinity, Parker (1996) found that although a hierarchy of "pupil-defined" masculinities existed, the violent and aggressive forms embodied by the "hard boys" were dominant, while scholarly styles embodied by the "victims" became subordinate. Likewise, Davison (2000) reported adult men's memories of explicit lessons in masculinity that took place during their sport-dominated PE classes. Collectively, these men felt they were being conditioned to be the right kind of boy, even though they did not "measure up" to the masculine ideal. Through the observation of PE lessons, Larsson, et al. (2009) scrutinized the heteronormative nature of PE that upheld and supported the dominance of some boys and found that although teachers were aware of the unequal power relations, this dominance was viewed as "normal" and therefore managed rather than challenged. The sport-based model of PE dominated using "band-aid" approaches to make it work while ignoring the complex social imbalances that thrived as a result of viewing gender as a biologically normalized category, rather than as socially constructed.

These findings that team sports continue to dominate most school PE programs and do so in oppressive ways for boys who embody certain types of other masculinities are, to say the least, troubling given the supposed widespread rise in youth physical inactivity and obesity combined with recent calls imploring physical education to ride to the rescue (Thomas, 2004). Practically speaking, the totality of research in school PE suggests that at least a moderate proportion of boys (and most likely plenty of girls) find PE irrelevant if not destructive to their self-esteem and health. This becomes doubly concerning when we consider that the boys who are often dominated in school PE generally tend to be less physically active and fit, which means that the boys most in need of positive physical activity experiences, if our intent is to employ school PE as a broad obesity elixir, are in fact having the worst experiences.

However, despite this increased attention to the masculinity configurations that get enacted in school PE, we still know surprisingly little about what it means to survive those settings as a boy who embodies non-hegemonic masculinities. In other words, while researchers have produced ample accounts of the multiple masculinities that commonly operate in school PE along with their hierarchical configurations and functioning, what often gets overshadowed are the voices of those boys who face the oppression levied by dominant boys simply because they enact "boy" differently. This is a significant omission from the literature because, as Connell and Messerschmidt (2005) argue, the solution to oppressive conditions often lies in the embodied narratives, both those of pain and suffering as well as resistance, of marginalized groups. As a result, the remainder of this chapter utilizes a case study of two physical education programs to specifically examine the experiences and voices of boys who embody non-hegemonic masculinities, with a specific focus on the role of embodiment in their struggles to survive school physical education, as well as a contextually situated analysis of their broader life conditions.

Case Study

Over five months in 2008, we examined the physical education programs at two suburban middle schools (grades 6-8) outside a large urban city in the Midwestern United States. We chose these programs because through prior relationships we knew that both conducted sport-based programs consistent with the majority of formal school physical education programs. At the outset, we were concerned with several key questions: What kinds of masculinities were operating in these programs? How were they hierarchically configured? What social practices led to those configurations? And, how did boys who embodied marginalized masculinities experience and understand their positionalities, especially with respect to their broader life situations?

We started the research by observing and casually interacting with the teachers and students in both programs for the first month. We were keen to get an initial read of how they operated day-to-day, to better understand masculinity dynamics, and especially to identify boys who embodied non-hegemonic masculinities. We identified two boys at West Middle School and three boys at East Middle School who we believed met this criterion and proceeded to spend the next month building relationships with them and learning their perspectives through one-on-one meetings during their normal PE classes. For the remaining three months, we met with the boys at each school in small groups and used a variety of techniques (e.g., popular magazine exploration, physical activity, writing newspaper advertisements, drawing pictures, etc.) to get them to explore their impressions of their complex PE settings, status as boys, wider life experiences, and self-identities.

The Centrality of the Body to Boys' Masculinities in School Physical Education

The story of masculinity at these two middle schools tells a tale of the absolute centrality that boys' bodies and embodiment play in masculinity configurations, hierarchical ordering and maintenance; the lived, felt oppression that some boys endure in PE programs; as well as the resistance that boys employ as active agents in subverting oppressive conditions. While the embodiment of masculinity has begun gaining increased attention, the boys at these two schools show how important it is to begin developing a more comprehensive and nuanced understanding about the body in physical education if this school subject is to have a role in broader health movements. In a sense, physical educators and health professionals must disrupt the current paradigm for understanding the body and its existence in the physical education setting. Certainly, the most dominant discourses of the body in physical education center on performance (Tinning, 1997), physiology/fitness (Quennerstedt, 2008), and body health (Rossi, Tinning, McCauig, Sirna & Hunter, 2009). They see the body as an object, or rather a "project," in need of training, exercising, and manipulation. While attention to the physical development of the body through training or exercise is laudable, when it becomes the sole focus of attention and achieves hegemonic status, we forget that bodies are equally sociological human features functioning in the midst of power relations, regimes of truth and the nexus of social justice, equity, and freedom. It is only when we turn our attention to the sociological side of the human body in the context of physical education that we can begin to understand the limitations of training, physiology, fitness, and health discourses in achieving public health objectives, even dubious ones, such as obesity reduction. In a very real way, it is only through a paradigmatic shift that we can begin to understand how sociological bodies undermine the potential of more performative health discourses. As a result, in our case study, we were keen to specifically examine how bodies performed within the social matrix of two school physical education programs. We treated boys' bodies both as physical entities and simultaneously as manifestations and metaphors of the masculine self.

In both of these PE settings, multiple masculinities operated as mechanisms of reproduction. On one end of the spectrum, we saw boys enacting characteristics that commonly achieve dominant, hegemonic status in PE, physical activity, and sport settings (Bramham, 2003; Connell, 2008; Davison, 2000; Drummond, 2003; Gard & Meyenn, 2000; Griffin, 1985; Hickey, 2008; Humberstone, 1990; Larsson, et al., 2009; Light, 2008; Millington, et al., 2008; Parker, 1996; Pringle, 2008). These characteristics included athleticism, strength, speed, muscularity, fitness, competitiveness, extreme physicality, aggressiveness, popularity, and a lack of compassion towards those who embodied other forms of masculinities. On the opposite end of the spectrum, we found boys who embodied different kinds of masculinities, especially those that are typically marginalized in school PE. They included having the wrong body shape (endomorphic versus mesomorphic), less coordination, less popularity, slower, weaker, less athletic, less fit, effeminate mannerisms, and more subdued. A host of boys also embodied combinations of these and other masculinities. Some were endomorphic, but coordinated and athletic. Others were slower and less coordinated, but were strong and aggressive. The point is that the boys in these classes embodied a range of physical characteristics and skillfulness, but what was most striking was that in these social settings boys' embodied characteristics carried enormous weight in determining their social positioning and whether they were privileged or marginalized.

Bodies function in very complicated ways within social environments, especially school physical education where the body is of central focus. Although many stories of masculinities and bodies could be told from these physical education programs, the following analysis explores the complex and interconnected ways that boys who embodied marginalized, non-hegemonic masculinities lived and survived. It begins by showing how the content of physical education, teachers' pedagogies, and the relationships endemic to school physical education center on issues of the body, especially with respect to the ways that boys embody masculinities. The story then shifts to how boys "wear" their oppression through guarded bodies, but also conversely how their bodies resist and subvert the marginalizing social practices of their teachers and fellow classmates. The story concludes by illustrating the contextuality of boys' embodiment in physical activity, most notably the stark contrasts between embodiment in and out of school PE.

Embodiment and Physical Education Content

The selection of team sports (e.g., volleyball, basketball, and football) as the sole content taught in these physical education programs played a central role in elevating certain masculinities and bodies to dominant, hegemonic status, while relegating others to subordination. The embodied characteristics that are required for successful play within sport activities are: strength, speed, coordination (of various kinds), aggressiveness, and physicality. By the very nature of sport activities, these kinds of physical endowments meet the situational dynamics embedded in the activities, while individuals who embody less of each of these characteristics quite simply cannot perform as successfully. The fact that sport results in winners and losers, clearly a hierarchical ordering, complicates things further. In other words, the embedded requirements (need for certain types of physicalities) and nature of the activity itself (social comparison resulting in winners and losers) situates certain embodiments as superior to others.

The dynamics are quite different, however, in other forms of physical activity such as fitness activities (e.g., swimming, pilates, yoga, Bosu, fitball, aerobics, strength training, etc.), adventure (e.g., team building initiatives, ropes courses, climbing walls, hiking, biking, etc.), and dance (e.g., hip hop, salsa, country line, etc.). While physical characteristics like strength, speed, coordination, aggressiveness and physicality are still involved in these activities (albeit sometimes in different ways), participants need not embody them in high degrees to find success, contentment, or desirable outcomes (like bodily wellness). Also absent in these activities are social comparison and hierarchical ordering. A class using fitballs, for example, does not accord status on individuals based on their physical interaction with their equipment. In fact, in activities like adventure and dance, success is determined not by elevating individual performance over others, but by elevating collective performance and self-improvement.

Our intent is not to demonize sport, but rather to show that different types of physical activities have different situational requirements and focuses. Hence, when these teachers selected exclusively team sports as the exclusive content of their physical education programs, they directly privileged certain forms of embodied masculinities over others. Some bodies were given the advantage to succeed, and, worse yet, attained social status as better than others. Perhaps, by selecting a more diverse curriculum that incorporated multiple forms of physical activity to complement sport, the kinds of masculinity ordering and oppression (which will be explained later) may have been reduced if not eliminated.

This shows that, as a field, physical education must come to grips with the social, political and moral dimensions of the content we teach. Electing to teach team sports is far from value-free, apolitical, and trivial. In fact, that seemingly mundane decision carries with it enormous baggage in relation to issues of gender, masculinity, elitism, and body ontology. As Humberstone's (1990) and Gard's (2001, 2003, 2008) work shows, the vary nature of alternative content like adventure and dance position social actors within very different situational requirements, expectations, and relational frameworks. Some argue that the answer to improving school physical education lies not in questioning and/or altering the content we teach, but the ways in which we teach it, in other words, our pedagogies. While we cannot deny the importance of powerful, equitable pedagogy, the sociological dimensions of the content that physical educators teach must undergo the types of critical scrutiny done in classroom subjects like history, social studies, and civics education (e.g., Banks, 1996).

Embodiment and Sport Pedagogy

Beyond content, the pedagogical practices the teachers' employed to teach sports in physical education played an equally powerful and synergistic role in students' embodied experiences. We observed teachers promoting winning and losing, emphasizing competition, giving enormous positive feedback to skilled performers, letting students divide themselves into teams based on skill, not instituting rules to prevent high-skilled students from dominating lower-skilled students, and not stopping higher-skilled students from physically and verbally abusing and taunting lower-skilled students. In other words, not only did the inherent requirements of the sports privilege certain bodies over others and elevate them to esteemed status as winners, but teachers' pedagogies accentuated the process by not creating a more level playing field and not protecting some boys from violence, ridicule, and harassment. In a sense, the teachers intensified the "survival of the fittest," social exclusion, and hierarchical divisioning and ordering inherent in sport at the arbitrary expense of surely plenty of girls, but also boys who, through no fault of their own, embodied boy differently (e.g., slower, less rough and aggressive, enjoy non-competitive activities, etc.). Had these teachers de-emphasized winning and competition, focused class attention on learning and improvement, selected teams privately, promoted integration, engaged in equally positive interactions with high and low skill students, incorporated game modifications or rules that prevented higher skill students from dominating entire games, and sheltered students from physical and verbal abuse the inherent downside of sport may have been mitigated to some degree. Instead, the pedagogies that the teachers enacted reinforced and even expanded the embodied inequalities inherent in the sports themselves.

For the last decade and a half, sport pioneers in physical education have developed elaborate and robust curriculum models that fundamentally shift the focus of sport taught in physical education away from elite performance and winning, by integrating concepts such as a "sport for all" ethic, small sided games, peer coaching, peace education and personal/social responsibility (Ennis, Solmon, Satina, Loftus, Mensch, & McCauley, 1999; Kinchin, 2006; Siedentop, 1994; Siedentop, Hastie & Van der Mars, 2004). Research has shown that Sport Education, Sport for Peace, and hybrid Sport Education-TPSR models not only lead to sport learning and development, but do so while also promoting social development, equity, and inclusion (Carlson & Hastie, 1997; Ennis, Solmon, Satina, Loftus, Mensch, & McCauley, 1999; Hastie, 1996, 1998a, 1998b, 1998c; Kinchin, 2006; MacPhail, Gorely, Kirk & Kinchin, 2008; MacPhail, Kirk & Kinchin, 2004; Siedentop, 1994; Siedentop, Hastie & Van der Mars, 2004; Wallhead & Ntoumanis, 2004; Wallhead & O'Sullivan, 2005). It is only by abandoning elite, win-at-all-costs performance discourses emblematic of collegiate and professional sport arenas from the sports taught in K-12 physical education that more children will find meaning and value in these forms of content and more enthusiastically participate in them both in and out of school PE, thereby increasing the chances that they might realize the supposed health outcomes (read differently, obesity reduction) espoused by sport-promoting physical educators.

Embodied Relationships

Beyond determining success in competitive sports, boys' bodies played a significant role in the relationships among the students and teachers. The boys who embodied non-hegemonic masculinities, especially the ones that were most marginalized, did not feel cared for by their teachers and believed their teachers viewed their bodies as deviant and wrong. They felt that teachers did not interact with them often or positively, publicly criticized their bodies, did not provide assistance with skills, and did not protect them from other students. For example, in the presence of the student, one teacher said to us, "Take him. I have never had a student like him. He drives me crazy!" Also, Joe said, "Teachers don't step in and help us when we can't do skills. I could probably be good at it [PE activities] because I'd be learning and the teacher would be helping me. I'm sure they think I'm not capable of this stuff [sports]." These boys believed that most of the attention they received from their teachers about their bodies was negative, which further marginalized their masculinities. Jack said, "My teacher is usually disappointed in me [my body] for not being good at skills, and the other kids know it." They felt it was more likely for teachers to reprimand boys bodies for not participating and being adorned incorrectly, and much less likely to smile, get close to, and touch (e.g., high fives, hand shakes, pats on the back) cheerfully or constructively like they often did with boys who embodied hegemonic masculinities. These negative public interactions between these boys' bodies and their teachers further communicated and reinforced that the embodiment of non-hegemonic masculinities were not valued in these PE environments. Nike reported,

> The teacher gets mad at me for forgetting my clothes and calls me a liar when I say I don't feel good. This happens in front of my classmates a lot, and then they think I am a baby for trying to get out of PE. I don't want them to know I am trying to get out of it because most boys like sports.

These boys also felt that the ways that they "embodied boy" forced them into a culture of being ignored and treated poorly by their classmates. They reported and we observed them being ignored, ridiculed, yelled at, laughed at, pushed, and physically isolated in PE. During an observation, a student shouted, "you suck" when Joe served the ball out of bounds, while other students laughed. Similarly, while observing a weight training class, Mike was approached by a classmate who handed him a one-pound weight and said, "Here, take this, you need it. This is what you need to use." Another time, after not being picked by the team "captains," Nike was physically shunned from two groups when trying to join a volleyball team. One girl said, "We have enough players, we don't need you," which was numerically not the case, and another girl shoved him toward a different court when he attempted to join her team. Joe was similarly overpowered by a girl when,

> After a group session, Joe returned to the gym just before dismissal. A female classmate saw him, looked up and down his body, and laughed before loudly saying, "Oh, I didn't even realize you weren't in class today." He looked at me [the researcher] and then quickly looked down.

Joe also felt as though his peers treated him poorly as a result of his awkward skills. He stated, "When you aren't good at PE, the other kids pick on you a lot. Mostly everyday you get teased and all that stuff. When you [your body] don't have the type of skills that everybody else has, it is embarrassing."

In addition, they reported that their teachers did not protect them from classmates who enacted either emotional or physical violence on their bodies. Jack exclaimed, "You could cuss someone out and the teacher wouldn't even notice or care. The teacher is in their own little world, they don't want to come by us, so they don't care to see what they [other students] do to us."

Additionally, Joe said, "I wish I could say the teacher steps in when other kids say rude things about me [my body], but that doesn't happen."

Beyond bodies playing a key role in sporting performance, they also lie at the heart of the relationships and social dynamics inherent in competitive, sport-based physical education programs. Said bluntly, boys' bodies determine their social positioning through the social practice of engaging with content (sports), learning/playing that content (pedagogies), and interacting with others (teachers and classmates) within the PE setting. It is the body, its shape, size, speed, athleticism, and aggressiveness, that determines how teachers and classmates gaze at boys' bodies, interact with them and touch them.

Wearing Marginalized Embodiment

The body is a distinct site where masculinities are enacted and practiced, but also in a sense "worn" as embodied manifestations of one's sense of self-worth and social positioning. As we watched the boys in these two settings enact various masculinities, it was abundantly clear that boys who embodied marginalized masculinities spoke a subtle language of pain, guardedness and uneasiness in the ways they carried their bodies in physical education. Their guarded, insecure bodies stood in stark contrast to the confident bodies and behaviors of boys who enacted hegemonic masculinities and were therefore privileged and supported. Their guarded embodiment resulted from anxieties about participating in sport-based PE programs that, through high-stakes activities and insensitive pedagogies, marginalized them. We observed these characteristics and the boys talked about them regularly. In a very real sense, by keeping their bodies guarded they communicated their fear and discontentment toward PE that left them feeling "awkward," "embarrassed," "unhappy," "lonely," and the "wrong" kind of boy." We observed them making their bodies small by crossing their arms and legs, tightly wrapping arms around legs while cradling heads in knees when sitting; placing hands in pockets, looking down or away from others, physically positioning themselves far from their classmates and teachers, and rarely smiling. Each claimed that their closed and protective body language betrayed intense feelings about their bodies.

> Nike sits and quietly listens as the teacher explains a volleyball lesson. He is not smiling; both arms are wrapped tightly around his knees as he sits motionless. When the teacher tells the students that they will be picking their own teams, he looks toward the floor, pulls his legs even closer to his torso while cradling his chin in his knees. He is molding himself into a ball and making himself very small. (FN#2)

Nike explained, "I sit like that because I'm scared and I'm not glad about gym." Jack said, "Sitting like that means you are uncomfortable and don't want to be in there. It helps you feel safer and makes the others kids not notice you as much."

Their bodies also clearly revealed that some boys, mainly boys who embodied masculinities that were marginalized, found much of the teachers' humor offensive and hurtful. They reacted very differently to teachers' humor than did boys who embodied hegemonic masculinities. For example, one teacher demonstrated incorrect methods of jumping rope in an awkward, frankly absurd manner. Most students laughed or at least smiled at the "show" particularly boys who embodied hegemonic masculinities. Conversely, boys who displayed guarded embodiment were straight-faced or looked down. To them this humor was insensitive, and at the expense of low-skilled students. Mike said,

> It makes me feel bad because I'm not always good at that stuff. People that don't know how to jump rope probably felt embarrassed to jump after the teachers' demonstration. My way of jumping rope might look like the teacher's demonstration.

The following vignette illustrates common body guarding the boys displayed. The teacher tells the class that they will be doing push-ups in upcoming fitness tests. The teacher laughs saying, "Some of you do push-ups wrong. It is so funny to watch you do them with your butts way up in the air or with your hips sagging toward the floor." Many students laugh. Mike, however, does not smile or laugh when the teacher takes the humor a step further by having a peer demonstrate incorrect push-ups. Straight-faced he looks to the floor and hugs his knees tighter. (FN#3)

For us as researchers, it was gripping and painful to watch the many ways in which these boys' bodies communicated anxiety and fear. For us, it sparked a certain ethical dilemma. Do we watch and document this travesty, or do we intervene in some way? We felt like asking the teachers, "Do you not see what we are seeing? Have you noticed their bodies? Have you asked them why they hold themselves the way they do?" Watching these boys bodies during PE classes and talking with them afterward about what they were feeling and communicating with their bodies caused us to realized that bodies not only determine social positioning within cultural contexts, they also "wear" that positioning in very visible and communicative ways.

Embodied Participation

To be fair, however, it is quite easy, once researchers become emotionally involved with their participants, especially ones they feel are unjustly oppressed, to begin interpreting everything they do or that happens to them as forms of oppression, patheticness, and deviance, as having no agency or resistance to what is happening to them. In reality, however, although these boys felt their bodies were deeply marginalized in these PE settings and their bodies wore visible signs of that marginalization, we also saw them enacting resistance. To protect themselves from abuse and ridicule, we watched them and they described a host of strategies they employed to avoid activities, interactions, and situations that would further marginalize their bodies. In other words, in an attempt to conceal their awkwardness and dislike for PE, they used crafty methods with their bodies to avoid certain activities or entire lessons altogether such as pretending to tie shoes, taking longer than needed to retrieve equipment, faking illness or injury, literally vomiting, stopping participation when the teacher was not watching, deliberately forgetting PE clothes, skipping class, telling the PE teacher they needed to meet with another teacher during PE, and allowing other students to dominate games with their bodies. For example, Jack said, "Sometimes the athletic kids take over, but I don't care because then it means I don't have to do anything." They also avoided participating by becoming skilled bystanders. For instance, Nike revealed, "When we are getting into groups, I'm on the court but I'm not even doing anything. I'm standing around and walking this way and that way. Moving around makes it seem like I'm participating." Additionally, during a jump rope activity in which students were told to jump 250 times, Jack effectively avoided the task without the teacher noticing.

> First, he took an excessively long time retrieving a rope by slowly walking to the jump rope cart, taking a rope then putting it back and taking another one several times. After finally getting a rope, he slowly walked back to a work space, which was located far from the jump rope cart. He made a few unenergetic attempts before he put the rope down and went into the hall for a drink of water. When he returned, he picked up his rope, and stood there until his group was called to return their ropes (FN#3).

Homogenous ways of understanding "boy" flourished as one of the many taken-for-granted gender truths in the PE settings, specifically the expectation that "real" boys are skilled and take pleasure in PE and sport. This deep-rooted notion of boys' bodies added an additional layer of complexity when these boys enacted task avoidance strategies. They recognized the necessity of concealing their bodies through task avoidance not only from their teachers, but even more so from their peers in an effort to give the illusion they were at least somewhat "doing boy right" by masking their dislike for PE and sport and also circumventing having to display their deviant, awkward bodies. Mike said, "Boys are expected to like PE because boys are usually the ones that play sports and like sports, so I hide it [task avoidance] from my classmates so they don't make fun of me or laugh at me." Similarly, Joe said, "When people know boys don't like PE, they make fun of you right in your face. It makes you feel bad so you have to hide it when you try to get out of stuff."

At times, however, these marginalized boys were unable to escape participation and were forced to be involved. Making it through this type of situation required the enactment of different mechanisms of survival such as participating with little or no intensity. For instance,

> During a volleyball game, Nike stood in the back of the court. At times, he rotated positions but never attempted to hit the ball other than his few unsuccessful attempts at serving when he was forced to rotate to that position (FN#2).

Nike explained that participating with little interest and intensity concealed his uncoordinated body, which was important because he believed that poor performances resulting from not being interested or not trying were seen differently by his peers than poor performances from lack of skill or fear of the activities. He said, "If you look like you don't care or if you look like you are not trying very hard, they can't yell at you or make fun of you for doing it wrong."

At the beginning, we interpreted this task avoidance and guarded participation as yet another way in which these boys "wore" their oppression. However, as we talked more with them, we recognized the need to de-center or unsettle this impression. Again, once a researcher feels sorry for their participants, it is easy to slip into the pattern of seeing them solely through the lens of oppression, domination, and deviance, without recognizing certain behaviors and social interactions as forms of agency and resistance. In a sense, it becomes a matter of interpretation. Were these boys "wearing" their oppression through guarded, survivalist behaviors? Or, interpreted differently, were these boys enacting volitional agency and thwarting attempts by teachers and classmates to further marginalize their bodies? The ways in which researchers and teachers interpret this conundrum have fierce ramifications for social progress and promoting equity for these boys. As researchers, we can more adequately explain this social setting. We can avoid the conventional assumption that these kinds of boys enact guarded participation and behaviors because they are lazy and lack motivation for physical activity, much like both Griffin (1985) and Parker (1996). Their use of the terms "wimps" and "victims" betray the researchers' positioning of these types of boys as problematic, deviant, and pathetic. However, perhaps, as this study shows, there may be alternative readings of their behaviors. Instead, it may be more accurate to explain their participation and passive behaviors as agentic and enacting subtle forms of power inside a network of power relations that position them in oppressive ways. The upside of producing this counter-narrative, according to Connell and Messerschmidt (2005), is that we can begin to identify paths forward to more just and equitable institutions by better understanding how non-hegemonic masculinities subvert the hegemonic status of more dominant ones.

Contextuality and Activity Embodiment

Originally, our research plan was to examine how masculinities functioned within the context of two school physical education programs. After working with these boys, however, combined with reflecting on the basic idea in hegemonic masculinity theory that masculinity hierarchies and social practices may be differently configured across different social contexts (even similar ones), we decided to examine these boys' masculinity experiences in both school PE and other physical activity contexts (e.g., with friends, family, and the alternative PE we were offering as part of the research process). We wanted to determine whether the masculinity configurations in school PE had any bearing on whether and how the boys participated in physical activities outside of traditional PE (if for example negative PE experiences would sour them to activity in other areas of their lives) and whether the masculinity configurations differed between those two contexts and what bearing that contrast might have on how these boys understood masculinities and physical activity generally.

We found through our fieldwork that these boys' masculine embodiments in physical activities taught in school PE contrasted sharply with those in other areas of their lives. They viewed physical activity outside of PE as fun, primarily because the imperfect bodies and performances that were cruelly marginalized in competitive sport-based PE were more accepted in other settings. Outside of PE, mistakes occurred without ridicule and imperfect performances were acceptable, unlike school PE where elite athleticism was both promoted and seen as a prerequisite for enacting "boy" properly. Our findings challenge the often taken-for-granted assumption that boys who disengage from PE are lazy and unmotivated toward physical activity. Quite to the contrary, we found that when the purpose of physical activity is fun, less competitive and more cooperative, boys who displayed guarded embodiment participated very differently.

The boys reported enjoying physical activity with friends due to the fun, cooperative nature of play, as well as the diversity of activities. They did not feel pressured to perform as superstars, and when playing with friends and family, mistakes were accepted. Jack said, "When I'm playing with my friends, they don't get mad at me because we're playing for fun. In gym, the kids yell at me if I mess up or lose the ball or something." These boys were active outside of school PE and listed numerous physical activities, even sports, they played with friends and family such as swimming, football, basketball, biking, rollerblading, rock climbing, Frisbee, tag, walking, bowling, and self-designed games. They described the dynamics of physical activities with friends and family to be dissimilar from the social dynamics in PE. For example, Jack stated, "When you play with friends in the yard, you feel better than in gym because you know them better than the kids at school and you know they won't pick on you." Mike also shared,

> Some nights, we'll [he and his family] just start riding our bikes and we don't even know where we'll be going. We'll just ride our bikes like maybe to here [his school], something like that and some other times we jog and stuff like that.

While many of the activities the boys reported enjoying were individual, non-competitive activities, it should be noted that they did not completely avoid sports. The major difference between playing sports in and out of PE was the emphasis of fun over competition. Joe described the contrast,

> I play basketball and stuff like that in the yard. People make fun of you when you're here [PE] and if you screw up the other kids yell and scream at you and make fun of you. When you mess up at home, they don't blame you for it. They're just like, whatever.

During small group work during the research process, we asked the boys to draw two pictures: one playing basketball in PE and one playing basketball at home. They were asked to illustrate the thoughts and feelings of the characters in their pictures by using text bubbles. On the back of the paper, we asked them to write a description of their drawing and then explain it to the group. Each boy's drawing clearly portrayed the home basketball experience as pleasurable and gratifying, while the PE basketball experience as stressful and upsetting. These feelings were represented through the use of facial expressions (i.e., smiling at home & frowning in PE), and text bubbles above the characters. For example, text bubbles from home basketball expressed, "I wish it was like this everyday" and "This is so fun." Conversely, text bubbles from PE basketball included expressions such as, "I should fake sick" and "That kid is such a baby." In addition, they depicted themselves physically near others in their home basketball drawings, but far from others in the school drawings.

What Role for Physical Education in the Obesity Epidemic?

Sadly enough, bolstered by many others, our research suggests that the cheerleaders of physical education as an elixir for youth obesity and inactivity ought to proceed cautiously (Gard & Wright, 2001; Tinning & Glasby, 2002). We have plenty of research finding that girls' participation in physical education as well as general physical activity decreases as they approach and move through adolescence. Similar research suggests, that while many factors contribute to this general pattern, it can be at least partly attributed to the domination they face by boys enacting hegemonic masculinities in school PE and teachers who either reinforce it or fail to restrain it (Flintoff & Scraton,

2006; Penney, 2002). To make matters worse, our findings, along with the burgeoning body of work of others documenting the intersection of boys' masculinities, inequitable power relations, and the impact on boys' self-esteem and body health, should prove equally troubling for the cheerleaders of conventional physical education. Said plainly, during secondary schooling (grade 6), many girls and boys feel alienated by the competitive, elite sport and body-as-project ethics promulgated widely by school PE programs. Of course, this line of reasoning becomes even more concerning when we consider how issues such as sexuality (gay-straight, transsexual, transgender, heterosexism, homophobia, heteronormativity) (e.g., Clarke, 2006; McCaughtry, Dillon, Jones, Smigell, 2005; Sykes, 2004), fat phobia (e.g., Sykes, 2008), and (dis)ability (e.g., Fitzgerald, 2006, 2009) further complicate children's experiences in school PE.

While the last two decades have seen a dramatic increase in the volume and sophistication of critical, cultural theory and research in physical education, we contend that too little has practically changed in everyday classrooms that might help physical education become a site for enhancing the health of more young people, beyond those who are already skilled, fit and enjoy physical activity. We must create the conditions where teacher education programs and practicing teachers can undergo a paradigmatic shift from our elite sport and fitness training historical roots toward a more nuanced sociological envisioning of the body, health, and exercise settings (i.e., physical education, sport, community physical activity). Armour (1999) calls for a "body-focus" for physical education and McCaughtry (2009) for an increasingly critical understanding of the life of the child, both of which emphasize the centrality of a critical sociological reading of the body as the foundation for physical education reform. We can no longer ignore the fact that issues like gender relations, masculinities, femininities, (dis)ability, sexuality, race/ethnicity, body image fatness/fatphobia/obesity and others play out in real classrooms and have real consequences for many young people. Talking about body fatness reduction, activity compulsion, and skill acquisition might be seen as irrelevant, if not laughable, when considered outside the sociological context in which children make sense of their bodies, their overall health (read broadly as including emotional, psychological, spiritual, as well as physical), and their location within the social environment. Rather than hypothesizing or even touting ways that physical education can alleviate some supposed obesity crisis (the logic of which is tenuous at best), perhaps a more pressing global and public health concern ought to be how we might go about creating more equitable and empowering classrooms, where both teachers and students engage in and nurture more critical learning experiences. What might it look like, for example, if teachers were as equally concerned with embracing, encouraging and supporting the multiple masculinities that young boys embody as they are with developing sport skills? What might happen if teachers avoided surface-level explanations for some boys' uneager participation as resulting from biological incompetencies, lack of motivation or social deviance, and instead read their bodies as wearing and communicating feelings or looked at their lives outside the classroom for explanations and ways of reaching them? Frankly, it might be quite interesting to see a classroom where teachers and students embrace and work through tough social issues that underlie inequities and domination, rather than pathologizing difference as binaries of superior/inferior, biologically capable/incapable, or normal/deviant.

Bibliography

Armour, K. (1999). The case for a body-focus in education and physical education. *Sport, Education and Society*, 4, 5-16.

Atkinson, M., & Wilson, B. (2002). Subcultures, bodies, and sport at the millennium. In J. Maquire & K. Young (Eds.), *Theory, sport, and society* (pp. 375-395). London: JAI Press.

Banks, J.A. (1996). *Multicultural education, transformative knowledge, and action: Historical and contemporary perspectives*. New York: Teachers College Press.

Bramham, P. (2003). Boys, masculinities and PE. *Sport, Education and Society*, 8, 57-71.

Carlson, T., & Hastie, P.A. (1997). The student social system within sport education. *Journal of Teaching in Physical Education*, 16, 176-195.

Clarke, G. (2006). Sexuality and physical education. In D. Kirk, D. Macdonald, & M. O'Sullivan (Eds.), *Handbook of Physical Education* (pp. 723-739). Thousand Oaks, CA: Sage Publications.

Connell, R. (2008). Masculinity construction and sports in boys' education: A framework for thinking about the issue. *Sport, Education and Society*, 13, 131-145.

Connell, R.W. (1995). *Masculinities*. Cambridge, UK: Polity Press.

Connell, R.W. (1998). Masculinities and globalization. *Men and Masculinities*, 1, 3-23.

Connell, R.W. (2003). Masculinities, change and conflict in global society: Thinking about the future of men's studies. *Journal of Men's Studies*, 11, 249-266.

Connell, R.W., & Messerschmidt, J.W. (2005). Hegemonic masculinity: Rethinking the concept. *Gender and Society*, 19, 829-859.

Davison, K. (2000). Boys' bodies in school: Physical education. *Journal of Men's Studies*, 8, 255-262.

Davison, K. (2004). Texting gender and body as a distant/ced memory: An autobiographical account of bodies, masculinities, and schooling. *Journal of Curriculum Theorizing*, 20, 129-149.

Davison, K. (2007). Methodological instability and the disruption of masculinities. *Men and Masculinities*, 9, 379-391.

Demetriou, D.Z. (2001). Connell's concept of hegemonic masculinity: A critique. *Theory* and *Society*, 30, 337-361.

Drummond, M. (2003). The meaning of boys' bodies in physical education. *Journal of Men's Studies*, 11, 131-139.

Edley, N., & Wetherell, M. (1997). Jockeying for position: The construction of masculine identities. *Discourse & Society*, 8, 203-217.

Ennis, C.D., Solmon, M.A., Satina, B., Loftus, S.J., Mensch, J., & McCauley, M.T. (1999). Creating a sense of family in urban schools using the "sport for peace" curriculum. *Research Quarterly for Exercise and Sport*, 70, 273-285.

Fitzgerald, H. (2006). Disability and physical education. In D. Kirk, D. Macdonald, & M. O'Sullivan (Eds.), *Handbook of Physical Education* (pp. 752-766). Thousand Oaks, CA: Sage Publications.

Fitzgerald, H. (2009). *Disability and youth sport*. London: Routledge.

Flintoff, A., & Scranton, S. (2006). Girls and physical education. In D. Kirk, D. Macdonald, & M. O'Sullivan (Eds.), *Handbook of Physical Education* (pp. 767-783). Thousand Oaks, CA: Sage Publications.

Frank, B. Kehler, M., Lovell, T., & Davison, K. (2003). A tangle of trouble: Boys, masculinity and schooling—future directions. *Educational Review, 55,* 119-133.

Gard, M. (2001). Dancing around the "problem" of boys and dance. *Discourse: Studies in the Cultural Politics of Education, 22,* 213-225.

Gard, M. (2003). Being someone else: Using dance in anti-oppressive teaching. *Educational Review, 55,* 211-223.

Gard, M. (2008). When a boy's got to dance: New masculinities, old pleasures. *Sport, Education and Society, 13,* 181-193.

Gard, M., & Meyenn, R. (2000). Boys, bodies, pleasure, and pain: Interrogating contact sports in schools. *Sport, Education and Society, 5,* 19-34.

Gard, M., & Wright, J. (2001). Managing uncertainty: Obesity discourses and physical education in a risk society. *Studies in Philosophy and Education, 20,* 535-549.

Gard, M., & Wright, J. (2005). *The obesity epidemic: Science, morality, and ideology.* London: Routledge.

Griffin, P. (1985). Boys' participation styles in a middle school physical education team sports unit. *Journal of Teaching in Physical Education, 4,* 100-110.

Hastie, P.A. (1996). Student role involvement during a unit of Sport Education. *Journal of Teaching in Physical Education, 16,* 88-103.

Hastie, P.A. (1998a). The participation and perceptions of girls within a unit of sport education. *Journal of Teaching in Physical Education, 17,* 157-171.

Hastie, P.A. (1998b). Applied benefits of the Sport Education model. *Journal of Physical Education, Recreation & Dance, 69,* 24-26.

Hastie, P.A. (1998c). Skill and tactical development during a Sport Education season. *Research Quarterly for Exercise and Sport, 69,* 368-379.

Hickey, C. (2008). Physical education, sport and hyper-masculinity in schools. *Sport, Education, and Society, 13,* 147-161.

Humberstone, B. (1990). Warriors or wimps? Creating alternative forms of physical education. In M.A. Messner & D.F. Sabo (Eds.), *Sport, men, and the gender order: Critical feminist perspectives* (pp. 201-210). Champaign, IL: Human Kinetics.

Irwin, C.C., Symons, C.W., & Kerr, D.L. (2003). The dilemmas of obesity: How can physical educators help? *JOPERD, 74,* 33-39.

Jandt, F., & Hundley, H. (2007). Intercultural dimensions of communicating masculinities. *Journal of Men's Studies, 15,* 216-231.

Kane, J. (2006). School exclusion and masculine, working-class identities. *Gender and Education, 18,* 673-685.

Kehler, M. (2004). Masculinities and resistance: High school boys (un)doing boy. *Taboo, 8,* 97-113.

Kehler, M., Davison, K., & Frank, B. (2005). Contradictions and tensions in the practice of masculinities in school: Interrogating embodiment and "good buddy talk." *Journal of Curriculum and Theorizing, 21, 59-72.*

Kehler, M., & Martino, W. (2007). Questioning masculinities: Interrogating boys' capacities for self-problemitization in schools. *Canadian Journal of Education, 30, 90-112.*

Kimmel, M.S. (1990). Baseball and the reconstitution of American masculinity, 1880-1920. In M.A. Messner & D.F. Sabo (Eds.), *Sport, men, and the gender order: Critical feminist perspectives* (pp. 55-65). Champaign, IL: Human Kinetics.

Kinchin, G.D. (2006). Sport education: A view of the research. In D. Kirk, D. Macdonald, & M. O'Sullivan (Eds.), *Handbook of Physical Education* (pp. 596-609). Thousand Oaks, CA: Sage Publications.

Larsson, H., Fagrell, B., & Redelius, K. (2009). Queering physical education: Between benevolence towards girls and a tribute to masculinity. *Physical Education and Sport Pedagogy, 14, 1-17.*

Light, R. (2008). Learning masculinities in a Japanese high school rugby club. *Sport, Education and Society, 13, 163-179.*

Mac an Ghaill, M. (1994). *The making of men: Masculinities, sexualities and schooling.* Buckingham, UK: Open University Press.

MacPhail, A., Gorely, T., Kirk, D., & Kinchin, G. (2008). Children's experiences of fun and enjoyment during a season of Sport Education. *Research Quarterly for Exercise and Sport, 79, 344-355.*

MacPhail, A., Kirk, D., & Kinchin, G. (2004). Sport Education: Promoting team affiliation through physical education. *Journal of Teaching in Physical Education, 23, 106-122.*

Martino, W. (2000). Policing masculinities: Investigating the role of homophobia and heteronormativity in the lives of adolescent school boys. *The Journal of Men's Studies, 8, 213-236.*

Martino, W. (2003). Researching masculinities: The implications and uses of Foucauldian analysis in undertaking ethnographic investigations into adolescent boys' lives at school. In M. Tamboukou & S. Ball (Eds.), *Dangerous encounters: Genaeology and ethnography* (pp. 153-174). New York: Peter Lang.

McCaughtry, N. (2004). Coming to see gender: Implications of personal history and political pressures on identifying disempowerment for girls. *Research Quarterly for Exercise and Sport, 75, 400-412.*

McCaughtry, N. (2006). Working politically amongst professional knowledge landscapes to implement gender-sensitive physical education reform. *Physical Education and Sport Pedagogy, 11, 159-179.*

McCaughtry, N. (2009). The child and the curriculum: Implications of Deweyan philosophy in the pursuit of "cool" physical education for children. In L. Housner, M. Metzler, P. Schempp, & T. Templin (Eds.), *Historical Traditions and Future Directions of Research on Teaching and Teacher Education in Physical Education* (pp.187-198). Morgantown, WV: Fitness Information Technology.

McCaughtry, N., Dillon, S., Jones, E., & Smigell, S. (2005). Sexuality sensitive schooling. *Quest*, *57*, 426-443.

Messner, M.A., & Sabo, D.F. (1990). Toward a critical feminist reappraisal of sport, men, and the gender order. In M.A. Messner & D.F. Sabo (Eds.), *Sport, men, and the gender order: Critical feminist perspectives* (pp. 1-15). Champaign, IL: Human Kinetics.

Millington, B., Vertinsky, P., Boyle, E., & Wilson. B. (2008). Making Chinese-Canadian masculinities in Vancouver's physical education curriculum. *Sport, Education and Society*, *13*, 195-214.

NASPE (2002). *Shape of a nation*. Reston, VA: NASPE Publications.

Nilan, P. (2000). "You're hopeless I swear to god": Shifting masculinities in classroom talk. *Gender and Education*, *12*, 53-68.

Oliver, J.E. (2006). *Fat politics: The real story behind America's obesity epidemic*. New York: Oxford University Press.

Parker, A. (1996). The construction of masculinity within boys' physical education. *Gender & Education*, *8*, 141-158.

Penney, D. (2002). *Gender and physical education*. New York: Routledge.

Pringle, R. (2008). "No rugby-no fear": Collective stories, masculinities and transformative possibilities in schools. *Sport, Education and Society*, *13*, 215-237.

Quennerstedt, M. (2008). Studying the institutional dimension of meaning making: A way to analyze subject content in physical education. *Journal of Teaching Physical Education*, *27*, 434-444.

Rossi, T., Tinning, R., McCuaig, Sirna, K., & Hunter, L. (2009). With the best of intentions: A critical discourse analysis of physical education curriculum materials. *Journal of Teaching Physical Education*, *28*, 75-89.

Siedentop, D. (1994). *Sport education: Quality PE through positive sport experiences*. Champaign, IL: Human Kinetics.

Siedentop, D., Hastie, P.A., & Van der Mars, H. (2004). *Complete guide to Sport Education*. Champaign, IL: Human Kinetics.

Swain, J. (2005). Masculinities in education. In M.S. Kimmell, J. Hearn, & R.W. Connell (Eds.), *Handbook of studies on men and masculinities* (pp. 213-229). Thousand Oaks, CA: Sage.

Sykes, H. (2004). Pedagogies of censorship, injury, masochism: Teacher responses to homophobic speech in physical education. *Journal of Curriculum Studies*, *36*, 75-99.

Sykes, H. (2008). Unbearable lessons: Contesting fat phobia in physical education. *Sociology of Sport Journal*, *25*, 66-96.

Thomas, K.T. (2004). Riding to the rescue while holding on by a thread: Physical activity in the schools. *Quest*, *56*, 150-170.

Tinning, R. (1997). Performance and participation discourses in human movement: Toward a socially critical physical education. In J.M. Fernandez-Balboa (Ed.), *Critical postmodernism in human movement, physical education, and sport* (pp. 99-119). New York: State University of New York Press.

Tinning, R. & Glasby, T. (2002). Pedagogical work and the 'cult of the body': Considering the role of HPE in the context of the new 'public health.' *Sport, Education and Society*, 7, 109-119.

Wallhead, T.L., & Ntoumanis, N. (2004). Effects of a sport education intervention on students' motivational responses in physical education. *Journal of Teaching in Physical Education*, 23, 4-18.

Wallhead, T. & O'Sullivan, M. (2005). Sport Education: Physical education for the new millennium. *Physical Education and Sport Pedagogy*, 10, 181-210.

U.S. Department of Health and Human Services. (2001). *The Surgeon General's call to action to prevent and decrease overweight and obesity 2001.* Washington, D.C.: Government Printing Office.

Young, J.P. (2000). Boy talk: Critical literacy and masculinities. *Reading Research Quarterly, 35*, 312-337.

CHAPTER TEN

Australian Young Men's Meanings of Physical Activity and Health: An Exploration of Social Class and Schooling

Jessica Lee

Globally, young people's health has been in the spotlight across all interest areas including academia, government policy, and in the popular media. A growing concern for young people's health fuelled by epidemiological reports of increasing levels of chronic disease (including obesity) and declining levels of physical activity has manifested itself in the emergence of a number of public health, school curricular, and sport policies in which the promotion of health is a key objective. This chapter explores young men's meanings of health and fitness and how these are shaped by their experiences of a physical culture saturated by health promotion messages including the influence of school sport and physical education. The young men's own meanings are explored alongside interview data from their school physical education heads of department and information published on school websites. The experiences of young men from different schooling, geographical, and social class contexts are juxtaposed. This chapter draws on data from an Australian longitudinal study into the place and meaning of physical activity and physical culture in the lives of young people.

Historically, in Western culture sport has been framed as character building for young men, promoting courage, chivalry, moral strength and military patriotism (Dowling Naess, 2001) and a medium through which to learn values such as being competitive, successful, and strong (McKay, 1991). Indeed, in contemporary Western societies it is difficult, particularly for young men, not to construct their identity in relation to physical activity and/or sport, even if it is in rejecting it as part of one's social and cultural life. At the intersection of social class and the construction of masculinities it has been observed that young men from upper and middle classes valued intelligence and sociability as characteristics of masculinity, whereas working-class young men respected "male chauvinism and masculine showing-off" (Laberge and Albert, 2000, p. 201).

Much academic literature has focussed on the correlation between social class (or socioeconomic status) and participation in physical activities (Borraccino et al., 2009; Inchley, Currie, Todd, Akhtar, & Currie, 2005; Starfield, Riley, Witt, & Robertson, 2002) and health outcomes, particularly overweight and obesity (Harrington & Elliott, 2009; McLaren, 2007). The consensus being that lower rates of physical activity and higher rates of obesity are found amongst lower social classes. Geographical location has also been implicated in having an impact on health outcomes and rates of obesity (Moon, Quarendon, Barnard, Twigg, & Blyth, 2007; Riva, Curtis, Gauvin, & Fagg, 2009) such that rural populations have higher rates of obesity and poorer health outcomes when compared to their city and urban counterparts. This chapter aims to unpack this evidence from a sociocultural perspective to explore how schooling impacts on the ways in which health promotion and obesity discourses are taken up by young men from different social and geographical locations.

Approach to the Research

Seven young men from Malcos College,[1] an elite private school for boys; four young men from Greenvalley High, a rural co-educational government secondary school; and four young men from Homestead School, a school of distance education participated in semi-structured interviews over the course of three years. At the commencement of the project young men from Malcos and Greenvalley were recruited from the first year of secondary school (grade 8, 13 years old) and the final year of compulsory schooling (grade 10, 15 years old). The young men from Homestead ranged in age from 11 to 14 years old from grade six, grade seven (the final year of primary school) and grade nine. This age range allowed for examination of the young men's meanings and experiences of physical activity and health across different ages and life trajectories.

The interviews followed the schedule of the Life Activity Project (Lee & Macdonald, 2009; Wright, Macdonald & Groom, 2003) and asked young people to talk about their past and present participation in physical activity, why and how they became involved in various activities and why they continued to participate, or not. To capture a sense of what was important to them in relation to their participation, the young people were asked to describe what they remembered about their participation in different activities and also what their feelings and experiences were in those activities. Specific interviews also focussed on aspects of physical culture (e.g., sports brand clothing, sport spectatorship, elite athletes as role models, Olympics) and meanings of health and fitness.

An analysis of the schools' websites and their physical and health education and school sport policies was conducted to determine the ways schools constructed meanings around physical activity and health. In addition, one health and physical education teacher from Greenvalley High was interviewed about the way sport and physical education was conducted at his school, the importance placed on these at the school and his own meanings about school sport and physical education. He was selected for interview on the basis of his longtime employment at the school and his status as Head of Department of Health and Physical Education

A poststructuralist approach to the data analysis was used with a focus on discourse and power. Using Bourdieu's theories of field, capital and habitus also enabled a multi-level examination of masculinity. In this way structuralist concepts such as class, gender, and geographical location were analysed from a poststructuralist perspective to explore issues of difference, diversity and complexity. This approach is consistent with recent calls to retain our "structuralist memory" (Crotty, 1998; McLaren & Farandmandpur, 2000) in acknowledging the ongoing influence of structures such as gender and social class in the lives of young people. Critical discourse analysis (CDA) was used to examine how discourses of class, masculinities, and health and fitness were utilised and perpetuated for the young men by identifying the ways they understood and described health, fitness and physical activity and their participation in sports and physical activities. Their talk was then further examined for ways in which their understandings or actions were constrained or facilitated by their observances of particular discourses. Following Luke (1996), CDA was used to investigate how reproductions of discourses were affiliated with differing kinds of cultural capital and social power. CDA allowed for an exploration of how social class, physical culture, gender, and location shaped the young men's conceptions of physical activity and health.

Young Men Talking about Physical Activity and Health

The young men's talk around physical activity and health will be explored in two sections. Each section addresses the school contexts, the young men's experiences with school sport and physical education, and their engagements with discourses around physical activity and health. The first of the two sections covers these themes from the perspectives of the young men from Malcos College and the second, from the perspectives of the rural young men from Greenvalley High and Homestead School.

"If you don't do rugby or rowing then you're a wimp"

Malcos College, an independent boys' school, was located in an inner city suburb. The school has a mostly middle-class student body whose parents tended to be in managerial/professional occupations contributing to a strong "old boy" tradition and network. Malcos College students enjoy a newly refurbished sports complex, perhaps "one of the best school facilities available," housing a weights room "considered to be the best in [elite] schools in [the state], if not Australia," two basketball courts, specific gymnastic training area complete with dive pit and performance floor, and a rowing ergo room, and hosting a variety of sports including volleyball, basketball, gymnastics, and futsal (cited on school website). In addition to the indoor sports complex, the college has a number of tennis courts and fields as well as a 50-metre swimming pool. A wide range of competitive sports are on offer (including athletics, Australian Rules football, basketball, cricket, cross-country, gymnastics, mountain biking, rowing, rugby, sailing, soccer, swimming, tennis, volleyball, water polo), and it is strongly recommended that "each student be involved in at least one physical activity per year" (cited on school website).

The Malcos young men spoke of their experiences in sports and physical activities with ease and a sense normality and ordinariness. Participation in sports played a significant role in each of the young men's lives from an early age within a range of activities including karate, rugby union, rowing, Australian rules football, soccer, cricket, tennis, basketball, and golf. Mostly, participation in these sports began in the primary school years as part of clubs although due to expectations of participation at Malcos, school became the main provider by the secondary years.

David: When I was young I started off sport when I was about ohh 6, started playing basketball then and, bit of AFL (Australian football) as well, just you know with some mates outside and stuff like that. Then when I came to Malcos I started playing basketball and tennis when I was also in primary school and when I came to Malcos yeah, I started playing basketball and I was also playing club basketball and club tennis. Then in grade nine I started rowing and um, and also, and I was still playing club basketball then and was also playing normal basketball, school sport basketball and in grade 10 I started playing rugby as well.

Int.:   Yeah and is there a reason why you dropped club basketball?

David: Mainly the time factor, cause you know after school you'd have to, I'd have to race out to [training venue] and play there and train there on Wednesday but um, it just seemed a lot easier just to play it at school.

This process of club sport evolving into school sport was a result of the increasing need to balance time spent on sport and on school work which were seen as equally important.

Harry: 'Cause like you've got to concentrate on sport and at the same time concentrate on your school work cause you can't get side tracked from one or the other... 'cause if you get side tracked in sport then you let your team down, if you get side tracked in school work then you'll let yourself down and your marks.

A number of themes describing their experiences in school sport were present. First, many of the Malcos young men spoke of the competitive nature of their participation in school sport. The young men were very aware of the school's expectation to participate in sports. Due to the inter-school sporting culture, competition was an inherent part of the young men's participation. Indeed, the young men were required to "try out" for a place on school teams so were competing against each other as well as against other elite schools.

Darren: Ohh pretty much everyone does [sport] 'cause our policy is you must play a sport a term... you have to try out for it, yeah they encourage you to play... I chose tennis because it was more select and was harder to get into a team so it was better to play that... If you're like bad at sport you sometimes you can get ragged and teased, yeah.

Int.:   So your soccer is pretty important at the moment?

Aidan: Well yeah, I don't really have a choice in that so I've got to do that.

Int.:   How come you have got to do it?

Aidan: Well I'm captain of soccer here so I can't really pull out or
            anything. I've sort of made a commitment so I have to follow it
            through.
Int.:   So do you feel a bit of pressure because you are captain?
Aidan: Mm, mm.
Int.:   And so if you weren't captain would you still play?
Aidan: Yeah. If it wasn't in the 1st team though, I probably wouldn't
            play... I don't really like the people in the other teams.

Int.:   How important do you think sport and other physical activities
            are inside the school culture?
Seth: Oh very high... School places a big importance in sport and it
            defines you as a person a lot in schools... Macho man, if you don't
            do rugby or rowing then you're a wimp.

The element of competition and indeed, the prospect of winning and the
reward and recognition that goes along with it was certainly a motivation for
these young men.

Int.:   What keeps you playing soccer at the moment?
Ross: The fun and the glory when you win.

David: Highlight of the [rowing] season, most probably coming second at
            the Head of the River. That was pretty good.
Int.:   Did you get any awards, anything from school for your
            performances?
David: Yeah, we got half colours for that... Yeah, it's always a motivation.

It was clear that during their school years the Malcos College young men
mainly had their sporting opportunities provided for them by the school.
Through the school fees, the families invested in the physical culture of the
school and in a way contracted out the commitment to sport and physical
activity. This resulted in a very routinised and taken-for-granted experience of
sport which had an effect on their participation in the post-school years (see
later discussion).

Given the requirement of at least some participation in sport, it was
interesting to note that none of the Malcos College young men in the cohort
continued physical education after the compulsory years (in years 11 and 12).
They generally enjoyed physical education in their younger years because it was
perceived as easy and let them relax away from the "more academic" subjects.
The most cited reasons for not continuing physical education in the senior
years was that it would not contribute towards their career (e.g., "I won't be

needing it at uni") and that they already do enough physical activity (e.g., "I don't have the energy to do that because I'm also doing sport after school"). Therefore, despite being physically skilled as evidenced by their participation in various sports, the Malcos young men still did not find physical education appealing in their senior years.

As participation in sports and physical activities was taken for granted among the Malcos young men, so was an investment in health and fitness. Being healthy and fit allowed them to participate in the various tasks of their daily lives including sports, school work, socialising, and part-time work. In keeping with their approach to school and sport, staying fit and healthy required a balanced lifestyle and a consideration of physical and mental factors.

For Thanh, there were "two types of health, mental and physical. Physical being fit, not too overweight, you're eating in moderation, exercising in moderation. Mental I think is not being over-stressed; I think the main word is moderation." Keeping healthy and fit was important in his chosen sport of karate, "In a small tournament I can last for the whole tournament, but when I have to do six or seven fights then I'm usually tired if I get through to the finals, so I'm disadvantaged."

Like Thanh, David regarded health as keeping everything in moderation, "I'd say having everything in moderation, like physical activity and sport and your academic and your social life, all sort of in moderation... I guess social life is pretty good you know, you need to have friends." Fitness was an important part of his life as he said it generally boosted his confidence and allowed him to feel "more energized."

While consideration of body shape featured in some of the young men's talk around health and fitness, it certainly was not a main focus and tended to relate to the ability to succeed in sports and other aspects of life. Indeed, the young men tended to be fairly satisfied with their physical appearances. David was confident with his general appearance, describing himself as having "tanned skin, about 5' 11", fairly athletic," Thanh described himself as "[m]oderately tall, athletic, slim... Asian."

Harry: [Healthy is] I guess a good attitude, obviously fitness, how you look at life, I guess...Yeah you've got to have a healthy mind I guess. I think fitness helps with school work because you can concentrate more... I guess it's not good to have high cholesterol, um, I just don't want to be fat, I wouldn't want to be a wreck. If you are fit you've got more opportunities to do things in sport.

Aidan: Yeah, in the physical sense maybe that health goes with happiness as well. If you're sort of happy, then you're healthy as well. It's

	hard to say, I don't think you're always, I don't think healthiness is a great indicator of your lifestyle.
Int.:	Okay. So what sort of things, how would you know if someone was healthy?
Aidan:	Sort of no diseases... and also just contented with their life I think, it's sort of the key to being healthy.
Int.:	So what is the priority about being healthy?
Aidan:	Just being physically able, not having a disease... Being able to live your daily life...

At this stage for these young men, the imperative was to maintain a balance in sporting, social and academic endeavours as well as being happy and mentally sound.

A number of the Malcos College young men completed school and continued on to university throughout the course of the study. Due to social and cultural capital gained at school, sport was not a major priority immediately post-school. As a result of this transition they found that their lives in general and particularly their participation in sport and physical activities became a lot less structured (Lee, Macdonald & Wright, 2009). None of them continued competing in their respective sports.

David:	It's a little different, you've got to sort of motivate yourself to do stuff; you don't have anyone sort of relying on you to be doing this work if you don't want to. I guess I sort of prefer the way that school was organised because then you always had things to do like to do with sport; you know it was a lot easier to get into back then.
Thanh:	Because school was so routine I was able to fit everything in. But now everything just, even though I have more free time it's not as routine.

It was clear that the young men felt that their school experiences had set them up for very smooth transitions into the academic and social side of university but the structure of the sporting programme made it somewhat more difficult to continue in sport and physical activities post-school. Masculinity became more closely associated with lucrative careers. The "balance" in life had changed at this stage in their lives.

The Malcos young men's engagements with physical culture tended to be typical of the view that young people's lives are saturated by consumption particularly around sport for young men (Kenway & Bullen, 2001). For example, they valued sports brand clothing and felt that sports labels were the best for them when they were participating in sports. As Seth comments, the physical culture also pervaded the school culture with the dominance of sports brand clothes.

David: it's really just the good quality of the brand name... If I'm getting some stuff for training, like for basketball training, I'd go for Nike or something 'cause you know, or my sport shoes which are Nike and my good shorts.

Seth: Definitely, it's a real big thing in basketball, I mean with all the clothes in basketball, like the shoes especially, whose shoes you have on... it's a big influence on which clothes you have on, like for instance Nike or whatever.

Int.:   What about at the school here, is there...

Seth: Yeah I mean things like you can wear an ordinary plain shirt or if you've got one with a tick on it you know everyone's going to think you know you dress well. They can be exactly the same shirt but have nothing labelled on it, you know the label makes it and a lot of, and you know it costs a lot more just with that one logo, you know one tick or one little logo... just personally because of the image factor you'd probably go for the logo brand... when everyone's looking at you and that if you don't have you know the right clothes you will, everyone will be, pick on you.

Int.:   So what, what logos do you wear on your clothing?

Seth: I like Nike, like Nike's probably the biggest and I just, a lot of people put a lot of emphasis on shoes... what your shirt is, is it a Nike shirt? Well you know you're alright but if it isn't, well you're no good.

They were also regular spectators at major sporting events, often with high-priced, premium tickets. Like their physical activity participation in general, these young men's engagements with physical culture were very privileged and taken for granted.

David: [I] usually go to the State of Origin (rugby league), we're going to the Indy (major motor racing event) on Saturday ... we usually go 'cause we usually get a box at all the rugby matches at [the stadium]. I went to the Isle of Mann once where they have the motor cycle races ... the good thing about going to the Indy is that my dad usually can get pit passes as well so you get to go down into the pits and check out the cars as well.

"Driving the tractors is sort of rough; it's a boy thing"

The rural young men's school contexts were much different from those experienced by the Malcos College young men. Greenvalley High was located in a socially isolated, small rural town with a lack of local services and access to public transport between nearby towns and larger centres. Some of the young people attending Greenvalley High lived on residential housing blocks in the town, while others lived on properties up to 30 kilometres away from the school. The Homestead School caters for students who cannot, for various reasons, attend regular schools and, as such, has a high proportion of students who live in remote rural locations. The Homestead School students in this study were all rural young people who lived in isolated areas with difficult access to local schools. Distance education as carried out through the Homestead School entails students receiving hard copies of learning materials and guidance on daily work plans from teachers. Personal communication between students and teachers is usually via telephone, sometimes email (depending on access) and audio-tapes can be used for assessment. The young people studying with the Homestead School lived on farming properties in four different rural locations up to 600 kilometres from the state capital and between 20 and 60 kilometres from the nearest town.

The Greenvalley High and Homestead School students' experiences of school sport and physical education were quite different from those of the Malcos College young men. The rural schools and towns had somewhat limited formal facilities and opportunities. Due to geographical isolation Greenvalley High also had a very limited inter-school sport programme. The Homestead School had no inter-school competitive sport programme, although it did run optional sport/family days for activities such as athletics and swimming. As such, the rural young men's sport and physical activity participation patterns tended to be more club focussed (in the case of sport), less scheduled (with some exceptions) and featured more recreational physical activities with siblings, physical labour, and active transport (Lee & Macdonald, 2009).

When the rural young men were involved in sports, they were directly supported by their parents, and sporting events tended to be family events.

Brandon's mother: With Friday night is a thing where we go to swimming club...and Terrence [husband] helps with the barbecue or whatever you know. (Greenvalley High).

Lemming and Mouldy's mother: Well I'm quite involved in club cricket. I usually score and help [my husband] set up things, so pretty much the whole family is involved (Homestead School).

For the rural young men, physical labour on properties was a regular feature of their everyday lives, and farm chores were often considered part of their leisure time as well.

Tyrone: Bike riding, straight away. If Mum wants me to go and check the trough over there and make sure it's not overflowing or anything and I'll be back about an hour later, just checking the trough and I'll go up the road and up the other side there, coming down the other side there's good [tracks], I think it's eight kilometres or seven (Homestead School).

Wadiken: ...as I say I get a fair bit of physical activity like yesterday afternoon after I did my exams I went up for a ride [motorbike] up the front just to check on things... and I went up to a dry dam and there was three sheep stuck in there, in the mud. The mud would have sucked against them right? So it's really tough work; you've got to be really fit to pull them out... basically by myself and then we lifted them into the trailer and take them back here and wash the mud off them and feed and water them. So you know, it's a fair bit of fitness is needed to do things like that (Homestead School).

An advantage the rural young men did have was an abundance of space to participate in recreational sport and physical activities. In addition to using formal equipment in the home, some of the Homestead young people innovatively made their own equipment, along with their siblings and sometimes with help from their parents. This goes some way to overcome the barrier of lack of formal sport and physical activity facilities in their local areas.

Mouldy: ...we made a mini golf course... Well we just decided where we were going to put the holes, teed them, then we dug a hole and put a tin in the ground and covered it with some dust so the grass would grow through it and it's pretty good. (Homestead School).

The significance of recreational physical activity in the rural young people's lives was also evident in the school context. At Greenvalley High, the more formal subject, "Senior Physical Education" aimed at students interested in pursuing sporting excellence, had lower student enrolment than "Recreational Studies" which emphasised participation and enjoyment of non-traditional physical activities (e.g., orienteering, golf, archery, kayaking, lawn bowls). Recreational Studies attracted almost double the enrolment of Senior Physical Education (Greenvalley High Physical Education HoD, personal communication, September 9, 2004). The Greenvalley High students in this cohort did not choose to participate in Senior Physical Education although some were eager participants in Recreational Studies (also called "Rec Studies" or "Health and Rec" by the students and teachers). Brett speaks enthusiastically about Recreational Studies in the following quote:

Brett: Yeah, it's [Recreational Studies] going pretty good. We're doing lawn bowls at the moment, did kayaking last term. I got a B in kayaking, that was pretty fun. We're supposed to be doing a coaching session, coaching lesson for two terms. We've got to coach the primary schoolers across the road (Greenvalley High).

It appears that Recreational Studies suited the rural young people's lived experiences of sport and physical activities as demonstrated previously, more so than Senior Physical Education.

For the students of Homestead School, practical Physical Education work focused on traditional sports such as basketball, soccer, athletics and swimming. The absence of a class context made participation in these types of activities difficult however, for the participants of this study.

Lemming: I didn't enjoy it [Physical Education] much. I had to play basketball and dancing with my mum. I reckon it would have been better if I could do it with other kids instead of with my family... It's a bit hard by yourself too, I had to travel for an hour to get to the pool in swimming so that was hard, and we don't have any water around here. (Homestead School).

The above quote from Lemming highlights some of the challenges of Physical Education faced by remote rural young people such as having to participate with siblings and/or parents, and extensive travel to facilities such as pools. Restraints such as these often resulted in the students disengaging with physical education altogether. In contrast to the Malcos College students, the rural young people from Greenvalley High and Homestead School tended to experience sport and physical activities outside of school and where sport was played in clubs, this required a substantial parental time and financial commitment.

Mr Mason, the Greenvalley High Physical Education Head of Department described their PE and sport programme as focussing on participation and equality:

Mr Mason: Okay then, my view on the emphasis of our PE programs here at school is primarily that it's sport for everybody; it's not elitist;

we're into maximising participation so that's the thrust, that's the view point that we take. We try to offer the students as wide a variety of activities as we can; we try and balance the program so that they're gender neutral or at least a balance of the genders in the different sports we offer so I guess they're the two main things I look at as head of department when we're program writing and devising.

In terms of physical culture, the rural young people tend not to be as immersed in popular sports cultures such as brand-name clothing as their urban counterparts. Mr Mason also elaborates on this:

Mr Mason: ... the kids out here are not touched by that [sports clothing culture] and it's difficult for people who don't live out here to understand. Half an hour from [regional centre] doesn't seem much, but this area is very much geographically isolated; kids out here are not touched by any of those sorts of fashion conscious; we get the odd student who'll come from another school, that is, and because they stand out so much it's not very long before they tend to drift towards [trails off].

The young people themselves spoke of wearing clothing that was "sensible, protective from the sun" and "suitable for work," and sports clothing was perceived as expensive and not appropriate for rural areas (Lee & Macdonald, 2009). Furthermore, other aspects such as sport spectatorship played a very small role in their lives due to distance from venues and expense of travel. However, when the rural young men did travel to sporting venues to watch national competitions in cricket and rugby league, it involved generations of male family members.

Mouldy: Yes, I've been to cricket... I went with my father, grandfather, uncle, cousins and brothers.

Mr Mason also suggested that sports participation did not play a large role in the culture of the town of Greenvalley.

Mr Mason: There's an element that's keen to participate in anything; there's a lot of people that are from lower socioeconomic backgrounds so they're more engaged with the struggle of day to day life and don't have the time or the real focus to be interested in sport. I wouldn't say it's high, the sense of community commitment or involvement, overall it's not high.

While the saturation of sports culture did not appear to be present in the rural locations, mainstream messages on obesity and health were still highlighted by Mr Mason who saw his "job [as a PE teacher] getting bigger and bigger" as "obesity is becoming more and more prevalent." He felt that obesity was a problem at Greenvalley High and that this was something of a concern for the school.

Mr Mason: Yes, I think you'd be struggling to find a community that doesn't [have a problem with obesity]... it's still not an acceptable level. No, obesity even out here [rural area], too many kids are overweight; too many kids are I guess not healthy [sic] conscious, which is something we try to change but as I mentioned earlier, it's a tough job.

Indeed, in an early stage of the national project where participants were surveyed on their participation in physical activities and aspects of physical culture, the rural young men were significantly more likely to respond "I am more self-conscious about my looks when I exercise or play sport" than the other male cohorts (Macdonald, Wright & Lee, 2001).

The rural young men from Greenvalley High who completed or left school during the study continued to be active in sport or physical labour. Brett went on to further study at a technical college and part-time work while continuing to be involved competitively in pistol shooting with his father and grandfather. Brett's participation with his male family members contributes to the discussion on rural hegemonic masculinity.

Brett: I sort of do shooting on the weekends and that, but other than that, that's basically all I'm doing because it's [work] five days a week and I don't have time for anything else...Usually in Christmas shoots they're usually more fun shoots. So usually me, Dad, and Dad's two brothers and Grandad usually get in one squad and usually we throw cases at each other and play up and call at each other when they're about to shoot and just muck up. Usually at competitions it's a big mental game.

Adam began full-time work at a local supermarket and eventually joined the army. His notion of health and fitness remained tied to his work.

Adam: Basically the job I've got now I'm lifting fairly heavy objects anyway, so the more I work the fitter I get.

Indeed, work and sport/leisure tended to complement each other in terms of fitness and health in general for the rural young men. Being healthy and fit was instrumental to being able to accomplish life's tasks. As Wadiken from the Homestead School commented "being able to get around and do things you know like if you're pooped it's a nuisance... If you're not fit you're not much use." Health and fitness was gauged by what they could achieve on the land or in their other forms of physical employment. Furthermore, physical labour was seen as a masculine pursuit, "Well, not my sister, she doesn't drive the tractors... mainly because I suppose it's sort of rough, it's a boy thing" (Wadiken). This feature of the rural context is well documented in the academic literature and perpetuated through the popular media whereby the rural image is masculine with a gendered division of labour. For example, those activities most obviously linked to farm production and income are culturally understood to be men's activities, while women are recognised as helpers or supporters (Davidson, 2001). Other studies of the rural gender order have revealed that this hegemonic masculinity extends into leisure sites like public bars and social occasions (Campbell & Phillips, 1995) and popular rural physical activities such as camp drafting (Henry, 1998). Indeed, as Gard (2001) states "sport, masculinity and country life are concepts which come together easily" (p. 20).

Discussion: Young Men's Physicality at the Intersection of Masculinity and Social Class

In terms of participation in physical activity and physical culture, the young men from different schooling, social, and geographical contexts had contrasting experiences. Where the young men from Malcos College experienced privileged access to sports from a young age, the rural young men from Greenvalley High and Homestead School had more restricted access to formal sporting opportunities and participated more in recreational activities and physical labour. The Malcos young men accessed their sporting endeavours through the school within a culture that expected participation, favoured certain middle-class masculine pursuits such as rugby and rowing, and encouraged competition between students. In contrast, the rural young men relied heavily on family support for participation in a limited number of traditional male sports. Furthermore, physical labour played a large role in the lives of the rural young men, which was considered to be a masculine pursuit naturally requiring and developing health and fitness. Following a similar trend, the young men's engagements with a broader physical culture outside of the school were diverse at the intersection of social and geographical location. Once again, the Malcos young men had a more privileged and taken-for-granted access to aspects of physical culture such as sports brand clothing and spectatorship at major sporting events. The rural young men, on the other hand, found these aspects of physical culture less relevant in their lives due to cost and travel.

The young men's experiences of physical activity at school within their social and geographical spaces had an impact on their conceptions of health and fitness. Indeed, both groups of young men expressed the importance of health and fitness in their daily lives, however the role they played was somewhat different. The Malcos young men spoke of balance and moderation to achieve health, incorporating academic, social, physical and mental aspects of their lives. This coincides with others' descriptions of upper-class young men's development of masculinities, where they are socialised into management or leadership positions thereby emphasising a balanced existence lived in moderation, denoting composure and control rather than emphasising physical strength and sturdiness in the evaluation of maleness (Laberge & Albert, 2000). This was demonstrated further as the Malcos young men who finished school went on to university to study professional degrees such as business and law but discontinued formal physical activity. While they still considered health and fitness as important in their lives, the pursuit of physical activity became less of a focus at that stage. The Malcos young men tended to be satisfied with their physical appearance as trim and somewhat athletic, as this also demonstrated balance and moderation in one's life. Their school experiences of abundant access to sports, privileged practices of physical culture and an encouragement into "healthy competition" at school primed them well for smooth transitions into university and a "balanced" future trajectory.

Health and fitness was important for the rural young men in order to be competent in their physical forms of employment. If one could not work and demonstrate physical prowess, they were deemed "useless." It was common for the rural young men to gauge their health and fitness by what they could achieve physically on the land. Again, this trend coincides with previous research on young men's masculinities, which suggests that working class young men were more likely to value and display more exaggerated embodiments and verbalisations of masculinity in order to express power over others within a context of perceived powerlessness (Laberge & Albert, 2000). Strong and muscular, non-overweight bodies were seen as a sign of physical competence and a necessity for physical labour. Rather than being a marker of attractiveness or "the body for others," a strong physical appearance was a requirement for their every day work. For the rural young men, the school had a relatively small role in providing physical activity opportunities, although it was evident from the teacher's talk that popular messages around obesity and health encroached on the curriculum. The impact of this was perhaps observed in the Greenvalley young men's concern around their physical appearance when participating in sports as demonstrated by the earlier survey results.

The data presented suggests that these groups of young men from different social and geographical locations who experienced contrasting school cultures around physical activity, health and fitness, are developing different approaches to masculinity. As such, there is a need to consider masculinity as having multiple manifestations and therefore, the term "masculinities" is more appropriate. Connell (2000) uses the term "hegemonic masculinity" to describe the dominant or most powerful form of masculinity. In relation to the contexts observed in this study, however, it would appear that there is not *one* hegemonic masculinity but many, depending on the social/ geographical/cultural context in question. Thus, while the young men were developing different approaches to physical activity, health and fitness and bodies, they would appear to be conforming to the dominant masculinities of their respective locations. Bourdieu's notions of *capital* and *field* are useful tools, as they allow us to explain the existence of multiple dominant masculinities. *Field* is understood as a social arena and is characterised by struggles for dominant positions to determine what constitutes capital within that field and how capital can be distributed (Webb, Schirato & Danaher, 2002). The two contexts discussed in this chapter can be understood as two fields, a privileged middle-class inner-city field and a working-class rural field, each with their own social and cultural environments, particularly experienced within schools by the young men. The young men's experiences within their fields leads to a perpetuation of discourses around physical activity, health and fitness, bodies, and masculinity through the *habitus*, an embodiment of social rules, values and dispositions (Bourdieu, 1977). The habitus reflects a configuration of *capital* comprising aspects of social currency that individuals possess in varying degrees and are unequally distributed amongst social groups (Bourdieu, 1986). The unequal distribution of capital is the basis of the power struggles said to characterise fields and leads to a condition within this situation where certain forms of masculinity become dominant. It would therefore be erroneous in comparing these two cohorts of young men to assume that one will be subordinate or marginalised to the other in terms of experiences of health and fitness and bodies in the construction of masculinities if we acknowledge that each field held their own versions of hegemonic masculinity.

In highlighting the existence of multiple dominant masculinities and the subsequent effect on young men's experiences of physical activity, health and fitness between fields brings forth the question of the relevance and impact of mainstream physical activity promotion and obesity messages. It is clear that both groups of young men in this study were touched by such campaigns through school and the popular media. These messages however, are being reconceptualised within fields or settings. For the private school young men from Malcos College, messages around health and fitness are experienced in terms of balance, a successfully managed lifestyle with everything in moderation including an element of healthy competition. "Healthy" bodies (not overweight and somewhat athletic) are a sign of this "properly" managed lifestyle in order to avoid the undesirable (lax, lazy) overweight body (Rich & Evans, 2005). This perception is consistent with the moral panic associated with obesity discourses (Rich & Evans, 2005). In the rural setting, health promotion messages around obesity seem to be perpetuated through the school and are taken up by the young men, resulting in a body self-consciousness when participating in physical activities. The non-overweight, muscular body however was not desired as a marker of attractiveness or moral correctness; it was perceived as instrumental for a rural lifestyle of physical labour. This demonstrates how health promotion messages can be recontextualised and have different meanings between fields characterised by contrasting social, cultural and economic circumstances. The use of Bourdieu's notion of field helps us to understand how young men can develop differing masculine identities yet still conform to the dominant social expectations of their contexts.

Conclusion

This chapter has sought to explore young men's meanings of health and fitness and how these are shaped by physical culture, particularly in school settings at the intersection of geographical location and social class. It was observed how, through schooling and the recontextualisation of health promotion messages, young men reproduced dominant and stereotypical meanings and approaches to physical activity, health and fitness, the body, and masculinity.

Given the diverse meanings of physical activity, health, and fitness observed, this qualitative study provides the means to critique the relevance and impact of top-down, one-size-fits-all health promotion messages. Furthermore, we are encouraged to look more closely at participation statistics and epidemiology that suggest that rural young people are less physically active than their urban counterparts. The current study would suggest that while rural physical activity participation patterns are less formal, and perhaps more difficult to measure, they still appear to participate in other legitimate forms of physical activity. It must be acknowledged, however, that this study does not enable the examination of the impact of these discourses in the different settings for young men who do not conform to dominant images. It does, though, demonstrate the impact of obesity discourses on the idealisation of masculine bodies, albeit with different meanings between the different cohorts of young men. In order to acknowledge the different meanings of physical activity, health and fitness within young men's lives, health promoters should be encouraged to consult with their target groups to inform more equitable and sustainable programmes so that these processes can be informed from the bottom up rather than top down.

Notes

1. All names of people and places have been changed to protect participants' anonymity.

Bibliography

Borraccino, A., Lemma, P., Iannotti, R. J., Zambon, A., Dalmasso, P., Lazzeri, G., et al. (2009). Socioeconomic effects on meeting physical activity guidelines: Comparisons among 32 countries. *Medicine & Science in Sports Exercise, 41*(4), 749-756.

Bourdieu, P. (1977). *Outline of a theory of practice.* Cambridge: Cambridge University Press.

Bourdieu, P. (1986). The forms of capital. In J. G. Richardson (Ed.), *Handbook of theory and research for the sociology of education* (pp. 241-258). New York: Greenwood Press.

Campbell, H., & Phillips, E. (1995). Masculine hegemony and leisure sites in rural New Zealand and Australia. In P. Share (Ed.), *Communication and culture in rural areas* (pp. 107-125). Wagga Wagga, Australia: Centre for Rural Social Research, Charles Sturt University.

Connell, R. W. (2000). *The men and the boys.* St Leonards: Allen & Unwin.

Crotty, M. (1998). *The foundations of social research: Meaning and perspective in the research process.* St Leonards: Allen & Unwin.

Davidson, A. P. (2001). Farming women and the masculinisation of farming practices. In S. Lockie, & L. Bourke (Eds.), *Rurality bites* (pp. 204-213). Annandale, NSW: Pluto Press.

Dowling Naess, F. (2001). Narratives about young men and masculinities in organised sport in Norway. *Sport, Education and Society, 6*(2), 125-142.

Gard, M. (2001). Sport, physical education and country towns: Diverse enough? *Education in Rural Australia, 11*(2), 19-26.

Harrington, D. W., & Elliott, S. J. (2009). Weighing the importance of neighbourhood: A multilevel exploration of the determinants of overweight and obesity. *Social Science & Medicine, 68*, 593-600.

Henry, J. (1998). Bullriding into manhood. In C. Hickey, L. Fitzclarence & R. Matthews (Eds.), *Where the boys are: Masculinity, sport and education* (pp. 97-108). Geelong, Victoria: Deakin Centre for Education and Change.

Inchley, J. C., Currie, D. B., Todd, J. M., Akhtar, P. C., & Currie, C. E. (2005). Persistent socio-demographic differences in physical activity among Scottish school children 1990-2002, *European Journal of Public Health, 15*(4), 386-388.

Kenway, J., & Bullen, E. (2001). *Consuming children: Education-entertainment-advertising.* Buckingham: Open University Press.

Laberge, S., & Albert, M. (2000). Conceptions of masculinity and gender transgressions in sport among adolescent boys. In M. A. Messner & D. Sabo (Eds.), *Masculinities, gender relations, and sport* (pp. 195-221). Thousand Oaks, CA: Sage Publications.

Lee, J., & Macdonald, D. (2009) Rural young people and physical activity: Understanding participation through social theory, *Sociology of Health and Illness, 31*(3), 360-374.

Lee, J., Macdonald, D., & Wright, J. (2009). Young men's physical activity choices: The impact of capital masculinities and location, *Journal of Sport and Social Issues, 33*(1), 59-77.

Luke, A. (1996). Text and discourse in education: An introduction to critical discourse analysis. In: M. W. Apple (Ed.), *Review of Research in Education*, Washington, DC: American Educational Research Association.

Macdonald, D., Wright, J., & Lee, J. (2001). *Constructing identity in relation to physical activity and sport: as told by two young men.* Paper presented at the biennial conference of the Australian Curriculum Studies Association, Canberra, Australia. Retrieved from: http://www.acsa.edu.au/pages/images/2001_constructing_identity_in_relation_to_physic al_education_and_sport.pdf

McKay, J. (1991). *No pain, no gain? Sport and Australian culture.* Sydney: Prentice Hall.

McLaren, P., & Farahmandpur, R. (2000). Reconsidering Marx in post-Marxist times: A requiem for postmodernism. *Educational Researcher, 29*(3), 25-33.

McLaren, L. (2007). Socioeconomic status and obesity. *Epidemiologic Reviews, 29,* 29-48.

Moon, G., Quarendon, G., Barnard, S., Twigg, L., & Blyth, B. (2007). Fat nation: Deciphering the distinctive geographies of obesity in England. *Social Science & Medicine, 65,* 20-31.

Rich, E. & Evans, J. (2005) "Fat ethics": The obesity discourse and body politics, *Social Theory & Health, 3,* 341-358.

Riva, M., Curtis, S., Gauvin, L., & Fagg, J. (2009). Unravelling the extent of inequalities in health across urban and rural areas: Evidence from a national sample in England. *Social Science & Medicine, 68,* 654-663.

Starfield, B., Riley, A. W., Witt, W. P., & Robertson, J. (2002). Social class gradients in health during adolescence, *Journal of Epidemiology and Community Healthy, 56,* 354-361.

Webb, J., Schirato, T., & Danaher, G. (2002). *Understanding Bourdieu.* Thousand Oaks, CA: Sage Publications.

Wright, J., Macdonald, D., & Groom, L. (2003). Physical activity and young people: Beyond participation, *Sport, Education and Society, 8,* 17-33.

Contributors

Michael Atkinson is Associate Professor in the Faculty of Physical Education and Health at the University of Toronto. His central areas of investigation pertain to physical cultural studies; notably, body modification and masculinity codes, technology and bioethics in sport, pain and illness narration in sport, animal ethics and sport, and the dimensions of criminal violence in sport. He has taught substantive courses in the sociology of bodies, sport, health and wellness, deviance and crime, popular culture, subcultures, youth, and core courses in social theory and methodology (including undergraduate and graduate-level quantitative, qualitative and historical methods courses). Michael is principally dedicated to the production of contextually based understandings of body practices (in sport, health and exercise settings), discourses about bodies and bioethics (both human and animal bodies), and subjectivities through which active bodies become organized, represented and experienced in relation to the operations of social power in sport/health/leisure worlds. Since 2004 he has served on the editorial boards of the American journals, *Sociology of Sport Journal* and *Deviant Behavior*, and the Canadian journal *International Journal of Qualitative Methods* and as associate book editor at the British journal *Sport in Society*. He is author of *Tattooed: The Sociogenesis of a Body Art* (2003), co-author of a book with Dr. Kevin Young titled *Sport, Deviance and Social Control* (2008), author/editor of *Battleground: Sports* (2008), and co-editor of a book with Dr. Kevin Young titled *Tribal Play: Sports Subcultures* (2008). In October of 2004, Michael received the Aurora Prize from SSHRC, as the outstanding young scholar/researcher in the Canadian social sciences.

Michael Gard is an Associate Professor in Charles Sturt University's Faculty of Education. He teaches and writes about education, dance, sport and the science of human health. He is the author of two books: *The Obesity Epidemic: Science, Morality and Ideology* (with Jan Wright) and *Men Who Dance: Aesthetics,*

Athletics and the Art of Masculinity. His new book, *The End of the Obesity Epidemic*, will be published in 2010.

Michael Kehler is an Associate Professor in the Faculty of Education at the University of Western Ontario, Canada. His research interests include the counter-hegemonic practices of adolescent young men, literacies, and the intersection of masculinities, health, body image and schooling. His research has been published in a range of journals including the *Canadian Journal of Education; Discourse: Studies in the Cultural Politics of Education; McGill Journal of Education; Taboo;* and *The International Journal of Inclusive Education.* He has contributed chapters in several edited books: *Masculinities and Schooling: International Practices and Perspectives* (Althouse Press); *Boys, Girls and the Myths of Literacies and Learning* (CSPI/Women's Press), and was contributor and co-editor with W. Martino and M. Weaver-Hightower, *Schooling Masculinities: Beyond Recuperative Masculinity Politics in Boys' Education.* (Routledge Press) He is also co-editor with S. Steinberg and L. Cornish of the forthcoming *Boy Culture: An Encyclopedia* (Greenwood Publishing). His recently funded Social Science and Humanities Research Council project with Michael Atkinson and Kevin Wamsley is ongoing as part of a three-year Canadian study.

Jeanne Adèle Kentel is currently with Carnegie Faculty of Sport and Education at Leeds Metropolitan University. She has taught in five post-secondary institutions and in numerous elementary and secondary schools in Alberta and British Columbia, Canada. She completed her doctorate in Curriculum Studies at the University of Alberta. Her current research interests examine the significance of deep learning, Deep Ecology, bodily ways of knowling, and critical pedagogies.

David Kirk currently holds the Alexander Chair in Physical Education & Sport at the University of Bedfordshire, where physical education teacher education courses have been provided continuously since 1903. He has published on a range of topics relating to physical education and youth sport, and is Founding Editor of the *Journal of Physical Education and Sport Pedagogy.* His latest book, *Physical Education Futures*, was published by Routledge in 2010.

Jessica Lee is a lecturer in physical activity and health at Loughborough University in the School of Sport, Exercise and Health Sciences. Jessica's main research interests lie in the sociocultural understandings of young people's engagements with physical activity and the broader notion of physical culture. She employs a critical sociocultural framework to explore current health and physical activity promotion initiatives and to inform practices that are supportive, equitable and sustainable. Her research to date has been with Australian young people as part of the Life Activity Project.

Richard Light is the 75th Carnegie Anniversary Chair in Sport and Physical Education Pedagogy in the Carnegie Faculty of Sport and Education, Leeds Metropolitan University, and Carnegie Director of Research. Previously, at the University of Sydney and the University of Melbourne, Richard's research program is focused on the body and its role in learning in sport, physical education and other physical activities, with an emphasis on non-conscious, tacit, embodied learning. He works within a theoretical framework that integrates constructivist learning theory with some of the social theory used in the physical education, sport coaching and sport sociology fields. Working from a very broad perspective on learning as an ongoing, life-long process he has conducted research in physical education pedagogy and sport coaching pedagogy across a range of cultural and social settings including Australia, Japan, France, Singapore and the USA. Richard's PhD thesis comprised a comparative study on high school rugby and the embodiment of culture and class-specific masculinities in Australia and Japan. He was also guest editor for a special issue of *Sport, Education and Society* on Boys, the Body, Sport and Schooling published in May 2008.

Nate McCaughtry is an Associate Professor and Physical Education Program Coordinator in the Department of Kinesiology, Health and Sport Studies at Wayne State University in Detroit, Michigan. His research focuses on issues of equity, diversity, and emotion in the context of K-12 schooling. He examines social, cultural, political and economic forces in the context of school-based physical education and health programs. Prior to his academic career, Nate McCaughtry taught secondary physical education and coached numerous youth sports.

James W. Messerschmidt is Professor of Sociology in the Criminology Department and the Women's and Gender Studies Program at the University of Southern Maine. In addition to over thirty academic articles and book chapters, he is the author of *The Trial of Leonard Peltier* (1983), *Capitalism, Patriarchy, and Crime: Toward a Socialist Feminist Criminology* (1986), *Masculinities and Crime: A Critique and Reconceptualization of Theory* (1993), *Crime as Structured Action: Gender, Race, Class, and Crime in the Making* (1997), *Nine Lives: Adolescent Masculinities, the Body, and Violence* (2000), *Flesh and Blood: Adolescent Gender Diversity and Violence* (2004), and *Hegemonic Masculinities and Camouflaged Politics: Unmasking the Bush Dynasty and Its War Against Iraq* (2010). Currently he is working on a comparative study of transmen and genderqueers.

Brad Millington is a PhD candidate in the School of Human Kinetics at the University of British Columbia. His research examines issues related to identity, health, and social (in)equality in physical culture. Specific topics of interest include the production and use of commercial technologies for health promotion, media portrayals of gender and ageing, and sport and environmental sustainability. His work can be found in publications such as *New Media & Society*; *Sport, Education and Society*; and the *Sociology of Sport Journal*.

Todd G. Morrison, PhD, is an Associate Professor of Psychology at the University of Saskatchewan, Canada. He is the editor/co-editor of several books including *Psychology of Modern Prejudice* (Nova Science, 2008) and *Male Sex Work: A Business Doing Pleasure* (Routledge, 2007), and has published over 40 articles in peer-reviewed journals (e.g., *Psychology of Women Quarterly*, *Diabetologia*, *Journal of Cross-cultural Psychology*, *Journal of Men's Studies*, and *Sex Roles*). His research interests include: psychometrics; stereotyping, prejudice, and discrimination; male body image; gay and lesbian psychology; and pornography.

Cormac Ó Beaglaoich is currently completing his PhD on adolescent masculine ideology at the National University of Ireland, Galway. His research interests include: gender roles conflict, male body image, psychometrics, stereotyping, human sexuality, prejudice, and suicidology.

Travis A. Ryan, BA, Higher Diploma in Arts (Psychology), is currently completing his PhD on male body image at the National University of Ireland, Galway. This work is funded by the Lady Gregory Doctoral Research Fellowship Scheme of the College of Arts, Social Sciences, & Celtic Studies, National University of Ireland, Galway. His research interests include male body image; masculinity; scale development; human sexuality; and prejudice, discrimination, and stigma. He is the coauthor of studies published in *The Journal of Homosexuality*, *International Journal of Men's Health*, and the *Canadian Journal of Human Sexuality* and a chapter in the *Handbook of Assessment Methods for Eating Behaviors and Weight-Related Problems: Measures, Theory, and Research* (Sage, 2009).

Amy Tischler is a doctoral student in the Department of Kinesiology, Health and Sport Studies at Wayne State University in Detroit, Michigan. Her research includes studies of gender relations and masculinities in school physical education. She is the author of several research papers and presentations examining male embodiment and masculinity configurations in various physical activity settings. Before her academic career, Amy taught elementary physical education in Livonia, Michigan.

Brian Wilson is an Associate Professor in the School of Human Kinetics at the University of British Columbia in Vancouver. His research interests include media, consumer culture, youth, social inequality, social movements, the environment, and sport and leisure studies generally. He has published in such venues as the *Canadian Journal of Sociology*, *Youth & Society*, the *Canadian Journal of Communication*, the *Canadian Journal of Education*, the *Sociology of Sport Journal*, and the *International Review for the Sociology of Sport*. He is author of *Fight, Flight, or Chill: Subcultures, Youth, and Rave into the 21st Century* (McGill-Queen's University Press), and is currently leading a project funded by the Social Sciences and Humanities Research Council of Canada entitled "Corporate Environmentalism and the Canadian Golf Industry."

Index

American children, 13-14
Anti-gym, 73
Anti-jock, 73, 83
Anti-sport, 73
Australian, 6, 8-9, 11, 15, 25, 39, 41, 64, 133, 135-136, 140, 180, 201, 204, 225

Bodies
    Regulation of, 22, 24, 26-30, 32-33, 37-38, 41, 53, 56, 64, 66, 78, 82, 120, 124, 126, 136-137, 156-157, 159-160, 164, 167, 170-171, 179, 182-184, 187-189, 190-191, 216-217, 223
    Surveillance of, 7, 21, 23-24, 26-27, 31-33, 39, 53, 56, 64, 78, 81, 121, 126, 136-137, 154, 159, 160, 164, 167-168, 171, 186, 188-190, 218

Body
    Athletic, 25, 29, 41, 52, 86-87, 96, 100, 102, 104, 127, 136, 155, 163-164, 169-170, 179, 183, 188, 190, 192, 204, 207, 216, 218

Dissatisfaction, 23-27, 30-32, 36, 39, 41, 78, 126-127, 158, 162, 186-189
Satisfaction, 23-25, 31-32, 39, 126, 158
Internalization, 22, 28, 30-35, 37-41, 121,124
Schooling the, 17, 28, 51-53, 64, 74, 78-79, 103, 120-121, 124, 126, 135, 157-161, 168, 171, 181, 183, 186-190
Shape, 21, 23, 25-26, 28-29, 31-33, 38, 55-56, 80, 91, 154-155, 156, 160, 161, 170, 188, 194
Self-esteem, 26-27, 32, 35, 37, 39, 62, 181, 194
Social construction, 51, 66, 85, 87, 135, 179
Body image
    Anxiety, x, xii, xiv, 32, 38, 74, 189
    Evaluation, 21-30, 32, 36-41, 52, 56, 64, 78-79, 82-87, 91, 99, 120, 121, 126, 153, 154, 156-162, 166-168, 171, 179, 182-186, 188-190, 195, 216, 218
    Investment, 21-30, 32-33, 35, 39, 91, 126, 156, 158-160, 166-167, 194

Body weight, 3-4, 6, 11-15, 23, 25-26, 32, 38, 80, 154, 157, 177, 194, 218-219

Bodily performance, 26, 28-29, 31, 33, 35, 38, 41, 52, 61, 64, 74, 78-79, 120, 126, 136, 157-160, 162, 164, 168, 170-171, 179, 183-184, 187-190, 192, 216

Britain, 14, 41, 53-55, 58, 60, 62

Bullying

Verbal, 81, 104, 113, 116-118, 120-124, 126-127

Physical, 79-80, 104, 113-115, 118, 120, 122-124, 127

Social, 79-80, 86, 113-115, 117-118, 125-127

Emotional, 59, 77, 79, 187, 194

Mental, 77, 79, 113

Violence cycle, 80, 121, 124-125, 128-129

Policy, 17, 128

Bullied, 80, 86, 113-121, 123-124, 127, 180

Canadian, 9, 73, 76, 83, 87-88, 106, 153-155, 159-160, 171, 223-224, 226-227

Carnegie, 54-57, 59, 61, 63, 67, 224-225

Coaches, 58, 65, 74, 79, 85-86, 134, 136-143, 147, 186, 212, 228

Codes

of masculinity, 73, 76, 79, 87, 114, 115-119, 124-128, 157, 170-171

dominant, 79, 118, 121, 126, 128, 136, 139, 145, 157, 165, 169, 170, 180-181, 183, 217-218

Crisis, 8, 24, 67, 75, 77-78, 80-81, 154-155, 177, 194

Culture of cruelty, 127-128

Curriculum, 51, 53-54, 55, 58, 60, 63-67, 73, 76, 82, 86, 96, 103, 128-129, 142, 147, 159, 180, 184, 186, 188, 216, 224

Cultural physical education, 56

Discourses

Heterosexual, 76

Masculine, 81, 84-86, 133, 136, 142-145, 147, 164, 169, 204, 223

Popular, 3, 4, 91, 133, 136, 147, 169, 182, 217

Scientific, 3, 4, 155, 182-183

Critical, 5, 38, 99, 105, 155, 167, 182, 186, 203

Gender, 27, 134-135, 142, 145

Obesity, 3, 5, 12, 170, 177, 178, 202, 218-219

Embodied

Practices, 114, 117-118, 120, 124, 126-127, 129, 135, 186-187

Spaces, 118, 124, 135, 183, 187, 189

Masculinity, 113-114, 118, 124, 128, 136, 162, 178-185, 187, 189

Gender, 114-115, 128-129, 162, 180-181, 186-188

Relationships, 186

Participation, 189

Learning, 225

Fitness, 17, 29, 33, 35, 39-40, 73, 128, 153, 179, 182-184, 189, 194, 201, 203, 207, 214-219

Game sense, 141, 143, 145, 147

Gay, 24, 27, 34, 36-37, 41, 76, 129, 156, 159, 194, 226

Gender
Making, 4, 13-15, 27, 33, 51-53, 60, 64-67, 74-75, 84, 86, 92-98, 100-101, 103-106, 113-118, 121-129, 134-135, 142-147, 154, 157-160, 165, 167, 169, 170-171, 178, 180, 190-191, 194, 213, 215

Girls, 3, 4, 7, 10-11, 13, 16, 21, 26, 28, 30-31, 33, 52, 54-55, 59-60, 63, 66-67, 76, 80, 83, 87, 91, 95-96, 99-103, 114-120, 122-123, 125-129, 134, 143-147, 154-156, 166, 170, 178, 181, 185, 187, 193-194

Habitus, 78, 84, 139, 203, 218

Health
Crisis, 6, 8, 67, 154-155, 177, 194

Hegemony, 78, 80-84, 92-93, 128, 133-137, 139, 144-145, 147, 167-168, 178, 180, 192, 214-215, 217

Hegemonic
Ideal, 22, 24, 26, 29, 59-60, 62-64, 77, 79-86, 94-95, 97-98, 101-102, 105, 133, 135-136, 139, 142, 144-147, 165, 167, 178-189, 191-193, 214-215, 217

Heteronormativity, 194

Heterotopia, 73-75, 77-78, 80, 84

Heterotopic space, 75, 77

Heterosexual, 24, 34, 36-37, 56, 63, 76, 92, 95, 98, 100, 166

Homophobia, 162, 194

Hyper-masculine, 33, 51, 53, 61, 64, 66, 105, 168

Identity performances, 93-94, 96

Images, 4, 8, 91-92, 100, 118, 121, 153-156, 162, 169, 171, 194, 209

Images of masculinity, 21-35, 37-41, 87, 97, 106, 156, 159-161, 167, 170-171, 215, 218

Jock culture, 73

Jock masculinity, 73

Justice, 86, 103-104, 106, 128, 179, 182

Locker room, 73-81, 83-87, 162, 166, 169, 171, 180

Loughborough, 54, 55, 57, 63, 224

Masculine bodies, xiv, 153, 156, 219

Masculinity Vortices, 51

Masculinities, viii-xiv, 53, 63, 74, 76, 79, 91-92, 95-102, 134-135, 153, 157-160, 164, 166, 170, 178-184, 186-189, 191-195, 202-203, 216-217
Hegemonic, 95, 97-98, 101, 102, 105, 179-183, 186-189, 191, 193
Multiple, 83-84, 178, 181, 183, 217
Normative, xiii, 74, 81, 84, 159, 163, 168

Mass media, xii, 21, 28, 30, 37, 84, 156

Media, ix, xii, 4, 8, 11, 21-22, 25, 28-41, 64, 81, 83, 91-92, 94-102, 105-107, 133, 146-147, 154-156, 167, 201, 215, 218
Messages, xii, 28, 34-35, 38, 40, 91-92, 94-95
Images, 22, 28, 32, 38-39, 41, 92, 100, 106

Media literacy, xii, 39, 50, 92, 105, 107

Muscular, x, xi, 22-26, 28-33, 36-38, 40-41, 85, 156, 163-164, 167, 216, 218
   Ideal, 23-25, 28-30, 39
Muscularity, viii, xii, 21, 23-24, 26-31, 33, 35, 37, 40-41, 99, 108, 156, 159, 163-4, 166, 179, 183

Non-genderist pedagogy, xiii, 134, 145-147

Obesity, vii, x-xi, 3-17, 154-155, 170, 177-178, 181, 183, 186, 193-194, 201-202, 214, 216-219
Obesity pandemic, x-xi, 3, 5-6, 154, 193
   Inactivity, vii-xi, xiv, 11, 73, 87, 153-156, 160, 181, 193
Ontario, xii, 73-74, 79, 82, 87, 154
Overweight, 3, 5-7, 13-16, 23, 26, 154, 202, 216, 218

Panic, xi, 154-155, 177, 218
Panoptic, 79
Pedagogy, 74, 85, 134-135, 141-143, 145-146, 185
   Critical, 134, 145
   Feminist, xiii, 79, 133-134, 143-145, 157-158
   Hard, 134, 146
   Non-genderist, xiii, 134, 145-147
   Soft, 133-134
   Sport, 140, 143
Physical appearance, 21-22, 24, 27, 33, 38, 40, 207, 216-217
Physical education, vii, x-xiii, 51-67, 73-76, 80, 82-83, 85-87, 91-92, 96, 101, 105, 134, 145, 157, 153-154, 157-162, 165, 168-171, 177-186, 188, 192-194, 201, 203, 204, 206-207, 210-212

Teachers, xi-xii, 51-67, 78-80, 85-87, 97-98, 102-103, 116, 127-128, 160, 171, 180, 182-190, 192-195, 203, 210, 212, 214, 216
   Teacher education, xii, 53-54, 60, 63, 67, 194
Play, 9, 65, 75, 77, 79, 83, 95, 104, 116-117, 119-120, 126, 134, 136-147, 155, 163-164, 168, 178, 184, 190, 192-193, 206-208, 212, 214
   Risk-filled, 75
Policies, ix, xiv, 17, 74, 128-129, 170, 201, 203
Popular muscular boys, 85

Risk, 6, 8-9, 23, 36, 39, 75-77, 80, 82, 93, 95, 137-139, 141, 161, 179-180
Rugby, xiii, 55, 57, 61-62, 64, 133-147, 180, 204-206, 209, 213, 215,

Scapeland, 75, 78-79
Scottish, 8, 36, 51, 54, 60, 97
Social class, 52, 154, 201-203, 215, 218
Sociocultural, 23, 27-28, 30-31, 33-34, 37, 41, 202
Sport, vii-xi v, 3, 9, 16, 25, 33, 40, 51-52, 55-56, 58, 60, 63-67, 73-77, 79, 85-87, 95-96, 102, 115-119, 127, 133-136, 139-140, 142-147, 154-155, 157-161, 163-164, 168-170, 179-188, 190, 192-195, 201-217
Stereotype, xii, 3-4, 6, 8-11, 53-54, 57-59, 63-64, 66-67m 100, 104, 106
Surveillance, x, 31, 73-74, 81, 89, 139, 160, 165, 169

Technology/technologies, 4, 8-11, 16, 91
Teaching games for understanding (TGFU), 141-143, 146-147

United States, vii, x-xi, xiii, 7, 9-10, 12-14, 25-26, 113, 155, 181

Victims/Victimization, xii-xiii, 73, 106, 113-119, 121, 124-125, 128-129, 180, 191
Violence, 76-77, 80, 95-96, 105-106, 113-115, 121, 123-124, 127-129, 133, 144, 179, 185, 187

Weakness, vii, 39, 95, 100, 156, 164, 166, 168
Weight
Body weight, 3-4, 6-7, 11-14, 16, 169
    Control, 26
    Loss, 25, 29
Overweight, 3-7, 13-16, 18, 23, 26, 80, 154, 157, 202, 207, 214, 216, 218

Adolescent
Cultures,
School &
Society

Joseph L. DeVitis & Linda Irwin-DeVitis
GENERAL EDITORS

As schools struggle to redefine and restructure themselves, they need to be cognizant of the new realities of adolescents. Thus, this series of monographs and textbooks is committed to depicting the variety of adolescent cultures that exist in today's post-industrial societies. It is intended to be a primarily qualitative research, practice, and policy series devoted to contextual interpretation and analysis that encompasses a broad range of interdisciplinary critique. In addition, this series will seek to provide a pragmatic, pro-active response to the current backlash of conservatism that continues to dominate political discourse, practice, and policy. This series seeks to address issues of curriculum theory and practice; multicultural education; aggression and violence; the media and arts; school dropouts; homeless and runaway youth; alienated youth; at-risk adolescent populations; family structures and parental involvement; and race, ethnicity, class, and gender studies.

Send proposals and manuscripts to the general editors at:

Joseph L. DeVitis & Linda Irwin-DeVitis
The John H. Lounsbury School of Education
Georgia College & State University
Campus Box 70
Milledgeville, GA 31061-0490

To order other books in this series, please contact our Customer Service Department at:

(800) 770-LANG (within the U.S.)
(212) 647-7706 (outside the U.S.)
(212) 647-7707 FAX

or browse online by series at:

WWW.PETERLANG.COM